Elham Manea is Associate Professor in the Political Science Institute at the University of Zurich. She is a Fulbright Scholar and consultant for Swiss government agencies and international human rights organisations. She is the author of *The Arab State and Women's Rights: The Trap of Authoritarian Governance* (2011), *Regional Politics in the Gulf: Saudi Arabia, Oman, Yemen* (2005) and *Political Parties and Organizations in Yemen, 1948–1993* (1994). She has recently been appointed by the Swiss Federal Council as a Member of the Federal Commission for Women's Affairs.

'This is an important book for our times. Manea eloquently makes a politically incorrect and absolutely necessary Arabo-Muslim case for the universality of human rights. She reminds us that the concept of universality is anything but abstract and has significant consequences in the lives of women and men. Western academics and advocates who think that, by promoting cultural relativism or exceptions to human rights and legal norms for minorities they are defending the marginalized or enhancing cultural rights, should read this courageous book, and rethink.'

Karima Bennoune, UN Special Rapporteur in the field of cultural rights

'An incendiary attack on the tenets of legal pluralism by an Arab Muslim woman who writes as an uncompromising advocate of secular universalism, this study could hardly be more timely. Confronting the mass immigration of Muslims from the Middle East and North Africa, Europeans must cope with circumstances that will aggravate existing problems of accommodating cultural difference within a human rights framework. Based on scathing assessments of British multiculturalism, the author warns that cultural essentialism will inevitably have the consequence of engendering violations of the human rights of women, children, and LGBT individuals, staking out provocative positions that should be of interest to readers of various ideological persuasions.'

Ann E. Mayer, Associate Professor Emerita of Legal Studies and Business Ethics, The Wharton School, University of Pennsylvania

'An honest, theoretically clear book with a strong narrative based on best case law tradition.'

Adrian Loretan, Professor of Canon Law and Ecclesiastical Law; Co-director of the Center for Comparative Constitutional Law and Religion, University of Lucerne

'An extremely timely, thoughtful and thought-provoking book about how Islamist movements increase their political domination through the introduction of plural legal systems and Sharia Laws. Elham Manea bravely challenges essentialists' demands by looking at the context of legal pluralism, its actual practice and the consequences of introducing "special laws" for "specific groups", particularly women and children. This book must find its way to every lawyer, activist, feminist and those concerned with a defence of the universality of human rights.'

Yasmin Rehman

WOMEN AND SHARI'A LAW

The Impact of Legal Pluralism in the UK

Elham Manea

I.B. TAURIS
LONDON · NEW YORK

Published in 2016 by
I.B.Tauris & Co. Ltd
London • New York
www.ibtauris.com

ISBN: 978 1 78453 735 7
eISBN: 978 1 78672 022 1
ePDF: 978 1 78673 022 0

A full CIP record for this book is available from the British Library
A full CIP record is available from the Library of Congress

Library of Congress Catalog Card Number: available

Typeset in Garamond Three by OKS Prepress Services, Chennai, India
Printed and bound by Page Bros, Norwich

To my Husband, the wind beneath my wings

CONTENTS

LIST OF TABLES

ACKNOWLEDGEMENTS

I have written other books but this one is most dear to me. It is one that I wrote with a purpose. For it is an expression of more than two decades of frustration with a discourse of difference and identity that came to mark some postmodern circles. It was imperative to give this discourse a name – the Essentialist Paradigm – and hence write this book.

This book is a culmination of four years of research and an outcome of intensive discussions and deliberations with colleagues and friends. The list of colleagues and friends, who read and commented on this manuscript, is long. I am grateful to all of them. I specifically would like to thank my Swiss colleagues and friends Helene Aecherli, Professor Anke von Kügelgen, Professor Antonius Liedhegener, Professor Livia Schubiger, Dr Dorothea Weniger, and Professor Judith Wyttenbach for their invaluable critical feedback and comments on the book.

I had the good fortune of presenting parts of this book to colleagues of Witwatersrand, Bern and Basel Universities in Bern in 2014. I wish to thank them all for their critical feedback.

I remain in debt to many persons in the United Kingdom, who generously shared with me their contacts, time, knowledge and expertise. They facilitated my field research and enriched my stay in the UK with their discussions. Without them this book would not have been completed. I realise that some of them, for different reasons, may not want to be mentioned here and I will respect that. They know who they are and I am most grateful to them. I wish to give special thanks to Gita Sahgal for the priceless insights she shared with me. I appreciate the time Baroness Caroline Cox gave me during my research, and I am most grateful to Jenan Al Jabiri, Rashad Ali, Salma Dean, Shaista Gohir, Dr Usama Hasan, Habiba Jaan, Gina Khan, Tehmina Kazi, Maryam Namazie, Charlotte Proudman and Tahmina Saleem. In addition, I am indebted to Helen Snively, who accompanied me during this project, and professionally edited the manuscript... and I wish to ask for forgiveness of those whom I might have forgotten to mention.

    Finally, I am lucky to have my husband Thomas and daughter Selma by my side. It was their continuous love, encouragement and support – even at the many times of my physical and mental absence – that made this book possible.

INTRODUCTION

THE DEBATE

It all started with a media controversy in Switzerland. The book in your hands is its direct result.

The catalyst was a short article by a professor in social anthropology at Freiburg University. The Swiss Federal Commission Against Racism dedicated its December 2008 bulletin, TANGRAM, to the theme of 'multicultural society'. In that issue, Professor Christian Giordano published an article he titled 'Legal Pluralism: An Instrument for Multiculturalism?'

It took a couple of weeks before the media got its hands on the bulletin and with it the article. A respected Sunday newspaper, *NZZ am Sonntag*, discussed the implications of Giordano's argument, interviewed him, and published an article with the headline 'Shari'a courts for Switzerland: Freiburg professor demands special laws for Muslims and other groups'.

As a female Arab academic who considers Islam to be her religion and has extensively researched the conditions of all genders in the Arab Middle East and North Africa (MENA) region, as a women's rights activist who has been involved in various campaigns for gender justice, and as a woman who has seen the dire consequences of the application of shari'a law, I knew all too well what that suggestion would entail.

The next week, the same Sunday newspaper published my response to Giordano's suggestion in the opinion section with the title 'Islamic law in Switzerland would be devastating'.[1]

That debate led me to research the topic further and write this book.

This book is a critique of a paradigm of thinking that has become characteristic of Western academic post-colonial and post-modernist discourse: one that insists on treating people as 'homogeneous groups', essentialising their cultures and religions, calling for special laws and treatment for groups within a society, underestimating the human rights consequences of their academic discourse, and discarding the voices of people from these very 'cultures' as 'not authentic enough'. I call this the Essentialist Paradigm.

This is also a book about the *context* within which this discourse is taking place. Often, these Western academics have become the unwitting allies of Islamists who propagate an ideology of Islamism that seeks to essentialise Islam, who claim to be the sole entity speaking for Muslims. They insist that they be treated as a 'homogenous group', and assert that human rights are a 'Western imposition'; in the process they violate these rights with impunity. What the Western academics seem not to notice is the totalitarian content within the ideology of Islamism and its aim of oppressive political domination.

Both types of essentialists are arguing that Islamic law should be introduced into the Western legal systems in the name of multi-culturalism. Britain is one famous, and I dare say disastrous, example of this experiment.

In response to this demand, this book is both a critique of the essentialists' discourse and a defence of the universality of human rights.

I argue that to understand the seriousness and gravity of the essentialists' demand, we must look at the *context of legal pluralism and its actual practice*. We must also consider the *consequences* of introducing 'special laws' for 'specific groups'. It is the consequences that should matter. And again, the British case can provide ample evidence of these consequences.

But I am getting ahead of myself. Let me first introduce the debate that took place six years ago and explain why I became convinced that a paradigm change is necessary.

***

What did Professor Christian Giordano say in the first place?

I will translate a paragraph of his article that best illustrates his argument:

Given Europe's massive waves of migration, it stands at a turning point: it has the choice of insisting on the uniqueness and irrevocability of the existing legal system, which is based exclusively on the positive law; or to try to pluralise this legal system and with this [step] officially recognise the existence of different claims to rights and diverse legal cultures.

Of course, such legal pluralism cannot be based on the construction of complete and autonomous parallel legal jurisdictions. Obviously, a *strong* legal pluralism remains inacceptable in the Western world. The point is rather to integrate *other* legal mechanisms, in certain areas of the positive law, with the help of its cultural and social structures, and accounting for this diversity.[2]

Giordano was suggesting that Switzerland introduces what he called a *weak legal pluralism*,[3] i.e. allow some groups, from different cultural or religious backgrounds, to use their own laws in specific areas of jurisprudence. In his interview with the *NZZ am Sonntag*, he acknowledged that he was being consciously provocative by making his suggestion, but he was of the opinion that the time was ripe for such a debate in Switzerland. He argued that the presence of migrants from 'very remote cultural circles' demands this legal shift: 'The cultural distance is too great. And however much these migrants also assimilate, there always remains a difference; this is also true of our legal system.'

He then elaborated further and proposed the introduction of shariʿa, and other religious, courts. Such courts would deal especially with civil matters and also with offences and assaults. Of course, he could not accept the idea of Islamic judgments that lead to corporal punishment; in fact, he argued that under no circumstances should human rights be violated. He said that corporal punishment should be 'converted to fines. Naturally, human rights should be fully maintained in a Swiss shariʿa court'.

More easily said than done. In fact, it is not possible to fully maintain human rights in a shariʿa court.

Simply put, it is often women and children who pay a heavy and painful price for such well-intentioned suggestions.

Imagine a 36-year-old divorced mother in Yemen, standing alongside an imam who is phoning her 18-year-old son in the United States to get his permission for his mother to remarry. What if he says no? The imam will refuse to conduct the marriage ceremony. She needs the permission of her guardian to marry. Since her father has died, her son has become her guardian.

Imagine a religious jurisprudence that does not set a minimum age for marriage. If a girl is said to be 'fit' to be married, her guardian can marry her off and it won't matter if she is nine years old, or twelve, or thirteen. If she has gotten her period, and her guardian considers her 'fit' to be married, then she will be married off. All too often, with the re-awakening of a very conservative interpretation of Islam, imams will gladly give their blessing. 'The earlier the better', as one famous sheikh in a shari'a court in Britain said in a recorded video.[4]

Imagine a religious jurisprudence that tells you that as a wife, it does not matter how many years you have spent in your marriage. If you get divorced, your entire financial entitlement will be three months of maintenance. What if a woman was married for 30 years? If she did not 'secure' herself with property and accounts in her own name, she will still get three months' allowance. Three months of maintenance is the rule.

Imagine a religious jurisprudence that tells you that as a man, you can divorce your wife by uttering the word 'divorced' three times. Just like that. Your wife does not have a right to object, because you have decided. The power, the might, is in your hands. But if she decides to divorce, she will need to go through a torturous legal process until she finally gets her divorce. Because even in this situation she needs your permission to divorce, and without it, she will have to either prove harm or give up her financial entitlements.

Imagine a religious jurisprudence that deprives a mother of her rights to her children's custody if she decides to marry again after her divorce.

Imagine a system that tells you that as a daughter you are entitled to half of your brother's share of your parents' inheritance. He is entitled to double your share because he is male. His gender determines his share.

Imagine all this and then tell me: how are we supposed to *fully maintain human rights — which entail the equality of men and women and freedom from discrimination regardless of religion and gender — in a shari'a court?*

Notice that here, I 'consciously' — to use a word from Giordano — departed from an academic legal discourse. I deliberately used language that will bring into stark clarity the consequences of Giordano's suggestion. It is the consequences that matter in this whole debate: the consequences in the daily lives of women and children. And it is these consequences that most often affect the weakest and the least privileged within the diverse communities of Muslim women's groups.

An educated and emancipated Muslim woman will be in a position to fight for her rights. She will know that these 'legal mechanisms' are voluntary. She will know the loopholes in Islamic jurisprudence, and there are plenty. If she does not want Islamic arbitration, she can simply turn to the civil court system. She will be in a position to negotiate and use her own agency. But imagine a young woman, brought from her village to marry a cousin in a Western country, who speaks little of the language, is not aware that she has rights, and is stuck in an abusive marriage and a patriarchal family structure. This woman will not be in a position to negotiate, or to use her agency to gain her rights.

Similarly, a young woman who is brought up in a closed community that exercises social control over its women will be afraid to swim against the tide of the rules dictated by community's elders and leaders. All too often, this young woman is constantly told that God has ordained these unjust rules because *he knows better*, and who is she to dare question the fairness of these rulings? Will she really be in a position to reject the judgment of the 'judges' in these shari'a courts?

A system that allows the most privileged to grab onto their rights while perpetuating the discrimination and abuse of the least privileged is not a fair system. It is arbitrary and inherently biased. As such it will not guarantee respect for human rights. That is the core problem with the suggestion of introducing weak legal pluralism in the Western context.

***

But that is not all.

My response to Giordano's suggestion has three aspects. These pave the way for the deliberations I will present in this book.

First, the specific context of Switzerland and its migrants from Islamic countries make such a suggestion pointless. Giordano argued in the Sunday newspaper that Muslims cannot integrate because they are accustomed to legal systems that are culturally alien to the Swiss system. This statement is not only false; it contradicts legal facts.

The majority of Muslim immigrants come from Turkey and the countries of former Yugoslavia.

Turkey is secular and shariʿa is not part of its legal system. In fact, Turkish family law is based on Swiss family law. Moreover, Bosnia had not had a shariʿa court since 1946, when they were abolished by law. And Albania applies a mix of civil and common law that leaves no room for Islamic law.[5]

Given these facts, it is bizarre to demand that Switzerland introduce an abstract idea of a shariʿa law for groups of people whose countries do not even apply Islamic law in their legal systems. It also raises many questions about the paradigm prism used in this argument.

That prism is the *anthropological version of law*: a version of law void of any historical, political, or even legal context. This term was first introduced to me by Tahmina Saleem, co-founder of Inspire, the British Muslim women's organisation.[6] She was describing how British courts, when they deal with cases involving British Pakistani citizens, accept a version of Islamic law that does not even exist in the Pakistani legal system. I will return to this concept later, in Chapter 4.

Second, legal pluralism is applied in countries of the MENA region, with very minor exceptions. In countries such as Syria, Lebanon and Egypt, each community uses its own religious laws in family affairs. But this system is hardly a model to emulate, not when it concerns aspects of gender justice, equality and human rights. In fact, the Arab Human Development Report (AHDR), *Towards the Rise of the Arab Woman*, described the consequences of applying these religious laws as a form of 'legally sanctioned discrimination'.[7]

Arab experts – the best in the field – wrote the AHDR. Their critique testifies to a critical discourse in the MENA region on religious laws and Islamic law in particular. This discourse has often illuminated both the gender issue and the problematic nature of applying shariʿa law in family matters. Many Arab and Muslim intellectuals, writers and activists, both men and women, have addressed the gender issue, stressing that the emancipation of women is a condition for the development of Arab society. They also made it clear that this emancipation cannot be achieved without changing the family laws that govern the lives of women.[8]

It is interesting that those who suggest introducing Islamic law in the Western legal context often ignore this critical discourse and consider

Islamic law and shari'a as something given, and whole, just as Islamists do. This perception correlates with another, similar, assumption they make: that Muslims are homogenous and identify themselves first and solely as religious persons. Islamists make a similar argument. I will explain this point further and the role of Islamists in Chapter 5.

Significantly, my research on the political consequences of applying legal pluralism in the Arab context highlights startling consequences for the cohesion and national unity of a society. Simply put, the religious nature of applied family laws perpetuates the social fragmentation in their societies. In Syria, regardless of which religious family law we are taking about, all family laws make it practically impossible for members of different religious or sectarian communities to marry. These laws have been instrumental in preventing marriages between members of different sects, religions, and tribes. In fact, by hindering intermarriage, they have kept the society divided. In the process, in several countries, these laws have sabotaged the development of social cohesion and a national identity. Far from being an example to emulate, these experiences highlight negative political and human rights consequences of legal pluralism. I will elaborate on this aspect further in Chapter 4.[9]

In my response to Giordano's suggestion, I also mentioned the possibility that if Switzerland were to open the door to 'religious and archaic special rights' for Muslims, then other non-Muslim migrant groups would start to demand the same treatment. This possibility, as I learned later, has started to become a reality in the UK. Gita Sahgal, the director of the Centre for Secular Space and the founder of Women against Fundamentalism, explained to me that leaders of some segments of British Hindu and Sikh groups see what the British Muslims are doing, and they want the same thing: 'Already there are informal caste councils, which make decisions about all sorts of decisions of forced marriage, marriage, divorce [and] custody.'[10]

Third, I have pinpointed a common feature in the mindset of those supporting the introduction of parallel religious legal jurisdictions within a Western context, the so-called 'Winnetou Syndrome'.

Winnetou is a fictional Native American hero of several novels (later adapted to films) written in German by Karl May (1842–1912). The novels became best sellers partly because of their romantic portrait of an imagined simpler life in close contact with nature. This romantic perception of other cultures seems to me very dominant in the essentialists' paradigm; it leads them to fear they might offend those noble others and impose their own laws and values on them. The argument seems to be that we cannot force our own values on immigrants from distant cultures.

At the time of my response, I thought that behind the façade of seeming tolerance was an arrogance that reveals a sense of superiority. Today, I am less harsh in my judgement. Today what I see more clearly is the white man's (and woman's) guilt and the burden of a legacy of colonisation. I see a sincere fear of offending what people perceive as the 'other': persons they obviously do not understand. I also see a real belief that this other is different and thus should be treated differently. Hence the Winnetou Syndrome, an expression used by Thomas Kessler, the former delegate for Migration and Integration Issues in Swiss Canton Basel-City. He said he experienced it when he was dealing with the issue of forced marriage in his canton: 'One wants to leave the noble savage as he is in a reservation for as [long as] possible.'[11]

In all my arguments I emphasise one crucial point: *Swiss law is exemplary in its respect for human/women's rights and gender justice.* This is important. We are talking about a law that guarantees the rights of women in family affairs, one that is based on universal human rights and the application of core United Nations human rights conventions. It took the Swiss a while to get to this point – the family law was changed in 1988 and women got the right to vote in 1971 – but today we can pride ourselves on this achievement.

This is not the case with Islamic law. It does not conform to international standards of human rights and too often its jurisprudence application (*fiqh* rulings) violates these very rights. So we are talking about two very different types of law: one that guarantees and protects rights and another that does not. My argument only holds when we have a law that respects universal human rights and citizens' rights, because the absurdity of the suggestion becomes clear once we compare the two types of law. Proponents of legal pluralism are calling to introduce a parallel legal system that in fact violates women's rights, and then to use it to legitimise systematic discrimination against women and children of different faiths. I will return to this point in detail in Chapter 4.

***

I am very conscious of the expression I am usir
It was not an arbitrary choice – it was deliberate. /
it, especially as I do recognise that many in some a
outraged to be called essentialists. How cou
perspective they vehemently oppose orientalist d
believe that they stand as the anti-thesis of essᴇ⟋⟋⟋
motivation is clearly protection – i.e. the protection of minorities, or ᴛʜᴇ
oppressed and certainly of Muslims.

But as much as I am convinced of their noble intentions, I insist that
some postmodern discourse did not lead to protection – rather to
violation. I use *essentialist* to describe this paradigm because of the prism
through which it sees the world. It:

1. Insists that a group of people have inherent unchanging
   characteristics because of their very religion or culture.
2. Ignores that any group is *constructed* through various political, social
   and religious factors.
3. Maintains that a person is first and foremost a religious entity and
   part of another religious whole.
4. Fails to see the complex different layers of identity – that a person
   may not subscribe to this religious identity in the first place.
5. Fails to see the dynamic nature of culture, religion, society and,
   certainly, identity.
6. Fears *imposing* what it perceives as 'Western' values on the 'other' and
   legitimises in the process grave human rights violations. Because it
   considers international standards of human rights to be 'Western'
   values not applicable to other societies or groups living in Western
   societies, it ingeniously plays to the hand of authoritarian
   governments and Islamist fundamentalists, who use similar
   discourse to legitimise their shameful record of human rights
   violations.
7. Ignores the developments and struggles taking place in Islamic
   countries to change family laws that discriminate against women and
   children, to demand states that are representative of all their citizens,
   and to insist on respect of freedom of expression, freedom of/from
   religion, and separation of religion and state. Because it considers
   these demands as universalistic, it dismisses them as not authentic

...ough. In other words, it designates itself as the arbitrator on who should speak on behalf of 'Muslims' and 'Minorities'.

Given the consequences of this paradigm, my objective here is to deconstruct this type of Western postmodern discourse and show how it paves the ground for a discourse of indifference — one that has grave consequences on the lives of many.

CHAPTER 1

A CRITICAL REVIEW OF THE ESSENTIALIST PARADIGM

As you may have noticed from the way I outlined my argument, I went through a journey of transformation, of learning and research, and through it I learned that what we are dealing with is not only one person's absurd suggestion.

Giordano's suggestion is the tip of an iceberg. It is an expression of a paradigm of thinking – I call it the Essentialist Paradigm – and it has four specific ideological features. The first is a combination of multiculturalism and legal pluralism in a social context. The second is group rights, the third is cultural relativism, and the fourth is the white man's burden.

First Feature: Combining Multiculturalism with Legal Pluralism in a Social Context

The very title of Giordano's article, 'Legal Pluralism: An Instrument for Multiculturalism', contains two important terms: *legal pluralism* and *multiculturalism*. When combined, they lead to a relativist approach to fundamental human rights and gender justice. The call to combine the two terms within a social context is one fundamental feature of the Essentialist Paradigm.

I tend, like Kenan Malik, a left-leaning, Indian-born English thinker, to distinguish between two types of multiculturalism. One type he calls the lived experience of diversity: 'the experience of living in a society that is less insular, more vibrant and more cosmopolitan.'[1]

This type I welcome and embrace. This type appreciates people with different roots and origins living together on a basis of mutual respect and acceptance. No one's origin, colour, race, religion or gender is seen as lesser than another's. We are equal by virtue of being humans. Full stop.

To use the words of Anne Phillips, the British Professor of Political and Gender Theory, it is a type of multiculturalism grounded in the rights of the individuals, not those of the groups.[2]

But it is the second type of multiculturalism that I criticise and find problematic. This is what Malik calls multiculturalism as a political process. The aim here is to manage that diversity, and as such it entails a set of policies that try to institutionalise diversity. This type puts people into ethnic and cultural boxes, defines individual needs and rights by virtue of the boxes people are in, and uses those boxes to shape policy.[3] This policy is implemented in Britain.

Similarly, when multiculturalism as a political process is combined with the policy of legal pluralism, it tends to divide people into boxes: of origin, culture, religion and, ultimately, gender. It sets them apart, and places them into parallel legal enclaves. Each enclave is governed by a different set of rules: rules that may or may not subscribe to the same notions of law and justice dominant in the larger society. As a result, people are not defined as individual members of a larger society or a nation that applies the same rules and laws to all of its members. Instead they are defined primarily as members of a cultural or religious group. Each group has innate and essential cultural features that demand special treatment and hence special laws for it to survive. This last aspect is often referred to as group rights.

Second Feature: Group Rights

The notion of group rights is a second feature of the Essentialist Paradigm, a notion famously espoused by the father of legal pluralism, the Canadian philosopher Charles Taylor. I am aware that other philosophers and scholars have influenced the discourse on group rights. I am using his work as an example especially as his idea of the politics of recognition, introduced in his edited volume, *Multiculturalism: Examining the Politics of Recognition*, has permeated much of the thinking by proponents of legal pluralism. He, too, refers to the politics of multiculturalism. But he refers to it in terms of the demands that minority or subaltern groups make for recognition:

> The demand for recognition in these latter cases is given urgency by the supposed links between recognitions and identity, where the latter term designates something like a person's understanding of who they are, of their fundamental defining characteristics as a human being. The thesis is that our identity is partly shaped by recognition or its absences, often by the *mis*recognition of others, and so a person or group of people can suffer real damage, real distortion, if the people or society around them mirror back to them a confining or demeaning or contemptible picture of themselves. Nonrecognition or misrecognition can inflict harm, can be a form of oppression, imprisoning someone in a false, distorted, and reduced mode of being.[4] [emphasis in original]

Taylor uses several examples to explain his idea. He says that black people have suffered in white societies that projected a demeaning image of them – and that some black people have internalised that image. Similarly, women in particular societies have been induced to adopt an image of themselves as inferior and have internalised an image of their own inferiority. The self-depreciation of both groups becomes one of the most potent instruments of their own oppression. Therefore they must purge themselves of this imposed and destructive identity. Taylor says that a society's misrecognition of these groups' identities is not only a failure to give them the respect they are due. It also inflicts harm and grievous wounds that saddle the victims with crippling self-hatred: 'Due recognition is not just a courtesy we owe people. It is a vital human need.'[5]

Society may indeed project a demeaning picture on an individual by virtue of their colour, gender and/or religion, but the process is complicated and not as straightforward as Taylor describes.

I will give a personal example to illustrate this point.

I still remember how I felt when I came to Switzerland 21 years ago. Suddenly I was very conscious of my colour. I am an Arab, with Yemeni and Egyptian roots, and never before had I given a second thought to my colour, a bronze or light brown. In fact, I felt pride in my looks. You may consider it strange to read the word 'pride'. But I was raised in a loving family, one that gave me the feeling that I am both precious and beautiful. This feeling remained with me when I moved to Washington, DC, with a Fulbright scholarship, to pursue a master's degree. There I lived in a multicultural context and felt very much appreciated. I also realised that my colour, among other features, made me somehow 'exotic', which made me very popular as a young single woman.

In Switzerland it was not a matter of not being appreciated that made me feel conscious of my colour. My husband and I tended to live and socialise with Swiss people like us: educated people with professions that brought them in direct contact with the outside world. Our neighbours of nearly two decades are open and embracing. With some I nurture close and warm relationships. So the issue was not appreciation. Rather, what made me conscious of my colour was the feeling that I stood out among the others because of it. So what made me feel different was not an actual demeaning picture projected to me by society, but the fact of being 'coloured' in an all-white society. It took me a while to address this feeling of being uneasy about my colour: to recognise its roots, to internalise the knowledge that 'being different' does not mean 'being lesser', and to finally come to the conviction, yet again, that this is my colour, and it is beautiful.

By the same token, as a girl living in a Yemeni social context, some people tried to give me the impression that I was 'an inferior being' and 'should behave as other girls do.' It goes without saying that I was not behaving as they thought I should.

I said before that I was raised in a loving family. Both of my parents loved and respected me. More important, especially in North Yemen's patriarchal and tribal context, I had a father who did not subscribe to the notion that a girl has less worth than a boy. That was not a given; my father only came to that conclusion through a personal journey of education and growth. His education and then travels as a diplomat were certainly instrumental in this process. It was he who always gave me the feeling that I am a free person, and independent, and that I can strive to be whatever I want to be. This conviction was reflected in the way I was raised and in the fact that I was allowed to do things that other girls on his side of the family did not do.

The safe haven of my family sharply contradicted some of the messages I received from the wider society. I vividly remember an incident when I was 11, walking on the outskirts of our neighbourhood. A group of young boys started to throw stones at me, calling me a 'whore', because I was wearing trousers and did not cover my hair. These boys were conveying a message they had internalised from their own family and societal context: girls wear a headscarf and later they wear a *sharshaf*, the two pieces of black cloth that cover the woman from head to toe, complemented with another one that hides the face. And any girl who does not wear the headscarf and then the *sharshaf* is not a 'proper' girl. I can assume that their using the word 'whore' was an expression of their childish conviction of that message.

Despite the pain I felt from this incident, please notice that I deliberately used the word 'some' when I referred to the messages I received from the wider society. This is important because while some of these messages were negative – and very negative as in the incident above – others were positive, and still others were neutral. My family socialised with groups of families who shared the same norms about perceptions of girls and their rights. From this group I received the message of acceptance. Being a girl was not a source of shame or a burden. My father's side of the family, on the other hand, had learned to accept my 'otherness' in a way that made their message 'neutral': 'You may not subscribe to the way we believe girls should behave in our societal context, but we accept you.'

So I do agree with Taylor that sometimes society may project a demeaning image on the individual, but I also tend to see the situation as more complex. Society is not homogeneous; it is complex and often made up of subgroups. The message I was getting from the wider society was likewise not homogeneous or static, and it changed according to the subgroups within which I was socialising.

Most important, sometimes a religious, gender or cultural identity can be imposed on a person, even if that person does not perceive himself/herself as such. Consider the person who is called a Muslim, 'perceived' as a Muslim and 'treated' as a Muslim, despite the fact that this person may not be religious at all or may prefer to be called and identified by his or her nationality. Here in Switzerland I want to be perceived as a citizen, a Swiss person with Arab origins. After all, that is what we do with other people of other religions; we identify them by their nationalities, not their religion. So why insist on reducing me to a religious identity?

This does not seem to be the argument of Charles Taylor. And just as he considers the message of the overall society to be homogeneous, he tends to see identity and with it culture and society as something static, something that does not change – a whole that has inherent and given traits.

Identity to him is 'who we are, where we are coming from,' and thus 'the background against which our tastes and desires and opinions and aspirations make sense.' But in his paradigm, identity does not exist in a vacuum. It is very much intertwined with the concept of what he calls *authenticity*: 'There is a certain way of being human that is *my* way. I am called upon to live my life in this way and not in imitation of anyone else's life.'[6] This 'notion gives importance to being true to myself. If I am not, I miss the point of my life; I miss what being human is for *me*.'[7] [emphasis in original]

This notion of authentic identity has given rise to what he calls the 'politics of difference', making distinctions the basis of differential treatment:

> The aim is to cherish distinctness, not just now but forever. After all, if we are concerned with identity, then what is more legitimate than one's aspiration that it never be lost?[8]

Cherishing distinctions requires introducing policies of 'collective goals' designed for 'cultural survival'. He insists that a society with strong collective goals can still be liberal, if it is 'also capable of respecting diversity, especially when dealing with those who do not share its common goals; and provided it can offer adequate safeguards for fundamental rights.'[9]

Fundamental rights aside, Taylor considers it quite possible that the rights of individuals will be restricted if the state focuses on safeguarding the collective goals; he also acknowledges that the pursuit of the collective end will probably involve treating insiders and outsiders differently.

***

Charles Taylor's concept of identity is not concerned with identity at the individual level. He focuses on the collective identity of a cultural group. This cultural group may be aboriginal bands or French Canadians, especially Quebeckers. It could also be a group designated by its gender, for example women. It could be a religious group, like the Muslims. His main motivation in describing the politics of recognition and hence difference is the fear of 'imposing' a hegemonic culture on the culture of a minority. Taylor's aim, and this should be emphasised, is to protect and safeguard minority rights, and to insure they are not violated. So from this perspective his aim is certainly noble.

The problem lies in his attempt to ensure that the collective identity of a cultural group can survive. Here he falls into an essentialist trap: focusing on the authentic identity of a cultural group assumes that it has fundamental unchangeable traits. This assumption ignores the fact that cultures do change, that they are not static. What we yesterday considered to be part of our cultural norms and identity may today look quite abhorrent.

In addition, minority groups are not homogeneous, as he assumes. They do not represent one cultural block with similar and standardised features and traits. Often members of minority groups have a complex set of identities that they express differently in different settings. Taylor also ignores the power structures within minority groups, which further complicate matters, especially when some claim to be representatives of a certain cultural group and with it assume the right to define what is the authentic identity of their group and what is not.

Taylor was trying to protect a certain right for particular groups of people, but his effort led to a mess. Why do I use the word mess? Because when we propagate the concept of group rights, we also justify the violation of human rights within minority groups as an expression of different cultural concepts of rights and justice. Women's rights have been violated with impunity on this very ground. In fact, this very argument is being espoused on the international level by oppressive tyrannical regimes. So the consequences of propagating this model are felt not only on the national level but also on the international level.

Culture does change. If you have forgotten, let me remind you.

Consider the fact that between 1877 and the mid 1960s, the Jim Crow caste system was quite acceptable in Southern states of the United States. The system treated Blacks as a degenerate caste and second-class citizens; it excluded them from public transport and public facilities, from serving on juries, and from entering certain jobs and neighbourhoods. And it severely regulated social interactions between the races. During that period it was quite normal to have separate hospitals, prisons, schools, churches, cemeteries, and public accommodations for Blacks and Whites. These laws and policies were sustained and supported by a whole range of religious, educational and 'scientific' discourses. The mainstream Christian interpretation at the time taught that 'whites were the Chosen people, blacks were cursed to be servants, and God supported racial segregation.'[10] Scientists (craniologists, eugenicists, phrenologists, and Social Darwinists) at every educational level bolstered the belief that Blacks were innately inferior to Whites, intellectually and culturally. The media did their share by routinely referring to Blacks as 'niggers, coons, and darkies', and 'their articles reinforced anti-black stereotypes.'[11]

At the time both Blacks and Whites were governed by cultural norms on how they should interact. For instance, a black male could not offer his hand to shake hands with a white male, as such a gesture implied social equality. Under no circumstance was a black male to offer to light the cigarette of a white woman; this also implied intimacy, and any intimacy between a black man and a white woman could be punished by lynching.[12]

Fifty years ago, that culture of racial discrimination was quite acceptable in some Southern states. Many white people considered the Jim Crow caste system to be, in Taylor's words, 'who we are, where we are coming from'; as such, it was 'the background against which our tastes and desires and opinions and aspirations make sense.' When others began to demand changes in these laws – and thus in this element of the Southern way of life – white people perceived these demands as tantamount to imposing an 'imitation of anyone else's life' and corrupting a 'certain way of being human that is my way.'[13]

I know I am being provocative here. But if we are to take Taylor's argument about authenticity, identity, and culture at face value, that would mean that the white people in the Southern states were, and perhaps still are, 'born racist'. That was the 'way they are'. Racism and the belief that they are superior to Blacks was 'inherent in the way they give meaning to their lives' and as such we should cherish their 'distinctness, not just now but forever.' After all, 'that was their culture' – so should we therefore aspire to its 'survival'? How horrible would this argument have sounded?

But that is hardly true, right? People are not born racists. They are made to be racists. They are made racists by a whole range of institutions, including those of religion, science, the media, and education. These institutions and their discourses supported and maintained the Jim Crow system of racial discrimination. I mentioned them deliberately, because cultures do not function in a void. They may be sustained or altered depending on the contexts they are operating within and the systems that maintain them. Therefore it was no coincidence that once men and women, black and white, from Southern as well as Northern states, started to tackle and then oppose the intellectual foundations of discrimination, the culture of the caste system started to fall apart, and with it the norms that sustained it.

What holds true for the 'hegemonic' culture applies as well for the 'minority' culture: minority culture does change and it does not function in a void. It can be sustained or altered depending on the context it is operating within and the systems that maintain it. This idea will become clearer in Chapters 2 and 5 where I discuss the Pakistani and Bangladeshi South Asian communities in the United Kingdom, later dubbed Muslim communities.

Moreover, a minority group is not homogeneous. It does not represent one cultural block with similar and standardised features and traits. The diversity within a minority group comes to expression in different forms, on an individual level as well as the group level.

Consider the example of a young woman I met in London in January 2013 during a meeting with members of a small LGBT Muslim support group called Imaan, which means faith in Arabic.[14]

She is of South Asian heritage, an atheist and a lesbian, and she wears a headscarf-veil. I will call her Leila. She wears the headscarf because of community pressure in her neighbourhood in Birmingham. She does not want to wear it but she lives in a closed community, where breaking the imposed rules would cause harm to her and her family. So she takes the easy way out and wears it. However, wearing it immediately puts her into a religious box: Muslim. Her appearance as a woman with a headscarf transforms her from a woman into a Muslim woman, and usually a Muslim woman is a religious person. But she is an atheist. The larger society is unable to see this part of her. If she wears the veil, then she must be a believer. It goes without saying that her belief, or rather her lack thereof, is a secret she keeps to herself within her community.

On top of that she is a lesbian. How does this fit within the prism of our ethnic boxes? She does not fit into any of the cultural or ethnic boxes that we would like to place her in: not within her community that imposes its values on its members, nor within the larger society. She is a complex person with various identities. Yet all we will see as we look at her is a religious identity that she does not believe in.

On an individual level, then, an ethnic or a religious box often cannot describe a person for two reasons: because a given person has various identities, and because being a member of a religious group does not automatically make that person religious or a part of the group.

Moreover, on a group level, a minority is not homogeneous. Consider the Muslim community (singular) in Britain. In the 1960s these people were called South Asian communities (plural). They included waves of migrants from Pakistan, India and Bangladesh. Within these national groupings, they were still diverse in their religious denominations and ethnic backgrounds. At that time, as many interviewees told me, you would be hard pressed to find a woman wearing a veil, let alone a burka. At that time, they identified themselves by their nationalities and sometimes by their regional affiliation, such as coming from Mirpur, a district and one of the largest cities in Pakistan's Kashmir region. They may have practised their religion but it was not the prism through which they interacted with the world. It was not the mantle they carried around with them. Their religion was not the identity they stressed.

For reasons that I will explain in Chapters 2 and 5, Britain inaugurated a multicultural policy that in reality imposed a religious identity on communities (plural) and inadvertently facilitated the creation of the Muslim community (singular): an invented community, not an imagined one, to use Benedict Anderson's term. As the government created this invented community, it was not to celebrate diversity within a British context. Instead, a group of loud Islamists was elevated to become the chosen 'community leaders'. They did not represent the majority within their communities. Several people I interviewed, people knowledgeable about Islamism and extremism in Britain, emphasised this point. The 'community' did not choose these so-called leaders, nor did the leaders, at the time, enjoy the support of the members. Their demands reflected their own political agenda: spreading their line of political Islamism. But by elevating them to this status, the government placed them in a position to define their group's cultural and religious needs. They were the gatekeepers of the 'Muslim minority'.

The money, resources and support they received from the British government, in addition to those flowing from Gulf states, helped them create a plethora of educational, religious and charity institutions. Now they had the tools to spread their line of Islamism among members of their communities. Most important, they helped create what I call closed communities, with patriarchal power structures that exercise social control over their members and intimidate those who reject their designated social rules. Closed communities like the one Leila is living in. She wears a veil not because she wants to, but because she has to. She does not dare to come out as either a lesbian or an atheist because she knows that she will be made to pay dearly for such an act of rebellion against the way a proper Muslim woman is supposed to behave.

I am quite certain that Taylor did not know where his ideas would take him. He said it was possible that the rights of individuals would be restricted by the state's aim of safeguarding collective goals, but he did not expect that people would either invent a community or violate its members' fundamental human rights. But sadly, that is exactly the outcome of his theoretical approach, one that ignores the political and social contexts of what it describes. It simply suggests an idea void of its context, in the process ignoring the mechanisms and institutions that either sustain them or alter them. This brings me to the third feature of the Essentialist Paradigm: cultural relativism.

Third Feature: Cultural Relativism

Cultural relativism has become an ingrained feature of the Essentialist Paradigm. In his article Charles Taylor suggested that we approach the study of certain cultures with a presumption about their value. His premise is that we owe 'equal respect to all cultures' and this should be a 'starting hypothesis with which we ought to approach the study of any other culture.' He states that withholding the presumption might be seen as the fruit merely of prejudice or of ill-will. It might even be 'tantamount to a denial of equal status.'

Doing so, he says, is a logical extension of the politics of dignity: 'Just as all must have equal civil rights, and equal voting rights, regardless of race or culture, so all should enjoy the presumption that their traditional culture has value.'[15]

When I read this part of Taylor's chapter, its formulation unsettled me. But I was mostly startled at myself. I certainly agree that we should respect all cultures equally. But then I realised that in fact I have a problem with his point. While I do support the demand that we treat *individuals* from other cultures with respect and on a basis of equal value and dignity, I believe that studying or approaching *a culture* should not entail the same treatment. Yes, I will treat the subject of my study with respect, but I will refrain from placing a value on it before I study it and see what it means for people's lives within its social and political context. Then, when I understand all that, I will dare to make a judgement.

Consider the traditional custom of the 'twin curse' in Madagascar. In the town of Mananjary, on the isolated east coast of Madagascar, a set of taboos, handed down across many generations, controls the lives of tribe members. These rules are implemented and kept alive by tribal chiefs, or kings. One of these taboos says that twins are considered a curse, an abomination, because they bring terrible misfortune, even death. If a woman gives birth to twins, she is expected to abandon them. If she refuses, she will be ostracised by the community and forced to flee her home and village. In the past, newborn twins were left to die in the bush. Today, most are still abandoned. But several mothers have dared to resist this taboo and are living together in what the Channel 4 reporter Kiki King called a 'twin refugee camp'.[16]

As a social scientist, how should I approach this custom? I can explain the custom, its historical roots, its context, its system of values, and of course the power structures that sustain it: the tribal chiefs are the ones who enforce these taboos, and are believed to be able to communicate with dead ancestors and have their permission to change the taboos. I will certainly do all that. But should I also say that I value the custom? Frankly, I do not. I do not value this practice or the cultural norms that produced it because it leads people to abandon newborn babies, who then die. Here I will dare to make a judgement. But I will only make the judgement once I see its consequences. I will say it is a harmful practice that violates a basic and fundamental human right.

Please notice that I am not assuming a hegemonic ethnocentric position that looks down on others. I am just stating that there are many cultural practices that are harmful and are done in the name of religion, culture and tradition. The harm they cause is the reason I judge them. It is their consequences that matter.

These consequences do not seem to concern proponents of the Essentialist Paradigm. Group rights are often intertwined with two versions of cultural relativism: strong and weak cultural relativism. The strong cultural relativists hold that 'culture is the *principal* source of the validity of a moral right or rule [...] the presumption is that rights (and other social practices, values, and moral rules) are culturally determined.'[17] The weak cultural relativists, on the other hand, assert that 'culture may be an *important* source of the validity of a moral right or rule. Universality is initially presumed, but the relativity of human nature, communities, and rights serves as a check on potential excesses of universalism.'[18]

Both versions of cultural relativism permeate the demands for group rights and with them legal pluralism. In fact, Giordano's argument included both versions at the same time: On the one hand, he does not expect Muslims to abide by Swiss legal tradition because the *cultural distance* is too huge. On the other hand, he insists that universal human rights should not be violated when Islamic law is applied in civil matters. This double demand is hard to fulfil.

Again, it is the consequences that matter. By simultaneously promoting the concept of group rights and a cultural relativist approach to rights and dignity, the essentialists have justified human rights violations within minority groups and by authoritarian regimes – as an expression of different cultural concepts of rights and justice.

The ramifications, while dire, threaten to undermine human rights on an international scale. Consider the resolution spearheaded by Russia and passed by the United Nations Human Rights Council in September of 2012. It calls for 'promoting human rights and fundamental freedoms through a better understanding of traditional values of mankind'; it demands a survey of best traditional practices, and declares that 'all cultures and civilisations in their traditions, customs, religions and beliefs share a common set of values.'[19] When I read that resolution I realised why I had a problem with Taylor's demand that all cultures have equal status.

The significance of this resolution was not lost on Human Rights Watch. In fact, it prefaced its 2013 *Human Rights Report* with an article titled 'The Trouble with Tradition: When Values Trample over Rights'. It warns of the dangers of invoking:

a single, supposedly agreed-upon value system that steamrolls over diversity, ignores the dynamic nature of traditional practice and customary laws, and undermines decades of rights-respecting progress for women and members of the lesbian, gay, bisexual, and transgender (LGBT) communities, among others.[20]

Significantly, the article argues, traditional values can be 'corrupted, serving as a handy tool for governments in the business of repression.' Simply put, tradition, culture and religion have been used to undermine human rights in authoritarian regimes.

Examples are plentiful.

Consider Iran. It has often used a discourse of cultural relativism on human rights in its relationships with international human rights bodies and has asserted the right to cultural exceptionalism, invoking 'authentic cultural and religious' justifications for its shameful human rights record. The 1995 statement by the Iranian representative to the Commission on Human Rights illustrates its argument clearly:

> The Commission on Human Rights and other UN organs give no consideration to religious values; it can even be said that there takes place, under various excuses, a kind of struggle against religious values and beliefs. They do not take moral precepts seriously. Nor do they seriously consider the possibility of placing limitations on the individual's liberty for the sake of proper moral necessities that are also considered in the Universal Declaration of Human Rights (Article 29–2). No government would ever be reproached for providing unlimited liberties that are against moral precepts and correct religious values. However, if a government establishes limitations on its citizens for the sake of the protection of public morality, it will be questioned and blamed in UN resolutions.[21]

Iran may claim it protects 'public morality and correct religious values,' but Reza Afshari, who documented Iran's discourse on human rights and its actual record of violations in his authoritative study *Human Rights in Iran: The Abuse of Cultural Relativism,* showed convincingly that the issue is not about 'Islam as a private faith of individuals.' Instead, it is 'what state officials claiming Islamic authority might have to say about the state's treatment of citizens.'[22]

Researching Iranian government documents, human rights records and archives of the United Nations, he provided ample evidence that Iran has behaved as a remarkably authoritarian government in its human rights abuses: it has systematically jailed, tortured and executed dissidents without due process of law and has assassinated political opponents outside state borders and often defended these acts as 'authentic cultural practices.'

'Authentic cultural practices' and 'correct religious values' sound quite hollow in the face of the persecution endured by Iran's Baha'i minority – the largest non-Muslim minority in Iran. Since they are not recognised, and hence do not exist officially, estimates of their numbers vary from 150,000 to 500,000. The Baha'i religion, a monotheistic faith, originated in Shiraz in 1840, but is deemed in Iran to be a 'false' revelation and its followers are treated as apostates.

They are persecuted in a way that aims to destroy the conditions they need to survive as a community; individuals are attacked on all possible grounds and in all spheres of public life. Oppression includes execution, torture, arbitrary imprisonment, denial of education and employment, arbitrary seizure of homes and possessions, confiscation of community assets, and seizure, desecration and destruction of holy places.[23]

The goal of the harassment and persecution is to get Baha'is to convert to Islam. One revealing document is an official letter sent by an Iranian authority to a Baha'i, who was denied his pension after the Islamic revolution:

> Based on the information received, you are Baha'i and therefore not entitled to a pension payment. However, should you convert to Islam and demonstrate remorse for having been a Baha'i and further provide this office with proof that you have embraced Islam, steps will be taken to restore pension payments to you.[24]

Certainly no one can justify depriving a citizen of his/her pension with the argument that doing so will protect 'public morality and authentic religious values.'

Saudi Arabia is another regime that uses religion as a tool to justify any policy the government chooses to follow – a tool of legitimisation that is hardly original. For example, Saudi authorities have cited religious teachings and cultural norms to deny women and girls the right to participate in sports activities: one religious leader called them 'steps of the devil' on the path to immorality.[25]

This violation of a girl's rights was cited in the 2013 Human Rights Watch report. But thanks to both international and internal pressure, the policy changed in April of 2014. Suddenly, after decades of insistence that Islamic teachings prohibit sport for girls, those teachings miraculously changed: the government cited a religious edict by a dead mufti to justify its change of course.[26] While the new policy is to be applauded, this example clearly illuminates how religion and culture are indeed utilised as tools of justification.

By the same token, Saudi authorities have often invoked religion to silence political criticism of their authoritarian style of governance. The apostasy case against Saudi blogger and intellectual Raif Badawi is a famous example. In 2006, he created the Saudi Liberal Network: a platform for serious discussions of liberal ideas, religious authorities and the Wahhabi interpretation of Islam in the Kingdom. As a result, he was imprisoned in June 2012, and is serving a ten-year sentence, which also includes 1000 lashes, a fine of US $266,631 and a ban on travelling and expressing himself in the media for ten years after he finishes his sentence. He was accused of apostasy and, using the words of the Jeddah Criminal Court, was found guilty of 'producing what would disturb public order, religious values and morals,' facilitating 'sin, aggression and insulting Muslims' sanctities' in addition to 'ridiculing Islamic religious figures.'[27] An international campaign is working for his release; I am involved in it.

Note that Badawi never renounced his religion. Choosing, or not choosing, one's religion is a fundamental human right. But the issue here goes beyond the violation of this right: it is the strategy of the Saudi authorities to accuse any opposition figure of apostasy as a way to delegitimise him or her. Amnesty International called his sentence 'outrageous', and described him as a prisoner of conscience who is guilty of nothing more than daring to create a public forum for discussion and peacefully exercising the right to freedom of expression.[28]

***

Nowadays, countries like Iran and Saudi Arabia turn to traditional values, culture and religion to justify their human rights abuses and oppression. It might come as a surprise that in the mid-twentieth century it was the colonial powers that used the strategy of cultural relativism to deny that human rights are universal. As Iran and Saudi Arabia do today, they used it to justify violating the rights of citizens in their colonies.

Indeed, in the early 1950s, cultural relativism was mainly driven by the imperial powers and was strongly opposed by the delegates of the few developing countries then included in the United Nations. So it was the exact opposite of what academic proponents of cultural relativism hold as orthodoxy. This fact has been researched and documented by Roland Burke in his impressive book *Decolonization and the Evolution of International Human Rights*. He writes:

> In the opening years of the 1950s, cultural relativism was the language of the Western colonial powers, which resisted any attempt to extend human rights to their colonies. Diplomats from Great Britain, France, Belgium, and the Netherlands explained to the UN Third Committee why particular human rights treaties could not be applied to the colonies under their control. René Cassin, a Nobel laureate [. . .] exemplified this tendency when he complained during a 1950 debate on human rights covenants that it would be improper to subject 'countries inhabited by different peoples to uniform obligations' especially those 'at the lowest stage of development.' As the Belgian representative protested in October 1950, human rights were for advanced 'civilized' countries, not for Africans.[29]

Western colonial delegations attempted to evade their human rights obligations through a 'feigned reverence for the traditional culture of indigenous inhabitants.'[30]

This last observation is very important because it contradicts a major assumption of the Essentialist Paradigm: that human rights is an imposition of imperial powers. This brings me to the last feature of this paradigm.

Fourth Feature: The White Man's Burden

Earlier I said that Taylor's intentions were noble because his real motive was to protect the rights of minorities. This sense of justice is intertwined with a strong sense of guilt and shame: the burden of Western hegemony and the colonial past, i.e. the white man's burden.[31]

Taylor's text is clearly haunted by the white man's burden, and the two elements of desire to protect and sense of guilt come together when he justifies his notion of group rights, and equal recognition of the worth and value of different cultures:

> This brings us to the issue of multiculturalism as it is often debated today, which has a lot to do with the imposition of some cultures on others, and with the assumed superiority that powers this imposition. Western liberal societies are thought to be supremely guilty in this regard, partly because of their colonial past, and partly because of their marginalization of segments of their populations that stem from other cultures. It is in this context that the reply 'this is how we do things here' can seem crude and insensitive. Even if, in the nature of things, compromise is close to impossible here – one either forbids murder or allows it – the attitude presumed by the reply is seen as one of contempt. Often, in fact, this presumption is correct. Thus we arrive again at the issue of recognition.[32]

The combination of these two elements – the desire to protect the rights of minorities or people in former colonies, and the strong sense of shame and guilt over the Western colonial and imperial past and its conduct of politics – yields an assumption that underlies the Essentialist Paradigm: human rights is a Western enterprise and an imposition of the powerful.

And it is a Western construct with limited applicability, as Adamantia Pollis and Peter Schwab famously say in their 1979 edited book *Human Rights: Cultural and Ideological Perspectives*. To them human rights are not universal and efforts to impose these rights reflect a 'moral chauvinism and ethnocentric bias' and are 'bound to fail.' To them, doctrines of human rights as embodied in the Universal Declaration of Human Rights are not even relevant to societies with a non-Western cultural tradition or a socialist ideology; ironically, they include Spain, Portugal and Greece in their notion of non-Western countries. To these authors, economic, cultural and collective rights have had as much validity and legitimacy as individual civil and political rights.[33]

This is the mindset that pervades the Essentialist Paradigm. This mindset perceives the 'other' – whether a 'minority' or a 'Third World country' – as the 'oppressed', and sees human rights laws as 'tools' of the 'oppressor'. And the guilt, the burden of the Western colonial past and current imperialism, serves as the motivation to unshackle these minorities or cultures from Western hegemony. Looked at from their perspective, it is a fight, a struggle, and they are standing on the side of the oppressed against the Western oppressor.

Intrinsic to this mindset is the idea of authenticity and the question of who can serve as an authentic representative of the 'other'.

Pollis and Schwab had the audacity to categorically dismiss human rights as elitist and those who defend these values as Westernised: 'the Western–based notions of human rights, to the extent that they are articulated by third world political elites, reflect these elites' Westernisation. It cannot be assumed that the mass of people hold these concepts.'[34]

Taylor does the same thing, but more subtly, as he refers to Frantz Fanon's novel *Les Damnés de la Terre* (Wretched of the Earth). In it Fanon argued that the 'major weapon of the colonisers was the imposition of their image of the colonised on the subjugated people. These latter, in order to be free, must first of all purge themselves of these depreciating self-images.' This leads, Taylor says, to 'a struggle for a changed self-image, which takes place both within the subjugated and against the dominator.'[35]

Noble intentions aside, the essentialist mindset inadvertently articulates an ethnocentric obsession with their own 'self': the Western self. Ethnocentrism is a double-edged sword. Those on one edge see the world through the prism of racism. But that is not the prism of the essentialists. What they represent is the other edge, a state of mind so haunted by their preoccupations with themselves and their short-comings that they fail to see other people's hopes, aspirations and demands separately from their own.

Furthermore, the essentialist mindset borders on arrogance, if not superiority: essentialists assume that they know better than others about the needs of developing countries, and their cultures, and of ethnic minorities. On top of that they assume that they know who *should* represent these societies, someone who should fit their criteria for authenticity: a folkloric construct of an Indian native with a feather on his/her head. Just as their predecessors, the colonisers, treated the locals in their colonies as uncivilised people unable to decide for themselves, the essentialists do the same, though unintentionally: they assume that they know better what is best for the locals, treating those who contradict the prism of their paradigm as minors who do not know their own interests.

If the feature of the white man's burden was merely a theoretical academic discourse that is both ethnocentric and arrogant, I would not have minded. But it is not merely theoretical: this academic discourse has grave consequences. It has been used to justify both violations of basic human rights, and violence against women, minorities, LGBT persons and people with different political or ideological orientations.

The following two examples will illustrate my point.

Example one. In their heated attack against the imposition of Western values, and their insistence that human rights are not universal, Pollis and Schwab ended up providing a justification for totalitarianism. Focusing on colonies' need for economic development and a national identity, they excused nations that violated human rights with impunity:

> The conjunction of a traditional culture that defined the individual in terms of group membership, the need to transpose this group identity to the nation-state level, a definition of modernization in terms of economic development, and the evolution of the notion of a one-party state as the embodiment of the people facilitated the adoption of decrees limiting freedom of speech, the adoption of preventive detention laws, the outlawing of rival political parties, the placing of the judiciary under party control, and the incorporation of all voluntary associations under the rubric of one party. These actions were not viewed as antidemocratic but as requisites whereby ethnically diverse, extremely poor states could create the unified political framework essential for economic development. As Nkrumah and Nyerere often said, if political differences were permitted to rule the state the economy would be stymied as the unity necessary for development would be absent.[36]

Their use of economic rights in this context is very problematic: I do not see a choice between political rights and economic rights. In 1996, as part of a Swiss TV team documenting Yemen's water shortage, I met Amina, a woman living in a remote village on the outskirts of Taiz. For Amina, the freedoms of speech and association have no meaning. They are nonsense. For her, the priorities are water, food, health and education for her kids. A dignified life, based on economic rights.

But this does not deny the necessity to respect the freedoms of speech and association. Yemeni women like Arwa Othman and Amal Al-Basha, well-known civil and human rights activists, defend these rights because they guarantee their own protection from the tyranny of their government. They guarantee their ability to mobilise for transparency and good governance.

Nor do economic rights contradict the necessity of fair trials and prohibitions against torture. Feras Shamsan, a young Yemeni journalist, who was detained in an Egyptian police prison in 2014, knows quite well that these rights are neither superfluous nor theoretical.

Shamsan was detained for simply trying to stop a fight between two women arguing about Abdel Fattah Sissi, formerly Egypt's minister of defence and now its president. Shamsan was put in a small cell for 35 days with 30 other inmates. You can imagine the conditions within this cell. Actually, you cannot. He was forced to stand most of the time, was unable to spread his legs, and had to pay the strongest thugs in the cell to be given a space to sleep. Worse, along with his other activist inmates, he had to fight daily attempts by the thugs to rape the youngest and weakest among them. He was sandwiched between two forces: members of the Egyptian security apparatus, who interrogated him and threatened him with torture and rape if he did not cooperate; and a brutal power system within the cell ruled by criminal thugs.[37]

For Shamsan the absence of these rights means the difference between being raped and not being raped: nothing Western about that. For any detainees, whether they be American, Yemeni or Chinese, prison conditions that respect their dignity and rights are not discussions that can be postponed. For Othman and Al-Basha the absence of these rights means the difference between freedom and imprisonment. Again, nothing Western about that. For them, these are basic human rights for Westerners and non-Westerners alike, for all humans. For them the absence of these political rights is undemocratic.

That is not what Pollis and Schwab are telling us. They are saying that, by definition, if a population is African and poor, it will be necessary to violate its citizens' human rights. Dictatorship and authoritarian regimes are best suited to these developing countries because economic development takes precedence. It comes as no surprise that multiple authoritarian leaders have used the theoretical argument that Pollis and Schwab offer, from Marxist pan-African leaders like Ghana's Nkrumah, through the pan-Arab nationalist Jamal Abd al Naser in Egypt, to the military strongman Abdel Fattah Sissi in Egypt. All too often, these leaders failed to achieve either economic development or a democratic order that respects human rights.

This gross exploitation led Pollis to revisit her argument in 1996. Although she remained strongly convinced of the salience of her early claim that 'in many societies – Asia, Africa, Eastern Europe (including Russia), and the Middle East – the liberal doctrine of human rights does not speak to the people's world view',[38] she acknowledged that the 'cultural diversity argument often plays into the hands of the state and is used to rationalize the arbitrary exercise of power.'[39]

Example two. The idea of the white man's burden and the obsession with imperialism and Western hegemonic power have been often used to silence any voices that point out violence against women, minorities, LGBT persons and people with different political or ideological orientations.

Meredith Tax, an American writer and political activist and director of the Centre for Secular Space, expressed this eloquently in her book *Double Bind*:

> Any feminist in the UK or North America who raises issues of gender politics in Muslim-majority countries is likely to be called an orientalist [. . .] If she is white, she will be told she is colonialist; if she is a woman of colour or feminist from the Global South, she will be considered to lack authenticity. She will be accused of 'essentialising' political Islam and ignoring difference within it; of lacking nuance and failing to contextualise; of having internalised ideas of Western superiority; [. . .] of being traitor to her community and culture.[40]

Tax was quick to see the ramifications of this academic discourse, especially in the context of the US occupation of Iraq and the Iraqi insurgency.

The Iraqi insurgency includes groups allied with al-Qaeda. It is made up of Sunni militants who practice sectarian violence against the Shi'a; they plant bombs in marketplaces and civilian neighbourhoods, and enforce a reactionary code of behaviour in their zealous attempt to impose an Islamic state.

Although Iraqi leftists and feminists oppose the Iraqi insurgency, left-wing academics and some anti-war coalitions in the North have endorsed it on the basis that it is fighting foreign invasion and imperialism.

Yet the insurgency has mainly directed its violence at its own people, and less at the US, targeting women in particular. The atrocities committed by the Iraqi insurgency were made clear by Anissa Hélie, a feminist scholar with Algerian roots and the former coordinator of Women Living Under Muslim Laws. In 2005, she wrote:

> For example, an extremist group in Iraq called Mujahideen Shura (council of fighters) warned it would kill any woman who is seen unveiled on the street. The recent case of Zeena Al Qushtaini has shown this is not an empty threat. Zeena, a woman's rights activist and businesswoman known for wearing 'Western' clothing, was kidnapped and executed by Jamaat al Tawhid wa'l Jihad, another armed Islamist group. Her body was found wrapped in the traditional abaya, which she had refused to wear when she was alive. Pinned to the abaya was a message: 'She was a collaborator against Islam'. Muslim extremists have already moved on to assassinating male and female hairdressers whom they accuse of promoting 'Western' fashion. They also specifically target trade union leaders as well as gays and lesbians. Religious minorities are also under attack, such as Christians in the Northern city of Mosul where women from the Christian community were singled out in a rape campaign.[41]

These atrocities targeting a wide range of Iraqis – women, minorities, hairdressers and trade union leaders as well as gays and lesbians – were swept aside by Corinna Mullin, a lecturer at the School of Oriental and African Studies, as she responded to Anissa Hélie's text. Her argument embodies the essentialists' obsession with imperialism:

> It is unclear if Hélie's problem lies with armed resistance, in general, or specifically, with armed resistance carried out by people

who hold different beliefs to her own. She is certainly right that there 'are plenty of unarmed civilians, as well as groups of every political affiliation, that reject the US occupation yet do not engage in violence or human rights violations' as there were in the Algerian independence war, which she references. But as Hélie may also recall, the issue of indiscriminate attacks, or 'terrorism', was also criticised by many on the European left during that time who, like Hélie, were also weary of the 'by any means necessary' argument, perhaps because they didn't understand the nature of asymmetric warfare and/or had little experience with the type of desperation that is born out of the exploitative and brutal conditions engendered by colonialism/occupation [...] Granted, the sectarian violence is somewhat different in nature, but still it is an issue that must be seen, like 'terrorism', within the context of colonialism/neo-colonialism and occupation.[42]

Killing civilians for choosing their own dress code, for working as hairdressers, for being Christians, Jews or Yazidis, for being labour union leaders, for being lesbian or gay: killing these people cannot be justified under any circumstances. Using colonialism/neo-colonialism and occupation to intellectually justify such atrocities at an academic conference is to me beyond comprehension. But that is the point − is it not? It is just an academic discussion for those arguing for an understanding of such atrocities. But if these academics or their families were to be targeted by such attacks, it would immediately cease to be theoretical. The pain and horror would make such a discussion shameful. The consequences would become crystal clear.

Again, it is the consequences that matter.

It is worth mentioning here that human rights violations have both individual and collective impacts. The dichotomy of the individual versus group that is intrinsic to the Essentialist Paradigm is irrelevant here. Each affects the other.

As I mentioned above, Raif Badawi is spending ten years in prison: deprived of his freedom and his ability to see his wife and three children. Once out of prison he faces ten more years of a ban on travel or interacting with the media in any form, including writing and speaking. He and his family feel the impact when his right to expression is violated. But Raif Badawi is only one person among many prisoners of conscience in Saudi Arabia and the Gulf Region. According to the Gulf Forum for Civil Societies, around 40,000 prisoners of conscience are held in the prisons of the six gulf countries, most of them in Saudi Arabia and Bahrain. The majority of these prisoners are writers, doctors, political activists, etc.[43] The plight that affects each one of them mirrors a climate of fear and terror prevalent in these societies, and testifies to the despotic nature and abuse of power of their regimes.

***

As I said at the start, Giordano's argument represents just the tip of an iceberg; the paradigm that lies below it has dominated the post-colonial, post-modernist discourses for far too long.

It combines multiculturalism as a political process with the policy of legal pluralism, dividing people along cultural, religious and ethnic lines, setting them apart, and placing them in parallel legal enclaves. It perceives rights from a group perspective – the group has the rights, not the individuals within it – and it insists that each group has a collective identity and culture, an essential identity and culture, which should be protected and perpetuated even if doing so violates the rights of individuals within the group. It is dominated by a cultural relativist approach to rights, and argues that rights – and other social practices, values and moral rules – are culturally determined. And it is very much haunted by a white man's burden, one that is formed by a strong sense of shame and guilt over the Western colonial and imperial past and a paternalistic desire to protect minorities or people from former colonies. It is a mindset that perceives the other, whether a member of a minority group or an entire developing country, as the oppressed, and human rights as the tools imposed by the Western oppressor. It considers that those who are fighting for universal human rights in their own societies are not authentic representatives of their own countries, and in the process it ignores or justifies dire human rights violations committed in the name of group rights or cultural and religious rights.

It is the Essentialist Paradigm.

We see its footprints not only in academic circles, but also in the way policies are suggested and made. One example is Giordano's suggestion to introduce weak legal pluralism into the Swiss legal system and, with it, Islamic law to regulate the affairs of the Muslim minority.

CHAPTER 2

ISLAMIC LAW IN THE WEST: THE CASE OF BRITAIN

The essentialists' way of thinking lies at the heart of the call to introduce aspects of Islamic law into Western legal systems.

Proponents of this idea often point to Britain as a model to emulate. Giordano did not mention it explicitly; he only alluded to a lecture by the former archbishop of Canterbury, titled 'Civil and religious law in England'. Giordano argued that people rarely mentioned the possibility of officially recognising certain forms of legal pluralism – until Dr Rowan Williams made his famous speech in 2008 and suggested 'integrating elements and mechanisms of Islamic law into British Common Law.'[1]

In the controversy that ensued here in Switzerland after Giordano's article and statements, a leading legal expert interviewed on Swiss television referred to the British case as the existing example of this type of 'weak legal pluralism'. But note that she was not condoning it, merely referring to it.[2]

John R. Bowen, an American anthropologist and a proponent of weak legal pluralism who has written extensively on it, has often defended the British system and its shari'a councils, portraying it in a positive light:

Of all Western countries, Britain has the most developed set of institutions for Islamic dispute mediation. Muslims can find Islamic tribunals in London, Birmingham, and elsewhere. The four or five major tribunals provide downloadable forms on their Websites, charge set fees for service, and meet on scheduled days of the month. Most of them offer only non-binding mediation. Each has its own characteristics: for example, the council in Birmingham's Central Mosque is led by women.[3]

I will not dwell here on what he said. Suffice to say at this point that the last sentence was not totally accurate. The tribunal at Birmingham's Central Mosque is not led by women. It had two women, now one, in its panel – a commendable development especially in light of the traditional domination of all male councils – but that is not the same as being led by women.

But his key point is well taken: Britain is the example in the Western context. The fact that it was repeatedly mentioned at conferences and in the literature made me decide to research the British case. So I went to Islamic shari'a councils and Muslim arbitration tribunals in various British cities, and met their leading sheikhs, including the only woman on their panels. I also interviewed experts and lawyers, and activists in civil society and women's rights groups, especially from within the Muslim communities, in addition to politicians who are pleading for a reform of this 'model'.

Again I am getting ahead of myself. Right now, what is important to emphasise is one point. The British case has all the ingredients of the essentialists' paradigm: A multicultural context, cultural relativism, and group rights, all intertwined with the use of the white man's burden to justify policies that treat citizens of different national roots as ethnic groups.

Immigration, Racism and Plural Monoculturalism

Immigration is the context within which calls to introduce aspects of Islamic Law in Western legal systems developed. Waves of immigrants moved to Europe and North America for various reasons: they were helping rebuild a Europe ruined by war, they were citizens of earlier colonies or EU citizens now allowed free movement, or they were driven there by economic problems, civil wars and political upheavals.

The immigrants we are interested in here are people in Britain not of European Union nationalities, especially South Asians. They came to Britain under the British Nationality Act of 1948, which guaranteed all citizens of the Commonwealth the right to enter the country.

The open borders policy was neither a sign of a sincere welcome to 'non-white' migrants nor a response to the post-war labour shortage. Laura Muchowieck argues that Britain's source of foreign workers was Europe, not its former colonies. Under the labour scheme called European Volunteer Worker, more than 350,000 Europeans, mainly Poles, were allowed to enter the country's labour market on the same terms as British workers after just three years of residence. A similar scheme for 'non-white' immigrants was simply out of the question. To use the words of the Ministry of Labour, it was rejected because of 'the serious implications that the introduction of *other races* into the labour force would have.'[4] Instead, what drove the Nationality Act was political considerations about British foreign policy, which placed a priority on good relations with the Old Commonwealth. This pattern has repeated itself over and over again in British internal policies, especially with regard to policies concerning 'Muslims': the needs of foreign policy often took precedence.

In any case, the Commonwealth Immigration Act of 1962 effectively put an end to the unrestricted movement and settlement of Commonwealth citizens. By the time it was introduced, around 100,000 persons of Indian and Pakistani origins had entered, and settled in, the country.[5] Most of them found employment in industries such as metal manufacture, transport and catering as well as professional occupations like those in the National Health Service. Other waves of their dependents and relatives followed as part of family reunification, which was protected by law.[6]

It is important to emphasise here that the first waves of South Asian immigrants to the UK came amid widespread racist and ant-immigration sentiments. It is also imperative to stress that until the late 1980s, these immigrants were referred to and attacked as members of nationalities: Indian, Pakistani and Bangladeshi. Religion was certainly an undercurrent, but it was not the marker of either identity or racism.

For example, *Paki* was the derogatory label used in the 1960s for all South Asians, including people from India, Afghanistan and Bangladesh. It referred to subjects of former colony states in a racist way.

Ed Husain, a senior fellow for Middle Eastern Studies at the Council on Foreign Relations and a one-time Islamic fundamentalist, recounts in his revealing memoir *The Islamist* incidents of racism he faced as a child growing up in East London. His father was born in British India and his mother was from East Pakistan. He and his fellow South Asian pupils at Sir William Burroughs Primary School in Limehouse grew up in the 1980s oblivious to the fact that they were somehow different: 'we were Asians'. Thugs of the British far right party, the National Front,[7] made sure to remind them:

> 'Pakis! Pakis! F___ off back home!' the hoodlums would shout. The National Front was at its peak in the 1980s. I can still see a gang of shaven-headed tattooed thugs standing tall above us, hurling abuse as we walked to the local library to return our books. Ms Powlesland [his teacher] and other teachers raced to us, held our hands firmly and roared at the hate-filled bigots. 'Go away! Leave us alone', they would bellow to taunts of 'Paki lovers' from the thugs.[8]

The same holds for Indian-born British writer Kenan Malik. His memories of childhood were of racism shaped by his nationality, not his religion. He recounts in his much-acclaimed book *From Fatwa to Jihad*:

> What shaped my early experience was not religion but racism. I arrived in Britain as 'Paki-bashing' was becoming a national sport. 'Paki' was the abusive name for any Asian, and 'Paki-bashing' was what racists called their pastime hunting out and beating up Asians. My main memory of growing up on the 1970s was of being involved almost daily in fights with racists, and of how normal it seemed to come home with a bloody nose or black eye.[9]

'Paki' was also used, albeit to a lesser degree, to describe those who looked like South Asians, including Arabs. Similarly, *Black* was used in the 1960s as a racist label for immigrants to separate them from the white British communities, hence the word Black for the non-white population. It was quite common at the time to see signs on hostels saying 'No dogs, no blacks, no Irish'.

Precisely because of this racist connotation, a generation of South Asians assumed *Black* as a political badge – a leftist one. That group included Kenan Malik and Salman Rushdie. They were fierce in their opposition to racism, but equally hostile to the tradition that often marked immigrant communities, especially religious ones. At the time, as Malik contends, being radical did not mean being a religious fundamentalist; it meant being 'militantly secular, self-consciously Western and avowedly left-wing,' someone like Malik himself.[10]

It was within this context of widespread racism and anti-immigrant sentiments that the British multiculturalist policies started to take shape.

Britain was pulled between two extremes. At one end of the spectrum was colonial Britain, and people who had not yet grasped that the empire on which the sun never sets was in fact coming to an end. At the other end was post-colonial Britain, very much aware of its past, riddled with guilt and shame, more open to the immigrants but undecided about how to treat them.

At the two extremes stood two famous figures, who shaped British policies on migrants: Enoch Powell, a conservative member of Parliament (MP) from 1950 to 1974, and Roy Jenkins, a Labour politician and Home Secretary from 1965 to 1967. Each delivered a much-quoted speech on immigrants, and they diverged starkly in their perceptions towards integration.

Powell's famous speech, 'Rivers of blood', which he delivered to a meeting of the Conservative Association in Birmingham on 20 April 1968, was meant as a critique of the Race Relations Act of 1968, which was then being deliberated in Parliament. The act made it illegal to refuse housing, employment or public services to a person on the grounds of colour, race, or ethnic or national origin. Powell was adamant that this would discriminate against the majority, who 'found themselves made strangers in their own country.'

His speech left no room for speculation on where he stood regarding 'non-whites' and their place in society. He quoted a dissatisfied constituent, who complained that 'in this country in 15 or 20 years' time, the black man will have the whip hand over the white man'![11]

This is one of the most quoted sentences of his speech but it is not the part that I consider most crucial. Powell was also talking about an issue that would be of great importance: integration. From his perspective, 'to be integrated into a population means to become for all practical purposes indistinguishable from its other members.' That proved to be difficult in his opinion, first because of immigrants' 'colour', hence race; second because the immigrants 'never conceived or intended such a thing,' and third because 'their numbers and physical concentration meant the pressures towards integration which normally bear upon any small minority did not operate.'

Accordingly, Powell's concept of integration meant total assimilation, which was not feasible – not because of any social or economic obstacles, but because of an essentialist feature of the immigrants: their colour, their race, not to mention their lack of will and desire to 'integrate'. Obviously Powell did not consider that the racist sentiments he expressed in his speech might in fact be contributing to the situation.

Precisely because of its racist tone, Powell's speech led to his being sacked from his position as a Shadow Defence Secretary in Edward Heath's Shadow Cabinet. Nevertheless, he clearly was articulating sentiments against non-white immigrants and fears shared by a wider public, especially in the areas most affected by these transformations.

But there was another side to Britain, one that thought differently, represented by Labour Home Secretary Roy Jenkins, who considered integration from another perspective: that of inclusion, equal opportunity and tolerance.

He famously described what he meant by integration in his speech on race relations on 23 May 1966 to a London meeting of the National Committee for Commonwealth Immigrants:

> I do not regard it [integration] as meaning the loss, by immigrants, of their own national characteristics and culture. I do not think that we need in this country a 'melting pot', which will turn everybody out in a common mould, as one of a series of carbon copies of someone's misplaced vision of the stereotyped Englishman [...]
>
> I define integration, therefore, not as a flattening process of assimilation but as equal opportunity, accompanied by cultural diversity, in an atmosphere of mutual tolerance. This is the goal. [...] But if we are to maintain any sort of world reputation for civilised living and social cohesion, we must get nearer to its achievement than is the case today.[12]

This vision, if it was implemented as a living experience, might have provided a road map for post-colonial Britain. Instead, multiculturalism was implemented as a political process, gradually translated into a set of policies separating people into ethnic and cultural boxes. Roy Jenkins failed to account for the one indispensible element that could have made his vision work: common rules that apply to all.

Multiculturalism as a living experience is similar to a football game. Off the football field, each of the 22 players has a different style of life, each according to his choices and beliefs. One player might be a punk; he likes to express his sense of rebellion and individualism through his hairstyle and clothes. He has tattoos all over his body, and his piercings accent key features of his face and body; some are in places we cannot see and do not want to. Another player is religious. It does not make any difference whether he is a Hindu, a Muslim, a Christian or a Jew. He is pious; he follows strict rules in life; sex comes only with marriage; and food has to be kosher or halal, according to his religion.

The two players could not be more different. Yet on the football field they play together. They play together. This is important. When they play, they play according to the rules of the game. These rules apply to the two of them. Both have to follow them.

Now imagine that each of the 22 players chose not to accept this simple principle: that the game has rules and these rules should be respected and followed by all players. Imagine if each player decided to play according to his own rules. Let us go back to our two players. The punk says he would like to be different, so he will express his individuality by playing with his elbows, not with his feet. And the religious player says he will only play according to his religious beliefs and adds that he will not play with any players who are atheists or non-believers. He might consider that playing with his feet is against his religious principles and therefore decide to play with his head instead. Imagine this and tell me what would happen. Well, for one thing we will not have any more World Cups. Some of you might be thrilled at that. But the fact is that without the rules of the game, we will have no game.

This is how multiculturalism as a political process has developed in Britain: instead of a multiculturalism as a living experience, one that cherishes diversity in a setting that brings everyone together with common rules, it has turned into what the Indian economist Amartya Sen, winner of the Nobel Prize, called plural monoculturalism: 'having two styles or traditions co-existing side by side, without the twain meeting.'[13]

Sen, who has been living in Britain and the US since the 1970s, has become a vocal critique of the misuse and double standards of multiculturalism in the form of plural monoculturalism. He gave an example that is relevant because of its gender dimension: the consequences that separating communities have for women's lives, a point I address later. He said that if a girl in a conservative immigrant family decided to date an English boy, this would certainly be a multicultural initiative. The attempt of her guardians to stop her from doing this, a common enough occurrence, is a move toward monoculturalism because it seeks to keep the cultures separate. Sen points out the irony in this situation:

> [T]he parents' prohibition, [. . .] seems to garner the loudest and most vocal defence from alleged multiculturalists, on the ground of the importance of honouring traditional cultures – as if the cultural freedom of the young woman were of no relevance whatever, and as if the distinct cultures must somehow remain in secluded boxes.[14]

Plural monoculturalism thrives on the concept of separate rules for separate 'ethnic and cultural' groups. And separate rules for separate ethnic and cultural groups have been the essence of the policies adopted in Britain.

It all started in 1969, when Sikh bus drivers went on strike in Wolverhampton over company policy concerning facial hair and turbans. A group of practicing Sikhs considered the ban on turbans and beards to be a direct attack on their religion. The leader of the group, Sohan Singh Jolly, and 14 others, had vowed to set fire to themselves if their request was not granted. Not surprisingly, this action did not receive whole-hearted support from all of Britain's estimated 130,000 Sikhs. In fact, the Supreme Council of Sikhs in the UK stated:

> We are going to wage relentless war on the idea that individuals can take this sort of action involving the whole community and very likely lead to a worsening of community harmony in Britain.[15]

Nevertheless, the Transport and General Workers Union, the Indian High Commission in London, and the Parliamentary Under-Secretary for Employment and Productivity all urged the Wolverhampton Committee to change its rules. The committee decided to do so, and stated that in 'the interests of race relations we have taken the decision to relax the rule.'[16]

Certainly, wearing a turban while driving a bus is not something I would consider problematic, but to many observers this strike and its success created a precedent of communal exemption, which developed into Sikhs' right not to wear motorcycle helmets under a 1973 law;[17] in 1982 it was institutionalised in a high court decision that Sikhs were a 'distinct ethnic group', entitled to protection under the Race Relations Act.[18] Britain was just beginning to witness the birth of politics of difference and group rights.

At this point I should mention that Powell did criticise the issue of communal rights in his speech. In fact, to highlight his point he quoted Labour MP John Stonehouse, who said:[19]

> The Sikh communities' campaign to maintain customs inappropriate in Britain is much to be regretted. Working in Britain, particularly in the public services, they should be prepared to accept the terms and conditions of their employment. To claim special communal rights (or should one say rites?) leads to a dangerous fragmentation within society. This communalism is a canker; whether practised by one colour or another it is to be strongly condemned.

I mention this specifically because Stonehouse, and with him Powell, was making a legitimate point. The problem was that Powell's racist comments made everyone afraid to raise the issue for fear of being associated with him.

Instead of opening the debate on immigration, Powell's speech achieved just the opposite; it closed it off, leaving the public with an attitude of 'let's not discuss issues that prove sensitive.'

As a result, both the right and the left, by mutual, if unspoken, consent, maintained a political silence on the issue of immigration. Revealingly, it was Trevor Phillips, the chair of the Equalities and Human Rights Commission (EHRC), who expressed this opinion in his 2008 speech, 'Not a river of blood, but a tide of hope'. He argued that serious political debate about immigration has been suppressed in every part of the political spectrum. Conservatives feared being associated with Powellism and condemned as racist; they claimed that political correctness had unfairly silenced them. The left bore its share of responsibility as well. Convinced that immigration was an issue that favoured the right, they kept silent. They also feared that an open and free debate on this issue would release a 'caged beast of an essentially reactionary public opinion.'[20]

But that was not all. The left also helped to introduce the politics of difference and group rights. The old radical left, Kenan Malik tells us, slowly lost its faith in secular universalism and Enlightenment ideas of rationalism and humanism. Instead, they began talking about multiculturalism and group rights, decrying those Enlightenment ideas as 'Eurocentric': part of a Euro-American project imposed on other people. For decades, they had argued that everyone should be equal despite their racial, ethnic, religious or cultural differences. Now they pushed the idea that different people should be treated differently precisely because of such differences.[21]

The state played a crucial part in translating this ideological shift into reality, by introducing multicultural policies at the local and national levels. Urban riots and unrest during the 1970s and 1980s raised concerns about how to engage 'ethnic minority communities' in the political process. The deliberations led to a position sanctioning a multi-racial, multi-cultural approach, which would recognise the different needs and ethnic communities in society.

What followed were policies that emphasised the importance of 'different cultural backgrounds in determining people's identity,' and the necessity to 'engage with community groups on this basis.' A shift was occurring in the public space, from the 'liberal tradition of dealing with people in a "colour-blind" way' and 'towards differential treatment according to their cultural identities.' Equality would now require 'cultural recognition and respect'. That is, 'if a person's culture' were not 'affirmed and given status,' that would be 'considered to be a denial of equality.'[22] The ideas of Charles Taylor had found their home in the British policies of difference.

Gradually, local and national authorities adopted a range of services and moulded them to accommodate the supposedly different needs of citizens and clients all across society. In time the nation had ethnic housing associations and ethnicity-based healthcare, arts and cultural provision, along with voluntary support, radio channels, public broadcasting and policing units, all based on ethnicity.[23]

Ethnic and cultural groups were encouraged to make demands based on their differences and cultural exclusion from the mainstream. Their ability to gain resources from the public purse was often dependent on their being unfairly disadvantaged because of their 'difference'. Slowly but steadily, over the decades, ethnically or culturally specific lobby groups emerged, 'each arguing their own corner for more money, resources and support for their particular identity.'[24]

The outcome was a demarcation of people into visible cultural and religious 'communities', headed by state-picked 'leaders' of those communities. The communities rubbed up against and competed with each other, living apart, and looking at each other with suspicion, if not hatred.

The Birmingham Council's policies after the 1985 Handsworth riots illustrate this point clearly. The riots, which rocked Birmingham, saw Blacks, Asians and Whites taking to the streets *together* to protest against poverty, unemployment and police harassment. Instead of addressing these needs, the Birmingham Council responded by proposing a new political framework to engage minority communities.[25]

Nine umbrella organisations were created, based on ethnicity and faith, to represent the needs of their particular communities and help aid policy development and resource allocation. These included the African and Caribbean People's Movement, the Bangladeshi Islamic Projects Consultative Committee, the Birmingham Chinese Society, the Council of Black-Led Churches, the Hindu Council, the Irish Forum and the Sikh Council of Gurdwaras.

The aim was to draw these 'communities' into the political process. However, the process by which these organisations were created was anything but democratic. Simply put, these organisations had 'no democratic mandate, indeed no mandate at all.'[26] I presume that the way they were chosen must have fulfilled an authenticity test of some sort. Malik correctly highlighted the absurdity of these steps, which presumed that an organisation can represent a community, treating the latter as homogenous whole, imposing identities on people, ignoring internal conflicts, and empowering not minorities but the hand-picked community leaders, who owe their position to their relationship with the state.[27]

Instead of addressing the real grievances that caused the 1985 riots, the Birmingham Council created a new problem, dividing communities and separating them, in the process creating a new source of conflict. As Malik put it:

> The model of engagement through Umbrella Groups tended to result in competition between BME (Black and minority ethnic) communities for resources. Rather than prioritising needs and cross-community working, the different Umbrella Groups generally attempted to maximise their own interests.[28]

The outcome was another riot in October 2005. This time the fighting was not between youth and police, but between Blacks and Asians.

The shift was felt in British society as a whole. Trevor Phillips described it eloquently in a speech after the terrorist attacks in London on 7 July 2005:

> [L]azy officialdom [. . .] colluded with old guard ethnic leaders to warp a progressive and very British recognition of diversity in the early nineteen eighties into a bureaucratic version of multiculturalism which today keeps many communities *closed and separate*. We know the result – people who want to scale the cultural walls that separate them, are blocked by institutions, which insist on pigeonholing them by their race, colour and religion.[29]

The country was sleepwalking to segregation, Phillips warned in his speech, and with good reason. Ghettoes, he said, have been erected, and people are increasingly living with their own kind. Not all ghettoes were poverty stricken and drug ridden, but they were places where more than two thirds of the residents belong to a single ethnic group. Residential isolation had become a reality for many minority groups, especially South Asians. In fact, the number of people with Pakistani roots living in what were technically called ghetto communities trebled between 1991 and 2001. While some minorities were moving into middle-class, less ethnically concentrated areas, 'what is left behind is hardening in its separateness.' And separateness had spread to schools. For example, in 2001, among the primary schools in the Tower Hamlets, 17 schools had more than 90 per cent Bangladeshi pupils, and 9 schools had fewer than 10 per cent. Nor was segregation limited to the schools; it also extended to the playgrounds, which meant that not only were the children not meeting, but neither were their parents.[30]

If you think that Phillips was exaggerating, I suggest you go to Small Heath, Green Lane, and Alum Rock in Birmingham, something I took the liberty of doing thanks to the advice of a British women's rights activist and social worker, who is of Pakistani heritage. She said that no amount of interviews, statistics and books can communicate the experience of living in a 'closed community' and the isolation one feels there. She was absolutely right. In Small Heath on Coventry Road, which could be described as a Somali ghetto, I felt disoriented; for a moment I thought I must have been transported by mistake back to Yemen, my country of origin. Women were wearing the full head-to-toe black covering including the face, and men were wearing the short dress of Salafi Wahhabi Islam; the chaotic jammed street was left to manage on its own by the police, whose superiors told them 'not to offend them', meaning the 'Muslims', as one policeman told my friend. Even the restaurants were segregated.

It is within this context that calls are coming to introduce Islamic law in the British legal system. This is a context where the Essentialist Paradigm of thinking has taken hold, promoting a multicultural policy of group rights: a policy that has created or rather invented communities, imposed identities on their members, treated a community as a whole represented by handpicked 'community leaders', and eventually produced a plural monoculturalism, where communities are closed and separated.

Proponents of Islamic Law in the West: The Essentialists

Three general groups of people want to introduce forms of Islamic law, shari'a, into British (Western) legal system(s).

1. Islamic and Islamist organisations. The terms Islamic and Islamist have different meanings. *Islamic* organisations often represent a traditional if not conservative reading of Islam, are led by individuals of traditional/conservative religious background, and often seek to impose a religious identity on 'Muslim community' members. *Islamist* organisations espouse a political agenda that aims to Islamise migrant communities of Islamic faith; Islamising their Western host

country is also part of their agenda, but it's a longer-term goal. Some Islamic organisations have members who espouse the ideology of Islamism and some do not. Often they work together and support each other's religious demands. Together they often claim to be the sole representative and voice of 'Muslim communities' and experts on their 'needs'. Until the terrorist attack of 7 July 2005, the British policies of plural monoculturalism facilitated and reinforced this claim.

2. High officials, lawyers, judges or political personalities, who seem to be concerned about how Muslim communities are becoming integrated in their respective countries, and consider the move toward shari'a law inevitable if Muslims are to integrate 'successfully'. Dr Rowan Williams, the former archbishop of Canterbury, is one famous example; another is Marion Boyd, Ontario's attorney general. Some of these people may be calling for soft legal pluralism for pragmatic political reasons. They earnestly believe that combating Islamic extremism − a serious problem in Britain − will require giving small concessions to the Muslim community, such as allowing them to live by Islamic family laws. Britain's former Lord Chief Justice Baron Phillips of Worth Matravers (equivalent to the chief justice of the US Supreme Court) made a comment that might be understood in this light. It is no coincidence that Islamic and Islamist organisations in Britain make the same argument: 'Give us Islamic law in family affairs to curb extremism'.[31]

3. Academics in a range of social science fields, specifically legal anthropology, law and sociology, who are leading a theoretical and intellectual discourse about the state: does it have a monopoly on legal productions and norms, on minorities and multiculturalism? They maintain that legal centralism is a Western model of jurisprudence, that it ignores the experience of non-Western nations. They blame colonial powers for depriving people in developing countries of access to their own traditional and customary laws, imposing their version of positive law on their colonies. They cite a 'more complex' relationship between law and society, one 'where law is conceptualised as more plural, not located entirely in the state.'[32] Accordingly, legal pluralists hold that state law is only one of many levels of law; their idea implies a plurality of social fields and producers of norms, which interact somewhat with each other.

They also insist that legal pluralism is an adequate system that guarantees the protection of minorities' rights and of their entitlement to be different.[33] They insist that an even-handed sensitivity to difference requires an abandonment of the formal vision of equality, one that assumes that all citizens are inherently identical. Instead, the legal system should take cognizance of the identity and values of different sections of the population, no matter how distinctive these values may be.[34] Within the British discourse on *weak* legal pluralism, some strong advocates are the American John R. Bowen, mentioned above, who is Dunbar-Van Cleve Professor in Sociocultural Anthropology at Washington University in St. Louis, Roger Ballard, the Director of the Centre for Applied South Asian Studies, and Tariq Modood, a British-Pakistani professor of sociology, politics and public policy at the University of Bristol.

Members of these three groups will tell you that weak legal pluralism is just one out of many instruments for resolving conflicts, and that it is an extension of a right already given to the Jewish minority: a right to arbitration tribunals in a system called Beth Din. And, they say, since the Jews already have it, why not Muslims as well?

They will emphasise that this instrument of conflict resolution is voluntary, that they only support it with safeguards that ensure respect for human rights, especially for women's rights. They will also tell you that if a member of a religious minority does not want to be ruled by these laws, all she or he has to do is to opt out and leave the community.

And they will tell you that the Western legal tradition, which argues for legal centralism and state monopoly over legal productions and a monistic conception of law (the basic foundation on which liberal-democratic nations are instituted) is indeed Euro-American centric and hegemonic. And most importantly, they will say, it ignores the experience of non-Western nations.

The more they explain their position, the clearer it becomes that they all share the features of the essentialists' paradigm of thinking: demanding separate family laws for Muslims as an extension of group rights. Here Muslims are a religious group that should be protected from the hegemonic secular culture of the majority. And they are an oppressed group that should be allowed its freedom to conduct its own affairs according to its religious and cultural heritage.

Cultural relativism in its two forms, soft and hard, is evident in their position. Islamic and Islamist organisations will use a hard form of cultural relativism while insisting on respecting the 'universal right of religious freedom'. They will say something like this:

Yes of course, we respect human rights, but mind you, are not human rights a Western concept imposed on non-Westerners? And, after all, Islamic law is not just any law. This is God's order, God's word, and we – that is, Muslims – should follow it. One day, the West will realise the benefit of these laws and adopt them as well, but until then, our community has the right to apply our religious law in family affairs. We are exercising our right to religious freedom. If these rules from Islamic family law sound unfair, it has to do with our limited human understanding of God's will, for he (and God is always a He, never a She in this line of interpretation) knows what is best for his creations and their nature. Polygamy, unequal shares of inheritances, male guardianship of women, and child marriage: all these are God's laws, which should be respected.

This is a summary of arguments I heard repeatedly during my interviews and research, not only in Britain but also in the Arab MENA region. I will quote some of them in Chapter 4 to highlight their positions on the type of Islamic law they espouse. Double talk, which claims to respect human rights but violates them in reality, is an engrained feature of this type of Islamist/Islamic discourse. Because of that, I often tell my students: listen to what they *say* and then look at what they *do*; the discrepancy will indicate where they actually stand.

The second and third groups of proponents will use more of a soft cultural relativism, stressing the importance of safeguarding human rights, but insisting all the way that religious laws just tend to discriminate against women anyway. In this regard Islam is not really unique; and even if we see signs of discrimination, let us not exaggerate. This will remedy itself over time; after all, we are living in a liberal context. Are we not? This is how it works in a liberal context.

Absent from their discourse is any actual experience with legal pluralism in non-Western countries specifically with its political and human rights consequences. Also absent is clarity about the type of

Islamic law being used in this so-called method of conflict resolution. No one considers the social context within which this law is being implemented. The diversity and multitude of positions towards Islamic law, the critical discourse in Islamic countries among civil society actors and intellectuals, and their attempts to change Islamic laws: none of this seems to be relevant to their discourse. Indeed, the discourse is very academic and theoretical, ignoring the settings or circumstances within which women are living in closed societies. It is as if Muslim women, Muslims and Islam itself had been crafted and constructed separate from their historical, political, social and religious contexts. The constructs mirror the essentialists' own self-obsessed and self-centred image, assumptions, expectations and ignorance.

Also absent from their discourse is an awareness of the role that two forms of Islamism – societal and political – plays in promoting this development, or of their totalitarian agenda. In fact, if you are Muslim and you were to mention this fact, you would immediately be accused of being Islamophobic, a self-loathing Muslim, or worse, a secular Muslim, someone who is not 'authentic enough'.

Given the importance of addressing these aspects in detail, I will devote a chapter to each of them. Chapter 3 is dedicated to the actual practice of legal pluralism and its consequences from two perspectives: political and human rights. It argues that in countries practicing legal pluralism a wide range of rights is often violated with impunity: human rights, citizens' rights and the rights of women and minorities.

In Chapter 4 I look at the type of Islamic law that is being promoted. Often the essentialists will argue that Islamic law will only be used to consider 'minor' issues and will only affect family law. Yet it is precisely because this suggestion concerns family law that it should be rejected. A closer look at how Islamic laws are applied in family matters will reveal their discriminatory nature and the human rights consequences for the lives of women and children. In this chapter I will also show how the type of Islamic law promoted by some leading sheikhs of shari'a councils and Muslim arbitration tribunals remains inherently prejudiced and may in fact facilitate child/early and forced marriages.

In Chapter 5 I move to the political context of the issue. I first discuss the role the British government played in creating 'the Muslim community' and promoting unelected Muslim leaders as speakers for that community. I then look at how political and societal Islamism have been actively promoting the introduction of Islamic law into Western legal systems as part of their project of political domination and infiltration.

In the final chapter I contextualise the debate in women's reality. I discuss the social contexts of women in closed communities, using Britain as an example; and I show how introducing Islamic law will increase the social control exercised over these women by their patriarchal family structures, communities and religious leaders. I then highlight how these demands to introduce Islamic law are being contested by women activists from within South Asian communities in Britain. By the end of the chapter it will become clear that this critical discourse is by no means limited to Britain but reflects a wider movement within Muslim countries.

CHAPTER 3

LEGAL PLURALISM IN PRACTICE

In the last chapter I argued that the plural monocultural politics implemented by the British government served to segregate communities rather than unite them on a basis of equal rights and mutual respect and tolerance. I described the outcome as 'a demarcation of people into visible cultural and religious "communities", headed by state-picked "leaders" of communities. The communities rubbed up against and competed with each other, living apart, looking at each other with suspicion, if not hatred.'

I have a confession to make here. Although my description was based on the accounts of British reports and on interviews I conducted, I was also paraphrasing a description by Albert Hourani, a renowned Lebanese American specialist on the Middle East. But he made it in 1947. And he was not talking about Britain and its minorities; he was talking about the closed segregated communities of the Ottoman Empire — founded around the thirteenth century and considered one of the most powerful states in the world during the fifteenth and sixteenth centuries — about the minorities in the Empire.

At the time, the similarities between the two examples struck me as very odd. Yet the more I looked at the issue, the more it became clear that once the state starts to situate rights within the frame of a group rather than within the individual, the likely outcome will be *segregation, inequality and discrimination.*

Listen to how Hourani described the situation of religious communities within the Ottoman Empire:

[T]he Ottoman Empire was not a military state; it was composed of a large number of groups, local, tribal, linguistic and religious. On the whole, these groups formed closed communities. Each was a 'world', sufficient to its members and exacting their ultimate loyalty. The worlds touched but did not mingle with each other; each looked at the rest with suspicion and even hatred.[1]

Closed communities were in fact the legacy of the Ottoman Empire. And their segregation was inherently intertwined with the policy of legal pluralism the Ottomans adopted. The essentialists rarely see this policy as relevant to their support for weak legal pluralism. In fact, when they do mention it, they do so to highlight the *tolerance* of the Ottomans in comparison to the *inconsiderate* Western legal centralism that is hesitant to accommodate its minorities in a similar way.

The essentialists are more interested in the legacy of the colonial powers, which in their opinion distorted the diverse legal reality of colonised societies. Yes, the colonial powers did change the legal orders in the areas they controlled, but their policies varied from one area to another within their domain of influence, with different consequences for their state and legal formations. Sometimes a colonial power would use different styles depending on the area and region it controlled.[2]

That said, it is important to emphasise that societies in the pre-Ottoman or pre-colonial periods were already divided along ethnic, religious, tribal and/or sectarian lines; it was an existing social fact, not one created or imposed by either the Ottomans or the colonial powers. The degree of this fragmentation, however, may have differed from one society to another. As one would expect, the Ottomans and colonial powers did exploit these ethnic divisions to their advantage and set up institutional orders that mirrored, exacerbated and cemented these divisions.[3]

Given its relevance to our discussion, I will focus here on the *millet* system created by the Ottoman Empire. In fact, despite the clear difference in historical and institutional contexts, I cannot help but see some resemblance between the millet system and Britain's 'Plural monocultural' policies, its subsequent creation of 'communities', and the direction it is heading.

The millet system organised the population of the Empire on the basis of religion, rather than territory or language. Before the Tanzimat reforms of the late nineteenth century, people in the Empire were not considered citizens. They were members of religious communities. Accordingly, the system was composed of religious communities, each of which had its own internal organisation controlled by a religious hierarchy.

Under the millet system in regions such as Greater Syria, recognised religious groups, such as Christians, were organised into relatively self-contained autonomous communities. Each was directed by a religious leader, each had its own religious laws and customs, and each took on various social and administrative functions, including deciding on issues of marriage and divorce.[4]

The outcome of this system was the creation of uneven and divisive hierarchies: one within the Empire, one between the communities, and one within the 'recognised' communities.

Under the millet system, a minority was narrowly defined: any population that was not Sunni Muslims of the Hanafite school of jurisprudence. Many regions in the Ottoman Empire did not have majorities of Sunni Muslims. Even though non-Muslims were often the majority in a given area, under that definition they would still be treated as a minority, with second-class status. Muslims who were not Sunnis would be ignored altogether, often poorly protected and susceptible to persecution. Hence, the ruling community was the Sunni Muslims; every other community, whether non-Muslim or non-Sunni, was politically insignificant.[5]

Another hierarchy was created *between* the communities. The treatment of a minority within the Empire depended, among other things, on whether the Ottomans recognised a religious group as a community or a millet. In fact, Christians and Jews fared better than non-Sunni Muslims.

For example, in Greater Syria, the Ottomans did not recognise the Alawites, a heterodox sect which split from the Shi'a religious tradition in the ninth century, based on the teachings of Mohammad ibn Nusayr. In fact, they considered them to be 'non-Muslims', 'heretics', and 'idolatrous'. What set the state for this perception was a series of religious fatwas and the pronouncements of Sunni theologians, who made it a 'duty to kill them' and said that waging war against them was the 'greatest of pious deeds and the most important obligations' for a Muslim. The natural outcomes were devastating pogroms before and during the Ottoman period in 1317 and 1516 and continued persecution. The Alawites were able to survive and maintain their autonomy, including legal autonomy, by living in isolated geographic pockets in the mountains.[6]

A hierarchy *within* the communities was also visible. In fact, leaders of the recognised religious communities were given absolute authority over their groups. They were the gatekeepers of their communities, they spoke on their behalf, and they controlled the administration of their affairs, taxes and family matters. For example, the Syrian Christian and Jewish communities covered by this system lived in their separate parallel societies controlled by their religious leaders.[7]

The kind of authority given to Syrian Christian religious leaders can be discerned from the Exequatur, or patent, that Sultan Abd al-Hamid II (1842–1918) issued to the new Greek Orthodox Patriarch of Syria. In it the Sultan proclaimed that 'all members of the Greek denomination, large and small, must acknowledge' the new Patriarch; they were 'not allowed to follow "old ordinances" which contravene their millet's basics without his approval and permission'; if they did so they would face 'the necessary punishments'. Moreover, 'in case of the marriage or divorce of a member of the Greek Catholics [. . .] no one has the right to interfere or mediate other than the designated Patriarch and his agents.'[8]

No wonder Albert Hourani described these communities as closed. They were closed communities, living in isolation and fear; each community formed a socially and culturally separate entity, and each kept separate from the other. They lacked any experience of inter-communal solidarity or social integration within the Empire. Also lacking was a sense of belonging and unity. People did not feel they were part of an empire or citizens of a state. No, they were made to perceive themselves as part of their community, and each community was a world in itself.[9] What did Hourani say? 'The worlds touched but did not mingle with each other; each looked at the rest with suspicion and even hatred.'[10]

How does all this relate to the subject at hand?

The millet system had negative consequences, but it was part of a chapter of history; so why should this historical detail be relevant to our discussion of Islamic law in the West?

Good question.

The millet system should be understood within its historical context and in relation to what was being practised in other states and empires at the time. I am sure it will take a lot of imagination and ignoring of details to compare the millet system to the British plural monocultural system, especially as we are talking about two different political units operating in different historical and institutional contexts.

Yet I dare say it remains relevant. For one thing, the millet system's closed communities remind us of the segregated communities of Britain, described by the left-leaning chair of the Equalities and Human Rights Commission (EHRC), Trevor Phillips, as 'these marooned communities'.

He said that these communities, if left to their own devices, would 'steadily drift away from the rest of us, evolving their own lifestyles, playing by their own rules and increasingly regarding the codes of behaviours, loyalty and respect that the rest of us take for granted as outdated behaviour that no longer applies to them.'[11]

Now imagine that these 'marooned communities' were given the freedom to use their own 'ethnic or religious laws' to administer their own affairs. What would happen then?

Aside from cementing the segregation that already exists between these communities, a hierarchy within the communities would be created, giving power and control to the community's hand-picked religious leaders and elderly, considered the gatekeepers of the community. They and they alone will be entitled to speak in the name of their communities and to decide on and define what they consider to be their communities' interests and needs.

Another hierarchy will also be created, one within Britain itself. We will have two categories of citizens: one that enjoys the freedoms and rights stipulated by the common law, and another that is deprived of them, if only because the 'choice' they were given would entail succumbing to the pressure their community imposes on them to 'choose' the community's laws.

I am asking you to imagine this situation, although imagination is not really needed in this case. This situation is already taking shape in Britain, as I will show in Chapters 4, 5 and 6.

Again, and I will not tire of repeating this: The moment the state starts to situate rights within a group rights frame rather than an individual frame, the likely outcome will be segregation, inequality and discrimination. The weakest will be left vulnerable, subject to abuse and discrimination.

Now if you add to this situation religious extremism, which has become part of the scene in these segregated communities, you will find that a combination of political instability, home-grown terrorism and division is in the making.

Notwithstanding this current situation, the millet system is important to our discussion. In the last chapter I said that the essentialists would often argue that the Western legal tradition, based on legal centralism and state monopoly over legal productions, derives from Euro-American traditions and ignores the experience of non-Western nations.

The millet system has left a legacy in the Arab MENA region: the legacy of legal pluralism. Looking at this non-Western experience will show why secular legal centralism is a necessary foundation for a liberal-democratic system that treats citizens as equal before the law. In the following review I will show that far from being a model to emulate, countries applying legal pluralism often feature a stratified citizenry and the double discrimination syndrome. Violations of human rights are a daily reality there.

The Legacy of the Millet System in the Arab MENA Region

The millet system gave recognised minorities the right to regulate their family affairs according to their religious laws. The family legal systems adopted during that period simply mirrored the Empire's religious, sectarian, and ethnic divisions and had three features:[12]

- Sunni jurisprudence had hegemony over that of non-Sunni Muslims.
- Society was fragmented along religious, denominational and sectarian lines, as each community had its own family law.
- Tribes had autonomy as their customary laws – called *al Orf* – regulated their family affairs.

This Ottoman legacy still haunts the Arab region. Indeed, family laws in most Arab societies today reflect these same features.

The legacy has a political function: it hinders national unity and perpetuates the grip of authoritarian regimes by keeping their traditional base of power intact and their societies divided.

For my 2011 book, *The Arab State and Women's Rights: The Trap of Authoritarian Governance*, I conducted field research in three Arab countries, Yemen, Syria and Kuwait, to investigate the authoritarian features of the Arab states and how those features influence their gender politics.

What I discovered was that legal pluralism has a political function that intersects with divided societies in the post-colonial era. Put simply, legal pluralism exists when the state fails to treat its citizens, who are divided along religious, sectarian or tribal lines, as equal before the law.

From this point of view, legal pluralism indicates a state's deficiencies and also exposes how the society is divided into parallel social groups living within the same society. I also found that the system of legal pluralism in family laws, while discriminating against women, is the tool that has helped perpetuate the very social division of Arab societies: it has kept society divided, hindering intermarriage between Sunnis and Shiites, Christians and Muslims and Jews, superior tribes and inferior tribes, etc. In the process, in each country, it has sabotaged nation-building and the development of a national identity.[13]

If this argument seems too abstract, consider the following examples.

Example One: Legal pluralism in the Arab MENA region has been instrumental in Islamicising societies where other religious minorities live

While each religious and sectarian group is allowed to have its own religious family law, in cases of conflict, the religious law of the dominating ruling group, in this case Islamic law, serves as the reference. This fact has political significance.

Simply put, the supremacy of Islamic law in cases of conflict, inheritance, custody and guardianship has led to incremental effects that gradually led to non-Muslims converting. For example, the prohibition on marriage between a Muslim woman and a non-Muslim man has a political function: it ensures that the only Muslims who can marry outside of Islam are men, so their children will automatically become part of the Muslim community. In the case of divorce, however, the law forbids non-Muslim women from having custody of their children. They law also forbids them to inherit from their Muslim husbands unless they convert to Islam. Many will do exactly that for obvious reasons.

Children born in such mixed marriages are not allowed to choose their religion, and those who do choose to follow their mother's religions face persecution. Of course they will automatically be disinherited. One good example will be familiar from international headlines in 2014: the 27-year-old Sudanese woman, Meriam Yahia Ibrahim.

Ms Ibrahim was born to a Muslim father and an Orthodox Christian mother. Her father was absent during her childhood, so she was raised as an Orthodox Christian. In August of 2013, based on the report of a family member, Ms Ibrahim was arrested and charged with adultery because she married a Christian South Sudanese man.

Under classical Islamic law, a Muslim woman is not permitted to marry a non-Muslim man, and any such marriage is considered void and therefore an adulterous relationship subject to punishment. The court added the charge of apostasy in February 2014 when Meriam asserted that she was a Christian and not a Muslim.

On 15 May, Ms Ibrahim was convicted of adultery and apostasy after she refused to recant her religion. She was sentenced to death by hanging under Article 126 of the Sudan Criminal Code for apostasy, and to 100 lashes under Article 146 for adultery.

Ms Ibrahim was eight months pregnant when she was arrested and was imprisoned with her 20-month-old son. The son was not allowed to stay with his father because of his religion: only if the father was Muslim would he be allowed custody. Meriam gave birth with her legs chained; because this made the delivery more difficult, the new baby may never be able to walk.[14]

Despite this horrendous ordeal, Ms Ibrahim was lucky. Thanks to a combination of outrage across Sudanese civil society, an international outcry, media coverage and Christian solidarity, she was released, and after a long struggle was allowed to leave the country.

The issue, however, is not one person's ordeal. It is symptomatic of religious laws that divide people into religious boxes, treat them differently because of their religion, and deprive them of their basic right to choose and/or change their religion and to choose their partner regardless of religion. Given all she and her husband suffered – condemnation to death for choosing the Christian religion of her mother, flogging for marrying a non-Muslim, and denial of custody over their children because of his Christianity – an easier 'choice' for both of them would have been to convert to Islam.

Example Two: Authoritarian regimes, of many types, have exploited legal pluralism to perpetuate the ethnic nature of their societies

To do this they have used a 'divide and rule' strategy and thus kept intact their traditional base of power.

Syria and Saudi Arabia are good examples.

In Syria, the Assad regime was reluctant to change the pluralistic Syrian family law system because, among other reasons, it needed to preserve the division between religious and sectarian communities in Syria.[15]

The regime was able to survive by playing on the fear of minorities – the Christians, Shi'a, Druze, and Jews and its own Alawite minority – that the Sunni majority would return to power. This is a reasonable fear, as they had suffered from Sunni hegemony under the Ottomans. The regime used several methods to engender this fear and has constantly resorted to the principle of divide and rule. It must keep the sectarian and religious division intact in order to continue this survival policy, and the Syrian family law system, based on legal pluralism, is the instrument that preserves this division. To see this point clearly, one need only consider the legal provisions in all these religious family laws that treat the issue of interfaith marriage. Table 3.1, taken from my 2011 book, provides examples.[16]

Every one of these family laws makes interfaith marriage very difficult. Christian family laws make it very difficult for a Syrian Christian to marry a Syrian of another religion, although they make space for marriages between members of Christian denominations. For example, the Syrian Greek Orthodox Personal Status Law No. 23 of 2004 states clearly that marriage is forbidden in the case of 'differences in religion', but it still allows marriage with a Syrian Christian of another denomination. The Syrian Catholic Denominations Personal Status Law No. 31 of 2006 does not even consider the possibility of a marriage with a non-Christian, and only dictates the conditions that allow for an intra-Christian marriage. Likewise, the Jewish Personal Status Law, called the Book of Personal Status for the Jews, takes a very strict position towards interfaith marriage. Its Article 17 states that for a marriage contract to be valid, the partners must be of the same religion and denomination: 'If one partner is of another religion or

Table 3.1 Selected provisions on interfaith marriage according to selected Syrian religious family laws

Islamic Personal Status Law, no. 59, 1953	Syrian Greek Orthodox Law, no. 23, 2004	Syrian Catholic Denominations, no. 31, 2006	The Book of Personal Status for the Jews in Syria	Alawite and Druze
• The marriage of a Muslim woman to a non-Muslim is not valid. (Article 48: 2) • For a marriage to be valid the man must be competent. (Article 26) • Suitability or *kafaa* is defined according to the customs of the country. (Article 28) • If an adult woman marries without her guardian's consent, the guardian may invalidate her marriage unless the husband is suitable. (Article 27)	• Marriage is forbidden in several cases; one is differences in religion. (Article 17: K) • If one potential marriage partner is not an Orthodox Christian then s/he should provide a statement from the spiritual leadership to prove that s/he is committed to an engagement or marriage. (Article 20)	• It is forbidden for two persons, one Catholic and the other not, to marry without previous permission from the religious authorities. (Article 813) • The local church president may issue permission for such a marriage if the Catholic partner declares his intention not to deviate from his faith, and if the other partner is aware of the promises his Catholic partner must issue. (Article 814: 1, 2)	• The religion and denomination must be the same for the marriage contract to be valid. If one partner is of another religion or another denomination then it is forbidden to contract a marriage or the marriage is void.	• Articles 26 and 27 of the Islamic Personal Status Law apply to the Alawites and Druze.

another denomination then it is forbidden to contract a marriage or the marriage is void.'[17]

The same concepts apply to the Islamic law on personal status: Muslim women are not allowed to marry non-Muslims unless the latter convert. Most significantly, this law gives the guardian the right to annul a marriage if he considers the groom/husband not 'fit' or 'suitable', according to a concept called *kafaa* or suitability. This provision is repeated in all Arab family laws, except in Tunisia. The term suitability as used in the law is not defined, and is left to the 'customs of the country'. In essence, the male guardian can threaten to declare a marriage void, calling it 'not suitable', and can thus control the women in his family. In fact this law is meant to keep society divided along its sectarian and religious lines. This explains why this stipulation has been applied to all Syrians, whether they are Sunni, Christian, Shi'i, Druze, Jew, Alawite or Ismaili: it is the legal tool that has helped to preserve the fractious character of Syrian society. Within this equation, women and their rights are irrelevant; it is the political functions that matter.[18]

In Saudi Arabia, the religious and customary laws are meant to cement the sectarian tribal hegemony of the Wahhabi Najdi ruling families and tribes and to prevent intermarriage between people from different regions, from 'higher' and 'lower' tribes, and from different Islamic confessions.

The Kingdom of Saudi Arabia is often described as an outcome of a 'holy alliance' between the dynastic leader Mohammed ibn Saud and a preacher, Mohammed ibn Abdul-Wahhab. The former was the founder of the Saudi dynasty and an emir in a small town near Riyadh called Al-Diriyah; the latter was the founder of Wahhabism, the orthodox fundamentalist Sunni movement, based on the Hanbali School of Jurisprudence, which advocates for the strict practice of, and absolute obedience to, Islam — as he interpreted it.

The two men made the pledge in 1744, with the aim of creating a state according to Wahhabi principles, yet the state they created in the eighteenth century was short-lived due to a successful military campaign by the Ottomans and their Egyptian allies.[19]

The pledge was reinstated again in 1902 when a new leader, Ibn Saud, supported by his clan and an army of Wahhabi zealots, launched a military campaign that unified by force four previously separate regions:

- **Najd** is located at the heart of the Kingdom and is the home region and power base of the Saudi dynasty and the Wahhabi sect.
- **Hijaz** is located at the western side of the Kingdom and is home to the Islamic holy sites. Its population follows the Sunni Shafite School of Jurisprudence and well-established Sufi orders.
- **The Eastern Province** contains the bulk of the Kingdom's oil reserves and is home to most of the country's minority Shi'i population.
- **Asir** and **Najran** are located in the south of the Kingdom. They are tied to Yemen both historically and geographically, and their populations are Sunni Shafite and Shi'a Ismaili tribes.

The Kingdom of Saudi Arabia, established in 1932, was based on the supremacy of the Najd region over the three conquered regions, and the Wahhabi interpretation of Islam was instituted as the official religion of the state.

Legal pluralism is practised in Saudi Arabia in a way that ensures the hegemony of Sunni Wahhabi jurisprudence over other religious traditions, makes it difficult for members of different Islamic denominations or tribal lineages to intermarry, and situates male Sunni Wahhabis from Najd at the top of a hierarchy of citizenship.

Earlier I said that in a context of legal pluralism, when conflicts arise between the religious laws governing the various groups, the religious law of the ruling group would automatically determine the outcome. That is, in countries where Muslims and non-Muslims are living together, Islamic law supersedes all others.

On the other hand, in Saudi Arabia, the population is divided along sectarian, tribal, and regional lines. When conflict arises there, the Wahhabi jurisprudence of the ruling Najdi region and its tribal customary laws would automatically supersede all others.

For example, in the Eastern Province, there are only seven Shi'a judges serving three Shi'a courts: two lower-level courts and an appeals court. Significantly, the jurisdiction of all these judges is limited to cases involving personal status, inheritances and endowments. In August 2005 a royal decree significantly curtailed the already limited jurisdiction of the two lower-level courts. It gave Sunni courts the authority to supervise the Shi'a courts and take up cases pending there, and its other provisions give it even more power. Hence, the regular

Sunni courts would have jurisdiction over cases involving a dispute between two parties, and the Sunni courts would automatically have jurisdiction in cases where one party was not a Shi'a, even if the case were not disputed.[20]

By the same token, among Saudis, tribal and sectarian rules have long determined who can marry whom. A woman can only marry a man from a 'suitable' tribal line who belongs to the same religious denomination. People rarely cross these social boundaries. Inter-marriages between tribes of higher and lower 'lineage' are also frowned upon. If a woman decides to break one of these rules, her male guardian has the right to ask that the marriage be dissolved, and his wish will be granted.[21]

A clear example is Fatima 'Azzaz, a 34-year-old woman in the northern city of Jufy who was forced to divorce her husband.[22] After their father died, Fatima's half-brothers took legal action, claiming that her husband had misrepresented his tribal affiliation when he asked for permission to marry Fatima, and that in fact he belonged to a tribe that was genealogically lower than theirs. While Fatima informed the judge that she wanted to remain married, he ruled in favour of her half-brothers and ordered the divorce in August 2005. Fatima rejected the court's verdict and was imprisoned, with her children, for doing so.[23]

Even in cases where the families decide that sectarian differences are not important, the religious authority takes it upon itself to interfere and annul inter-sectarian marriages. An example, from the Asir Region, is the forced divorce of Laila bent Muhammad Fayez Assiri, who is Sunni, from her husband Ala Allah bin Hassan bin Fnis al-Fnis, who is Shi'i/Ismaili.

Although the couple, and the wife's father, consented to the marriage, in April 2006 a judge passed a sentence ending their marriage of one year because of the sectarian difference. The sentence is based on Wahhabi religious edicts that prohibit inter-sectarian marriage, and consider such marriage contracts 'invalid for the reason of religious incompetence since Shiites are not as competent as Sunnis'.[24]

These provisions, I repeat, are instrumental in preserving the sectarian and tribal hegemony of the Najd region in the Kingdom, for they have kept its tribal lineage intact and prevented its members from marrying people from other regions. The fact that the state actively intervenes to dissolve marriages that transcend these boundaries highlights the political function these provisions play.

The tribal customs and traditions for preserving blood purity also play a role in cementing the state's enforced social segregation. They also reflect which tribe stands at the top of society's hierarchy. Hence, 'pure-blooded' Najdi men can marry women from other tribes or regions but their sisters and daughters will not be allowed to marry outside their group. These strict rules reflect negatively on the more open traditions of other regions.

Mai Yamani remarks in her book, *Cradle of Islam: The Hijaz and the Quest for an Arabian Identity*,[25] that in the late nineteenth and early twentieth centuries Hijazi marriages were more flexible and paid little attention to origins. Being a Muslim, regardless of one's origin, was a strong enough basis from which to enter a marriage. But this openness changed after the Kingdom was established, and it was replaced with strict rules to match those of the Najdi.

Yamani observes that 'Najdi marriage was, and remains within, the same lineage, with bonds among the tribal families usually reinforced by patrilineal parallel-cousin marriages.' But she stresses that a distinction should be made between marriages that are *khadiri* (non-tribal and hence not pure Najdi) and those that are *gabili* (tribal 'pure-blooded' Najdi):

> This strict patrilineality allowed 'pure blooded Najdi' [men] to marry outsiders, such as Egyptians, but their female relatives have never married outside the tribe. In principle, then, men from the Hijaz would not have been able to marry into a 'pure-blooded' Najdi family, while women would, although Hijazi women were not, as a rule, given in marriage to Najdi families, nor were they asked.[26]

It comes as no surprise that marriages between Hijazis and Najdis are very rare. The latter refrain from marrying Hijazis because they consider their linage not pure enough. Yamani contends that the rarity of such intermarriages is the 'most significant expression of the social boundaries between the regions of Saudi Arabia,' demonstrating the fractured nature of the Saudi state.[27]

Again, within this equation, women and their rights are irrelevant; what matters is the political function.

The Consequences of Legal Pluralism from a Citizenship and Human Rights Perspective

It is the political function that matters.

That is what struck me when I researched legal pluralism in the Arab MENA region between 2006 and 2009. As a political scientist I was naturally more concerned with its political implications but I certainly did not expect them to be so fundamental.

This period of research entailed travelling to the region and conducting more than 60 in-depth interviews with diverse groups of elites: high government officials, opposition members, intellectuals and women activists. It had a profound impact on my perceptions. I went there convinced that religion is the primary element that causes discrimination against women in the region but I came back with a more nuanced and complicated picture. Yes, religion is part of the problem. Regardless of which religion we are talking about, more often than not, the religious interpretations prevalent in the Arab MENA region discriminate against women. But I found another more basic, and pressing, question: Why is it that religion still matters at all?

That question necessitated a closer look at the type of state prevalent in the region. It is certainly an authoritarian state. Yet this authoritarian Arab state has another feature, one that was repeatedly emphasised during my interviews: it is *pre-modern*.

One Syrian intellectual put it to me this way:

> What we have is a pre-modern state. We do not have a state of citizens, with free and equal individuals. What do we have? What is the citizenship that we have? [Are we] Syrians? No. that is not my fundamental legitimacy. No, I am Muslim, I am Christian, I am Shiite, I am Alawi, I am from Houran, [and] I am from Aleppo: a pre-state. These are the references of the state. Individuals are not individuals. Even in the elections, this is the candidate of so-and-so clan, or so-and-so tribe. No citizenship, no freedom and no equality. Then where is the modern state? In fiction. This is the Arab state. Give me one example of a *modern* Arab state? There is none [...] This is the problem [...] If the state's reference is citizenship, [then] the woman and the man [are] equals. [They will be] individuals, her brother and father

have no business with her. She is free once she reaches a certain age, free with her religion, free with her denomination, where to live, equal.[28]

The state is pre-modern.

A term like that is bound to make people uneasy. I understand that in the post-modern and post-colonial discourses the terms modernity, modern and modernisation are almost dirty words. Or let me use the words of Gita Sahgal, the Indian-born British director of the Centre for Secular Space and the founder of Women against Fundamentalism. In these types of discourse, she says, 'if you say the word modernising, it will be as bad as [saying] colonialism.' This is a pity, she says, because people seem to have forgotten 'that the anti-colonial movement was a modernising movement and a huge movement for equality.'[29]

Yet I continue to believe that several aspects of modernity are important if we are to have a state that treats citizens as equal before the law: a single, *secular, democratic legal order based on respect for civil and human rights*. The essentialists would flinch at my use of 'secularism', but I insist that a state that is not secular is in no position to be neutral in its treatment of its citizens. A state that is secular but not democratic and does not respect civil and human rights will ultimately abuse its power. And a secular state that is democratic and respects human rights but introduces plural legal orders will ultimately discriminate against some groups of its citizens. Hence, these qualities are mutually dependent: a single secular democratic legal order must be founded on norms of civil and human rights.

Rather than engage in a philosophical discussion, I suggest that we examine what that Syrian intellectual was saying. He was pointing out the intrinsic connection between the type of state that prevails in the Arab MENA context, and the situation of women there. What he was saying corresponded with what I was hearing from others I interviewed: the Arab state was and still is rarely a state composed of citizens. It is a state composed of ethnic groups.

It is a state of ethnic groups, not of citizens, and it is a state that does not treat its citizens as equal, not officially and not in reality. Indeed, the state has often come to represent the interests of a dominant group: a religious denomination, a sect, a tribe, a region or a cliental elite.

Other social groups have been pushed to accept the institutional reality of a state that has rarely considered them equal citizens. In fact, the state that was supposed to be impersonal, and treat its citizens as equals, has been acting as an ethnic bodyguard for the interests of the ruling elites. The lack of any solid institutional foundation has made it possible for the 'ethnicised' elites to hijack the state's institutions for their own benefit.[30]

Family laws mirror these features of the Arab state: they are divided, separate, ethnic and paternalistic, and they are also the tool that has helped perpetuate the very authoritarian nature of the Arab state. They have kept the society divided, hindering marriage between Sunnis and Shi'is, Christians and Muslims and Jews, superior tribes and inferior tribes, etc. In the process, in each country, these laws have sabotaged the development of a national identity. In other words, they have served to keep intact the elite's traditional base of power in all its fragmented sectarian, religious, tribal and regional forms.[31]

Is it a coincidence that there is no such thing as a civil marriage in any of the Arab MENA region countries? It simply does not exist. Even in countries like Israel and Lebanon, where the authorities grudgingly accept a civil marriage between members of different religious backgrounds, even there, the couple has to marry outside of the country, often in Cyprus, and then register the marriage in Israel or Lebanon. Is this situation a coincidence? The fact that civil marriage does not exist across religious or ethnic lines mirrors the religious/ethnic divisions I have described. It also reflects the absence in these countries of citizens who can stand as independent and equal regardless of their gender, religion or ethnicity. I am using the word divisions here though some might call it diversity. But the way it is lived and practiced there turns diversity into divisions; diversity becomes a source of instability, a source of fear. In fact, I dare say that the harder it becomes to marry across religious lines in a given state, the more susceptible that state is to political instability.

Stratified Citizenry and the Double Discrimination Syndrome

This political function of legal pluralism within the context of an 'ethnicised' Arab state, one that treats its citizens not as individuals but as members of ethnic groups, has consequences for both citizen's rights and women's rights.

I will again use Saudi Arabia and Syria to illustrate this point.

In Saudi Arabia the way legal pluralism is applied reflects the power equation in its political structure. It tells us clearly which ethnic/religious group dominates the political landscape: the Wahhabi Najdis. Other ethnic/sectarian groups in the society are considered secondary. Consequently, citizenship is stratified, organised around religious and regional references. It is a hierarchy: at the top stand the Sunni Wahhabi Najdi tribes as first-class citizens; Sunni Hijazis of the Shafite denomination follow behind, and the Sufi Hijazis are officially considered to be followers of a deviant denomination.

Those who belong to different and frowned-upon Islamic denominations, such as the Shi'a population of the Eastern Province, stand at the bottom of the citizenship ladder. The Wahhabi establishment and the religious police publicly call them heretics, followers of an 'evil' sect, and 'the greatest enemy and deceivers of the Sunni people.'[32]

Not only are they prevented from practising their religion openly; even their religious festivals are banned. Discrimination runs across all sectors: in employment and state services, and in the ability to join the army or diplomatic service or climb the political ladder on an equal footing with their Sunni counterparts. Very tellingly, they are prohibited from teaching either religion or history. This comes as no surprise, as the school curricula reflect the Wahhabi world view and condemn the Shi'a as a corrupt form of Islam whose adherents are condemned to hell.[33] In fact, these curricula do more than that. They reflect the hierarchy of citizenships I mentioned above. For just as they 'condemn and denigrate Shiite and Sufi Muslims' beliefs and practices as heretical and call them polytheists,' they also 'condemn and denigrate the majority of Sunni Muslims who do not follow the Wahhabi understanding of Islam, and call them deviants and descendants of polytheists.'[34] And school children in all regions of Saudi Arabia are told that.

The legal pluralism practiced in Syria also mirrors its sectarian/religious divisions and is also used to cement these divisions. But in Syria, it's the minorities who stand at the top of the citizenship hierarchy. At the top of the citizenship ladder is the Alawite minority, composed of four main tribal sections. They fill the ranks of the army, the security apparatus, the judiciary and the ruling party. Second on this ladder are the other minorities, including the Christians and Druze. They have been courted by the Syrian regime and have often filled secondary positions in the government and army. At the bottom have long languished the majority Sunni Muslim population, constantly humiliated and reminded that they are marginalised in the system. And you may remember that this hierarchy is exactly the opposite of the one that prevailed in Syria during the millet system of Ottoman times, reflecting the different power equations within the system now and then.

We should also note that the Syrian minorities have been drawn to this alliance almost reluctantly, out of simple fear. They have been pushed to believe that their own well-being is synonymous with the survival of the regime. Indeed, my research in Syria revealed that the regime has encouraged and supported 'societal Islamism' among Sunnis, through groups that advocate for conservative Sunni Islamic teaching and preach hate against minorities. This support has 'raised the ire and panic of other groups.' What some Syrian intellectuals have called the regime's 'industry of panic' has facilitated a 'crisis of national confidence'.[35] This crisis is obvious on several levels, especially the religious. As one interviewee told me, 'Christians are afraid of the majority Muslims; as a result they are increasingly solidifying their religious identity.' Meanwhile, 'the Muslims are suspicious of the Christians' because they think they 'identify with the West.'[36]

And the regime plays the role of the guarantor, which can ensure the safety and protection of the minorities against the 'tyranny of fundamentalism'.[37] And while this system has been falling apart over the past years of raging civil war, the strategy is still key to the regime's ability to survive.

Indeed, the hierarchy of citizenship, as we see in both the Saudi and Syrian cases, is often based on fear: the minority's fear of the majority and vice versa, and various groups' fear of other groups. It is also based on membership in a group, whether that group is based on ethnicity, religion, a sect or gender. As such, an individual citizen's position on the hierarchy is dependent on his/her membership in the various groups. Discrimination has many shapes and factors. But when the state starts to treat a citizen as a member of a group rather than as an individual, it paves the way for discriminatory treatment.

The Syrian intellectual I quoted at the start of this section turned out to be quite accurate when he said that the Arab state is pre-modern: in such a state an individual is not treated as citizen, as someone free or equal, but as a member of a group. Such a state plays the role of a bodyguard that serves the interest of an ethnic ruling group, and treats each citizen differently depending on the groups he or she belongs to.

In such a state, women face *double discrimination*. In Saudi Arabia, a citizen is a male Wahhabi Sunni from Najd. Across the hierarchy of Saudi citizenship, women always stand after the males, regardless of their denomination. In other words, while she faces the state's systematic discrimination, she also has to endure the control of her male guardian. Male guardianship, a system instituted by the state, treats women as perpetual minors and infringes on their basic human rights. A 2008 Human Rights Watch report put it this way:

> The Saudi government has instituted a system whereby every Saudi woman must have a male guardian, normally a father or husband, who is tasked with making a range of critical decisions on her behalf. This policy, grounded in the most restrictive interpretation of an ambiguous Quranic verse, is the most significant impediment to the realization of women's rights in the kingdom. The Saudi authorities essentially treat adult women like legal minors who are entitled to little authority over their own lives and well-being.[38]

While, as I described above, male guardianship over women is instrumental in preventing intertribal, interregional and intersectarian marriages, it has a second function: it literally creates chains around women's daily lives, as every adult Saudi woman, regardless of her economic or social status, must obtain permission from her male guardian to work, travel, study, seek medical treatment or marry. This system is maintained by the imposition of rigid sex segregation, which prevents women from participating meaningfully in public life.[39]

In Syria, a woman stands trapped between her ethnic/religious group – which demands her ultimate loyalty against the other groups – and her own aspirations for equality and justice as a woman and a citizen. I call this situation the *double discrimination syndrome*. Legal pluralism has meant that women must endure several levels of discrimination.

First, general discriminatory provisions apply to women in all Syrian groups. For example, all Syrian women are subject to male guardians, either their fathers or husbands or other male relatives. This means that women are always in dependent and secondary positions.

Second, each Syrian woman faces other discriminatory religious provisions, based on her own group's family law. These often enshrine a conservative patriarchal perception of women and their roles in the family. For example, as in Islamic law, the Christian personal status laws expect obedience from the wife. According to the Personal Status Law of the Syrian Greek Orthodox community, a woman must live with her husband in their residence; if she is required to live elsewhere, she must have his consent (Article 22). The equivalent law of the Syrian Catholic denominations declares a woman disobedient 'if she leaves her husband's house, if she prevents her husband from entering it, or if she refuses to travel with him without a legal reason.' And it decrees that a 'disobedient woman has no right to her husband's financial support' (Article 127: 1,2). The equivalent law of the Armenian Orthodox community reflects the same patriarchal conception of a marriage. Article 46 states that 'the man is the head of the family and her legal and natural representative. The man should protect his wife, and the woman should obey her husband.' And that of Syrian Jews, called the Book of the Provisions of the Personal Status of Jews, is no different. Article 73 reads: 'Once the wife is wedded to her husband, she has to obey him and follow his orders and legal prohibitions.'[40]

It is an arbitrary system. Arbitrary is the right word here because, depending on a woman's membership in a group, she may enjoy more rights than her counterpart in another group. But by the same token, the laws that govern her group may lead to violations of her rights while the laws governing other groups do not.

Accordingly, child marriage, or early marriage, is allowed in some groups and not in others. The Book of Personal Status for Syrian Jews sets the girl's minimum age for marriage at 13, while the Islamic Personal Status Law, no. 59 of 1953, sets it at 17 and the Catholic law sets it at 18. While Islamic law discriminates against women in inheritance rights and is applied to all religious groups, it is not applied to the Alawite group, whose customary law in rural areas deprives women of any inheritance rights.[41]

Let me repeat. This is an arbitrary system that grants some rights and withholds others while holding all groups hostage to their precarious positions on a gendered and ethnicised hierarchy of citizenship, where citizens are certainly not equal before the law.

***

These examples are not limited to the contexts of Saudi Arabia and Syria. In states that offer no clear separation between religion and politics, legal pluralism has been used as a tool that expresses the hegemony of the stronger ethnic group over the weaker in all areas: religion, socio-economic matters, tribal matters and gender.

In the Arab MENA region all the national constitutions declare that Islam is the religion of the state; thus Muslims are automatically placed in a privileged position vis-à-vis other religious groups. Some of these constitutions may state that citizens are equal regardless of religion, gender, race, etc. But the reality is different.

For instance, in Egypt the constitution guarantees equal citizenship, but state officials have often turned to customary law, based on shari'a norms, to resolve religious clashes between Muslims and Copts (Christians) in rural villages. The way it has been applied reflects a biased preferential treatment of the Muslim side and a tendency to administer measures of collective punishment against the Coptic side.

Often, religious tension will flare up for mundane reasons, like a Muslim's shirt being burned while it was being ironed at a laundry owned by a Christian. Sometimes the reason will be more serious, like a love affair between a Muslim girl and a Christian boy or the reverse. Violence erupts, the houses and shops of Christians are torched, and the Christian families are forced to leave the village. The use of customary law has never addressed the underlying causes of this religious violence, nor has it brought the perpetuators to justice or held them accountable. In fact what it does is deepen Egyptian Christians' sense of persecution and humiliation.

Consider a recent case of arbitration, which the Egyptian media have dubbed the Al Mataria case. On 11 February 2014 a fight started between an Egyptian Christian owner of a furniture shop and two Egyptian Muslim dealers in building materials who left bricks, cement, and sand in front of the store. It ended with the two dealers hitting the owner of the furniture shop. A meeting to resolve the situation ended in a bigger fight, this time involving families and outsiders, Muslims and Christians. Shooting erupted between them, and a Christian killed one person there, a Muslim.

Next, 15 members of the Christian family were arrested; some had not even been present during the fight. The police ordered the closure of their businesses for five months and forced them to arbitrate using customary law, based on shari'a.[42]

According to customary law, when someone is killed, the family of the perpetrator either pays a sum of money, or donates a piece of land, or pays in cattle. A member of the perpetrator's family should also carry a shroud (grave clothes) to the family of the victim, a custom symbolising an end to the blood feud. Then the killer will not be jailed or killed.

In the Mataria case the verdict was a showcase of how customary law has been used to express the domination of one religious group over another. All of these measures were administered, plus collective expulsion.

The verdict included the following. The Christian family was expelled from the village. They had to sell their property and stores, pay 1 million Egyptian pounds (about 110,000 euros), give 100 camels to the family of the deceased, and donate a piece of land of 234 square meters for a mosque to be built. Five members of the Christian family were ordered to carry five empty coffins, rather than one, to the family of the deceased and five calves were slaughtered. A penalty of 5 million Egyptian pounds was set in case the contract was breached.

The collective punishment of Christians, including elements like expulsion from their villages and selling of their property, has been a common part of the 'arbitration' in such cases. When a Muslim is killed, as in the Mataria case, arbitration does not mean an end to the state criminal process. The Muslim family declared that in accepting the deal, they did not abandon the criminal process that could lead to the perpetrator being imprisoned or executed. In cases where a Christian is killed, however, arbitration signals an end to the state criminal process. The perpetrator is set free.[43]

If you are thinking that customary law must have it its own sense of justice and cultural logic, I suggest that you take some time and listen to what Egyptian Copts are saying in this regard. Look at the issue from the perspective of the weaker party in this power equation.

The Coptic Church has continuously taken a firm position against the use of customary law in such conflicts, arguing that state law should be applied to all:

> The church sees that the provisions of customary arbitration sessions are unjust; [these sessions] equate the perpetrator with the victim; degrade the state's status and rule of law, and leave citizens feeling they are part of a tribe governed by customs in a context shadowed by the passiveness of security forces in protecting citizens.[44]

The Egyptian Initiative for Personal Rights, a human rights organisation advocating for civil rights for Copts, has repeatedly denounced the state's reliance on customary law, saying it leads to 'collective punishment against Egyptian Christians.' It has stressed the need to restore the rule of law, which the customary law sessions often bypass, and called on the Egyptian government to stop the forced evictions and displacement of Christian families, which are officially sanctioned by such arbitration sessions.[45]

Other advocacy and political organisations representing Egyptian Christian citizens, such as the Maspero Youth Union, Copts United and the Coalition of Egyptian Copts, have repeatedly articulated the same opinion. They all call on the state to bring the perpetrators to justice and refrain from collective punishment. They frequently use the word humiliation in these calls for a rule of law that will protect equal rights for all citizens:[46] 'We are being forced to submit to sessions of humiliation!' Customary law, as one human rights lawyer put it, has the aim of 'humiliating one side, namely the Christians.'[47]

***

Earlier I said that legal pluralism, in states that do not clearly separate religion and politics, has been used as a tool to express the hegemony of one dominant group over the weaker in many respects: religious, socio-economic, tribal and gender. I should emphasise that this practice is hardly limited to Islamic or Arab states. That legal pluralism is also practised in Israel, a Jewish democratic state, and Pakistan, a non-Arab Islamic state, only reinforces my argument.

Let me start with Israel, where legal pluralism, combined with the state's treatment of citizens as members of groups rather than individuals, has a clear political function: preserving the Jewish nature of Israel and fragmenting other religious communities into separate entities.

Israel was established in 1948 as a Jewish and a democratic state. Its Declaration of Independence had a liberal vision of a new democratic state that would 'uphold the full social and political equality of all its citizens, without distinction of race, creed or sex'; 'guarantee full freedom of conscience, worship, education and culture'; 'safeguard the sanctity and inviolability of the shrines and Holy Places of all religions'; and 'dedicate itself to the principles of the Charter of the United Nations.'[48]

However, the tension between the Jewishness of the new state and its democratic nature has cast a shadow on its dedication to equal citizenship. Passionate debates have circled around this point, with some claiming that the two concepts are compatible, and others countering that they are inherently at odds. Meanwhile a third camp insists that the apparent tension between the two concepts could be made consonant through interpretation.[49]

In reality, however, the state's institutions have been geared to favour one religious group – the Jews – over other religious groups.

In fact, as Sarah Slan, who wrote her master's thesis on Arab-Jewish couples in Israel under my supervision, argued, the state:

> distinguishes between national (Jewish) and non-national (non-Jewish) citizens, prioritising the national citizens and perceiving that non-national citizens are a threat to its survival and ethnic integrity. This leads to policies and regulations in various spheres of life that discriminate against non-Jews, especially against the Arab minority.[50]

The founders of the Israeli state have consciously applied the tool of legal pluralism to preserve the Jewishness of their state while maintaining the separateness of other religious groups.

Israel inherited the fragmented confessional personal status systems of the Ottoman millet system. After independence, Israel integrated the religious courts of 14 state-recognised ethno-religious communities, and their family laws, into its legal system; since then its government has directly executed their decisions.

Since the founding of the state over 60 years ago, Israel has largely preserved this fragmented confessional structure and refrained from introducing changes that would normatively or institutionally unify its personal status system.[51] Why?

Yüksel Sezgin, in *Human Rights under State-Enforced Religious Family Laws in Israel, Egypt and India*, offers some answers. He argues that Israel's leaders have maintained this variant of the Ottoman millet system for two reasons: first, to homogenise and preserve the Israeli-Jewish identity by creating a uniform and homogenous Israeli-Jewish collectivity, and second, to segregate and bolster communal divisions among the country's non-Jewish inhabitants.

On the one hand, Jews of different sectarian backgrounds had to be able to marry one another without wondering whether their future spouses were 'proper' Jews. This was imperative, to maintain the 'purity of the nation' and to avoid splitting 'the house of Israel into two.' Consequently, all marriages among Jews had to be in consonance with *halakhah*, Jewish religious law. On the other hand, preserving religious family laws for the different communal groups was instrumental in preventing 'non-kosher interfaith marriages' and creating a sense of separateness. The father of the Israeli state, David Ben-Gurion, famously supported the establishment of Druze religious courts, saying they were necessary to 'foster among the Druze an awareness that they are a separate community vis-à-vis the Muslim community.'[52]

Looked at from this perspective, the 'founding ideology was innately exclusionary as much as it was theoretically inclined.'[53] Hence, the country simultaneously undertook two opposite processes of nation-building, which Sezgin calls homogenisation and differentiation:

At the first level, the Zionists aimed to minimise the cultural, linguistic, sectarian and ideological differences among the Jewish immigrants by melding them into a modern Israeli-Jewish identity known as Sabra. At the inter-ethnic level, a complementary process of differentiation was undertaken to accentuate cultural, social and religious disparities between the Palestinians and the Jews. That is to say, even though non-Jews were granted full citizenship on paper, in reality Israel has never aimed to create a civic sense of citizenship or Israeli nationality (leumiut yisrailit) on equal terms, but rather has opted for a stratified citizenry. In fact, the preservation of the old millet system has enabled the Israeli regime to simultaneously pursue the goals of homogenisation and differentiation by institutionalising confessional divisions among the subjects of the Jewish state.[54]

Israel was created as a land for the Jews. In the same year, Pakistan was created as a land for Muslims. A non-Arab MENA state, it was carved out of India. From its very inception in 1947, Pakistan was confused about its nature. Or in the words of Werner Menski, in *Comparative Law in a Global Context*, the country's legal structures on independence 'were confused about whether God's law or men's law was supreme and raised critical questions about Islamisation.'[55]

The country's founding leaders were not in a position to secularise its legal system, as those in Turkey did, for fear of a backlash from their own constituents. Nor were they eager to follow the Indian model of secularism that guaranteed equal treatment for all members of the new state. What they wanted was a 'Muslim state mainly for Muslims', and this has meant following a path 'centred on the Islamic identity of the country and most of its people.'[56] This choice, and the role of Islamisation, had a profound impact on the country's legal structure and gradually led to an erosion of the boundaries between politics and religion.

The religious nature of the state was articulated in the Objectives Resolution of 1949, which was turned into the preamble to all of Pakistani's constitutions, of 1956, 1962, and 1973. It stated that 'sovereignty over the entire universe belongs to Almighty Allah alone, and the authority to be exercised by the people of Pakistan within the limits prescribed by him.' Principles of 'democracy, freedom, equality, tolerance and social justice' were to be strictly followed within the framework of Islam.[57] 'Adequate provisions' were to be made for the minorities to freely 'profess and practice their religion and develop their cultures.' However, fundamental rights (including equality of status, of opportunity and before the law, social economic and political justice, and freedom of thought, expression of belief, faith, worship and association) were to be 'subject to law and public morality.'[58]

Together, these provisions and subsequent amendments to the constitution paved the way for violations of fundamental human and minorities' rights. A Machiavellian style of political opportunism led politicians and military dictators, eager to win over the public and secure the support of conservative Islamist movements, to launch a process of Islamisation; that process has ultimately criminalised women and minorities and led to 'massive abuses of law and legal procedures,' all of which continue today.[59]

Legal pluralism, combined with the state's treatment of citizens as members of groups, rather than as individuals, provided the setting to create a stratified citizenship pyramid.

From Britain, Pakistan inherited a hybrid system that applied English common law, Islamic law, customary tribal laws and religious laws – Christian, Hindu and Parsi (Zoroastrian) – that govern the family affairs of these minorities. The Islamisation process led to laws being passed that specifically targeted the frowned-upon religious groups.

One good example is the treatment of the Ahmadiyyah minority, followers of a modern Islamic Sufi sect founded in 1889 by Mirza Ghulam Ahmad. Like the Baha'i and Alawite faiths, it holds to the belief that other prophets came after Muhammad. Throughout its history, it has been persecuted by Sunni Muslim legalists, who opposed mystic Sufism in general, and considered blasphemous its questioning of Muhammad's role as the last prophet of God.[60]

After Pakistan became independent, the Ahmadiyyah community was legally considered a Muslim community – and that is how it perceived itself. However, a combination of political opportunism and the Islamisation process led to a 1974 amendment to the constitution declaring the community to be non-Muslims. The state has engaged in considerable persecution, especially since 1977, when General Mohammad Zia ul-Haq came to power through a coup. Since then, the community has been denied any semblance of Islamic character and its people have been denied positions in the civil service and the military.[61]

Members of this minority have been routinely imprisoned for engaging in the minor daily behaviours common to most Muslims: saying 'Muslims, peace be upon you', citing the Quran, calling their worship places 'mosques', and simply 'behaving like a Muslim'. These points were included in the Penal Code (298–C), which declares:

An Ahmadi who refers to his faith as Islam, or preaches or propagates his faith, or invites others to accept his faith, by words, either spoken or written, or by visible representations, or in any manner whatsoever that outrages the religious feelings of Muslims, will be punished with up to three years in prison and is liable to pay a fine.[62]

And in both Israel and Pakistan, women are left vulnerable to the double discrimination syndrome caused by the system of legal pluralism. In Israel, just as in Syria, Saudi Arabia and Egypt, women are sandwiched between their own needs for equality and justice as women and as citizens, and the needs of their ethnic/religious communities – which often feel that their very existence is threatened within the state and hence demand ultimate loyalty from their members.

Family affairs are regulated by religious laws, which inherently discriminate against women in the areas of divorce, child custody, maintenance and alimony. But family laws have been interwoven with the concepts of nationality and identity. To demand a change in these laws is considered an attack on the religious groups themselves.

Yüksel Sezgin has masterfully shown how women in Israel are left treading on thin ice as they claim their right to justice and equality. Both Israeli Jewish and Muslim women have their fair share of problems under state-enforced religious laws. Yet because matrimonial affairs have been viewed as a pillar of Palestinian autonomy and identity, Muslim women have often remained silent. When they do try to break away from this double bind and work together with their fellow Jewish women citizens, they risk being perceived as a tool that can undermine the 'national, cultural and institutional autonomy of the Arab minority in Israel.'[63] Worse, they risk being labelled, and attacked as, traitors.

Israeli Jewish women also feel the burden of their religious family law. Although they fare better than their fellow citizens from other religious groups, they too face discrimination within this system. They cannot help but feel they are being betrayed and discarded by their own state, as the statement below, from an Orthodox Jewish woman, shows. The woman wanted her husband to grant her a *get*: a document that would allow a divorce. He refused, and she said:

This is not Tehran [...] this is Jerusalem. This is supposed to be a democratic country, not a theocracy [...] I have nothing against the religion. I believe in God [...] And God is fair and compassionate [. . .] He has nothing to do with what is happening to me right now [. . .] I blame it on those judges who side with that awful man [her husband]. And I hold no one responsible, but the government which pays their [rabbinical judges] salaries, and never fails to reward them for their intransigence.[64]

The double discrimination syndrome is also prevalent in Pakistan. Women in all Pakistani religious groups face different kinds of discrimination. They too stand sandwiched between their patriarchal religious group and a state that discriminates against them by virtue of their gender. For example, Christian marriage laws, left untouched since 1869/72, make divorce an ordeal for both men and women. The Divorce Act of 1869 states that a husband may seek to dissolve his marriage on the grounds of adultery by his wife. A wife, on the other hand, cannot request a divorce simply on the ground of her husband's adultery. She must prove either 'incestuous adultery, bigamy with adultery, adultery coupled with rape, sodomy or bestiality, adultery coupled with cruelty, or adultery coupled with desertion without reasonable excuse, for period of two or more years.'[65]

Not surprisingly, most Pakistani Christians who seek a divorce base it on false charges of adultery. In addition, as Islamic law has precedence in the Pakistani legal system, most Christians would rather convert to Islam to get a divorce. When a Christian man converts, he can divorce his wife by pronouncing the divorce unilaterally, and when a Christian woman converts, her marriage to her husband will automatically be dissolved because, according to Pakistani law, a Muslim woman cannot marry a non-Muslim.[66]

Customary law is another source of discrimination against women in Pakistan's pluralist legal system. According to Hindu customary law, sisters and daughters cannot inherit at all. The state does not interfere to remedy this injustice, despite a constitutional clause that prohibits discrimination on the basis of gender alone (Article 25.2).[67]

Most significantly, the double discrimination syndrome is acutely felt through the jirga tribal system, which has introduced constant fear into the lives of women in Pakistan. The jirga is the traditional system of justice, actively practised in several regions of the country. It exercises both judicial and executive roles that cover all aspects of economic, social and political life in tribal society. It is a council composed of two or more persons, who sit together in a circle and arbitrate. They are often family elders and the groups are dominated by the powerful tribal and feudal leaders in their area. It has a comprehensive system of tribal codes, rules, regulations and mechanisms.[68]

Where it concerns women it operates with a twisted understanding of honour and justice. If you are flinching because of the word twisted, I apologise. The problem is, it is twisted.

According to a tradition called *karo kari*, a family whose honour has been offended should kill any man and woman who have either become involved in an illicit relationship or married against the will of their families. Often the woman in such a case is the one who ends up being killed.

But that is not all.

In fact, the logic of the jirga system turns the concept of victim and perpetrator upside down. The women who are killed are not seen as the victims. They are the guilty parties. The woman – the wife, sister or daughter – belongs to the man, and he 'has to kill to restore his honour.'[69] According to this logic, the killer is the victim and should be compensated.

The family or tribe of the guilty individual has to ask for a tribal jirga to counter the wish of the aggrieved party to take revenge. When the jirga is making a decision against any woman accused of breaching a family's honour, it does not give that accused woman any right to appear before the council or to defend herself. It takes the statements of her father, brother or other relatives on her behalf. According to this system, just the evidence of the husband is enough to declare that a woman is *kari*, that she has committed adultery. If a woman is unmarried, then the testimony of her father or brothers would be enough to declare her *kari*.[70]

When a man kills his wife in a case like this, the tribal jirga ensures that he will be compensated because he is 'sustaining the loss of a woman.' Compensation, which is given by the family of the killed woman or the lover of the woman, can be in the form of money, land, or women. Yes, women!

The standard price is one girl above the age of seven or two under seven. In order not to have to give up two of their girls, families are known to have knocked out the child's milk teeth to pass her off as older than she really is. But sometimes the compensation has to include two women regardless of age because [as a jirga member explains], 'if her paramour [lover] escapes, he has to pay two khoons [blood money], one for the loss of a wife or daughter and one because the paramour's life was spared.'[71]

It is important to mention the jirga system here because it highlights one important aspect of my discussion of legal pluralism. Proponents of legal pluralism often argue that customary laws, while they may be flawed, are the only legal system available to people in rural areas in states that are corrupt and have weak institutions. Hence, they argue, one should accept the system as a reality and work with it. And while they are correct in describing the problem, their suggested remedy does not solve the problem; it simply preserves the status quo, cements the system's inherent inequalities, perpetuates the feudal and tribal abuse of power, and makes a cynical joke of women's daily struggles.

Perhaps a better suggestion would be to take the hard way suggested by some courageous Pakistani men and women. They are the ones fighting these arbitrary systems of 'justice'.

Mukhtar Mai, a village woman in southern Punjab, has become the Pakistani face of the campaign against this abusive system. In 2001, she was gang raped by members of the powerful Mastoi tribe on the orders of a jirga council the tribe controlled.

Members of the tribe claim that her brother, then 12 years old, had an affair with a woman from their tribe, who was then 20. Mukhtar Mai's tribe, which is lower in status, claims that members of the Mastoi tribe sodomised the boy, and were trying to cover up their crime; in fact this charge was later confirmed in a state court. After she was raped, Mukhtar was forced to walk home, almost naked, before a jeering crowd. Instead of committing suicide as is expected in such circumstances, she went to the police and reported the rape. Although the system eventually failed her, she, and Pakistani human rights organisations, have continued to campaign for an end to this arbitrary system.[72]

In fact, the Pakistani Human Rights Commission issued a joint statement in 2013, criticising the Pakistani government for failing to take measures to fight violence against women and girls, including sexual exploitation and honour killings and for letting Tribal courts (jirgas) continue to issue highly discriminatory judgements against women unhindered.

Tellingly, when the commission made this recommendation, it was determined to solve the problem rather than perpetuating the system by working with it. In fact, it called for an outright end to these parallel legal systems of arbitration. The statement called on the government of Pakistan to 'Take measures to establish a unified judicial system, and eliminate all parallel legal systems and informal dispute resolution mechanisms which discriminate against women'; it also asked it to 'make the public more sensitive on the importance of addressing violations of women's rights through judicial remedies rather than parallel justice systems.'[73]

***

So far I have presented cases of legal pluralism practiced in states with two characteristics: they do not separate politics and religion, and they treat their citizens as members of groups rather than individuals. In all these cases we have seen the same three results: a stratified citizenry, outright violations of citizen's and womens' rights, and the double discrimination syndrome.

A different form of legal pluralism is often practiced in democratic states that do separate politics and religion, and do respect human rights, but still choose, for historical or political reasons, to grant group rights to a certain ethnic/religious group. The group applies different laws and rules in a way that separates it from the state's legal system. This jeopardises respect for human rights and gender equality.

This type of plural legal order exists in countries such as Canada, the United States, Australia and New Zealand, where indigenous peoples, who were historically discriminated against, are accorded legal orders which are recognised as law.[74]

For example, in Canada around 1.4 million people (4.3 per cent of the total population) are indigenous, commonly called aboriginal. Half of these people are registered as 'status' Indians, members of First Nations. In addition, there are 617 First Nations or Indian bands in Canada, representing more than 50 cultural groups and living in about 1,000 communities, as well as elsewhere across the country.[75]

The general statute governing registered Indians/First Nations is the Indian Act, first decreed in 1876. It regulates most aspects of aboriginal life and governance on Indian reserves and deals with such issues as who may, by definition, claim Indian status in Canada, the rights and duties which accompany that status, the structure of Canada's reserve system, and the nature of aboriginal self-government.[76]

Canada is undoubtedly committed to protecting its indigenous people. The 2014 *Report on Canada*, by the special rapporteur on the rights of indigenous peoples, made sure to mention that repeatedly.

I do understand the complexity of the issue and I applaud the government's efforts to amend the suffering caused by centuries of discrimination. But I question the response to this injustice. Is it a valid solution to keep these people separate in 'reservations', where their membership is connected to a defined, if not frozen, category of identity? It certainly has not helped to improve their situation so far. In fact, they remain stranded at the bottom ladder of the human development index, living in Third World conditions as indicated in the report mentioned above.

Moreover, the double discrimination syndrome appears in this system as well. The 1981 case of Sandra Lovelace versus Canada is a good example. In 1970, Lovelace, a Maliseet Indian, married a non-Indian and left the reservation. Following her divorce, she sought to return to live on the reservation. However, under section 12(1)(b) of the Indian Act, she had lost her rights and status as an Indian by marrying a non-Indian. Lovelace pointed out that an Indian man who marries a non-Indian woman does not lose his Indian status, and argued that the Act is discriminatory on the grounds of sex.[77]

Her case is hardly insignificant or individual. According to Canadian statistics, each year between 1965 and 1978, an average of 510 Indian women married non-Indian men; compare this to the 590 Indian women who married Indian men of their same band each year.[78] Apparently many Indian women choose to marry non-Indians, despite the hard choices that could result if they lose their right to live in a community and enjoy the benefits of that status.

But Lovelace's case was both exceptional and historical. The Canadian court system was reluctant to interfere with a domestic issue within the First Nations, so Lovelace brought her case to the UN Human Rights Council. It decided in her favour but not from a perspective of gender rights. It addressed her case specifically as a minority rights issue, and considered the act discriminatory because it denied her the 'right to culture'. The case did force the Canadian government to repeal the gender-discriminatory provisions in Canada's

Indian Act, but unfortunately, the amendments did not go far enough, and the act continues to protect some gender discrimination.[79]

***

Thus we see once again that in settings of legal pluralism, women are left vulnerable to discriminatory laws, customs and norms. In fact, they face double discrimination and are left to themselves as a secondary category of citizens. This is why I insisted, at the beginning of this chapter, that states should situate rights within an individual framework. They should treat their citizens as individuals, not as members of groups. Otherwise they will end up stranded in a pyramid based on a stratified citizenry. I have presented different cases of 'non-Western' legal pluralist orders and have shown that far from being an example to emulate, they all violate a wide range of rights with impunity: human rights, citizens' rights and the rights of women and minorities.

These examples highlight a point I will continue to emphasise: protecting citizens, especially women and minorities, on an equal basis requires *a secular, democratic, and singular legal order based on respect for civil and human rights*. These features are mutually dependent.

In states that are secular and democratic, and respect human rights, but that introduce plural legal orders, like Canada, the double discrimination syndrome and a stratified citizenry are likely outcomes. Here, the minority within the minority is left subject to abuse and discrimination.

Which brings me to the topic of this book: Islamic law in the West.

In Britain, in the province of Ontario in Canada, in Australia, and elsewhere, people have recently been demanding that religious arbitration be recognised in family matters and other 'minor' civil matters.[80]

Self-proclaimed community leaders and well-intentioned politicians and personalities, in addition to academics, have argued that religious laws should be applied in family affairs. They have articulated these demands using the essentialists' discourse: group rights, identity politics, rights to difference, the white man's burden, and multiculturalism.

This is only one mechanism for conflict resolution, they would argue. And it would only affect the minor affairs that are governed by family law. Yet it is precisely because this suggestion concerns family law that it should be rejected. Why? Because the key issue here is legally sanctioned discrimination against women and children.

Ironically, when the essentialists talk about arbitration, legal mechanisms, and conflict resolution, they often seem to evade and circumvent the one vital question: What kind of law will be used in this arbitration?

Good question. Which law is being used in arbitration?

And when we pose the question in this way, it will become clear why applying this law will lead to legally sanctioned discrimination and why its use should not even be considered. I am afraid there is no politically correct way to say this: when it concerns women, children and fundamental rights, Islamic law violates human rights standards with impunity.

In the next chapter I will look at the question of Islamic law and human rights. I will then look at the type of Islamic interpretation of shari'a law that is dominant in the leading shari'a councils and in Muslim arbitration tribunals in Britain.

CHAPTER 4

ISLAMIC LAW AND HUMAN RIGHTS BETWEEN THEORY AND REALITY: BRITAIN AS A SHOWCASE

Islamic law discriminates against women. I think we can accept this as a fact. But this is only half of the problem. When we focus only on the discrimination, we miss the other half of the picture: the political function of Islamic law. Looked at from this perspective, allowing weak legal pluralism into the Islamic legal enclaves in Western democracies may undermine the very foundation of those democracies.

So we should never consider one of these two aspects – the discrimination caused by Islamic law and the political function of weak Islamic legal pluralism within Western democracies – without also considering the other. This chapter is dedicated to the first aspect: Islamic law and human rights. In Chapter 5 I focus on two forms of Islamism and the political function of Islamic legal enclaves.

In the next section, I first discuss one argument within the essentialists' paradigm that supports the idea of integrating Islamic law within a Western legal order, showcasing the 2008 speech on that topic by former Archbishop Rowan Williams. In the section after that, I offer a universalistic response to his argument. I then move to argue that the essentialists, along with acquiescent British officialdom, are in fact opting for what Tahmina Saleem, co-founder of Inspire, the British Muslim women's organisation, called an 'anthropological version of law' – which I define as a version of law void of any historical, political or even legal context. In the last section I outline the areas where the suggested Islamic law contradicts universal human rights, and women's rights, and then present the type of weak plural legal system now operating in Britain. I will argue that the dominant interpretation of Islamic law being espoused within British Islamic shari'a councils and Muslim arbitration tribunals is inherently discriminatory against women.

An Essentialist Argument for Islamic Law: Rowan Williams and Religious Groups Conscientiously Opting out

Sometimes I wonder why Rowan Williams, the former Archbishop of Canterbury, chose to talk about Islamic law, knowing quite well what was likely to ensue. I am referring to his famous 2008 speech entitled 'Civil and Religious Law in England: A Religious Perspective'. Even when he was dazzling us with a fine-grained differentiation between shari'a as 'the universal principle of Islam' and shari'a as the 'particular concretisation of it at the hands of a tradition of jurists,'[1] he was well aware that he was stepping into a minefield, and one full of discrimination against women.

Yet the more I re-read his lecture, the more I became convinced that he was actually protesting the secular encroachment into religious space, using the issue of Islamic law as a stealthy, sophisticated way to do so. I am not alone in this opinion. Bernard Jackson, a world-renowned expert on Jewish law, has suggested that in giving his lecture, Williams's primary interest was in building 'a religious coalition, led by the Church of England (as the 'established' Church),' that would 'favour [. . .] exemption from secular law on grounds of religious conscience.'[2]

From this perspective, I found his speech utterly irresponsible.

Notwithstanding this irritation, I still see Williams's lecture as a fine, well-articulated piece of philosophical deliberation, one that has all the trademarks of the essentialists' paradigm: multiculturalism combined with a demand for group rights, and a weak cultural relativism permeated by an apologetic sense of the white man's burden.

Dr Williams would like us to 'think a little harder about the role and rule of law in a plural society of overlapping identities.' He used his lecture as an opportunity to carefully discuss and 'tease out some of the broader issues around the rights of religious groups within a secular state' and to offer 'a few thoughts about what might be entailed in crafting a just and constructive' relationship between Islamic law and the statutory law of the United Kingdom.'[3]

He accurately identifies three objections raised 'when there is a robust affirmation that the law of the land should protect individuals on the ground of their corporate religious identity and secure their freedom to fulfil religious duties.'[4]

First objection: It 'leaves legal process (including ordinary disciplinary process within organisations) at the mercy of what might be called vexatious appeals to religious scruple.'

He gives two examples of such vexatious appeals. In the first, a Muslim woman employed by Marks and Spencer, the department store chain, reportedly refused to handle a book of Bible stories. The second example is forced marriages; he reminds us that it is crucial to distinguish between cultural and strictly religious dimensions.

These examples, he argues, suggest the need for 'access to recognised authority acting for a religious group' to help determine 'the relative seriousness of conscience-related claims.'

In the case of the 'Muslim community' in the UK, Williams knows to whom we should turn. He identifies the 'recognised authority': the Islamic shari'a council:

> There is already, of course, an Islamic Shari'a Council, much in demand for rulings on marital questions in the UK; and if we were to see more latitude given in law to rights and scruples rooted in religious identity, we should need a much enhanced and quite sophisticated version of such a body, with increased resources and a high degree of community recognition, so that 'vexatious' claims could be summarily dealt with.[5]

Second objection: 'recognition of supplementary jurisdiction in some areas, especially family law, could have the effect of reinforcing in minority communities some of the most repressive or retrograde elements in them, with particularly serious consequences for the role and liberties of women.'[6]

He highlights the inherent problem in recognising the 'authority of a communal religious court to decide finally and authoritatively' about such issues. Not only will it allow an 'additional layer of legal routes for resolving conflicts and ordering behaviour.' In addition it 'would actually deprive members of the minority community of rights and liberties that they were entitled to enjoy as citizens.'

He does not dispute this, or see anything wrong in it. In fact, accepting this objection, he says that:

> Were any kind of plural jurisdiction [...] recognised, it would presumably have to be under the rubric that no 'supplementary' jurisdiction could have the power to deny access to the rights granted to other citizens [regardless of faith affiliation], or to punish its members for claiming those rights.

Dr Williams is very aware of the validity of such danger and gives several examples of how conflict could arise, such as in cases of forced marriage (which he again emphasises is a cultural practice), the inheritance rights of widows, and Islam's prohibition of apostasy.

Having pointed out these areas of conflict, he comes to what he calls the same conclusion:

> So the second objection to an increased legal recognition of communal religious identities can be met if we are prepared to think about the basic ground rules that might organise the relationship between jurisdictions, making sure that we do not collude with unexamined systems that have oppressive effect or allow shared public liberties to be decisively taken away by a supplementary jurisdiction. Once again, there are no blank cheques.

Third objection: The third objection in fact addresses Dr Williams's own objection to what he calls 'legal universality' and his argument that it should be possible to *opt out* of this legal perception on religious grounds.

He writes about the Enlightenment's claim to 'override traditional forms of governance and custom by looking towards a universal tribunal,' saying it was 'entirely intelligible against the background of despotism and uncritical inherited privilege which prevailed in so much of early modern Europe.'

The most positive aspect of this historical development was 'its focus on equal levels of accountability for all and equal levels of access for all to legal process.'

Nevertheless, Williams insists that this alone 'is not adequate to deal with the realities of complex societies.' He argues that 'it is not enough to say that citizenship as an abstract form of equal access and equal accountability is either the basis or the entirety of social identity and personal motivation.' Instead, he says this:

> Societies that are in fact ethnically, culturally and religiously diverse are societies in which identity is formed [. . .] by different modes and contexts of belonging, 'multiple affiliations' [. . .] This means that we have to think a little harder about the role and rule of law in a plural society of overlapping identities [. . .] the rule of law is thus not the enshrining of priority for the universal/abstract dimension of social existence but the establishing of a space accessible to everyone in which it is possible to affirm and defend a commitment to human dignity.

Rowan Williams comes to the core purpose of his lecture:

> One of the most frequently noted problems in the law in this area is the reluctance of a dominant rights-based philosophy to *acknowledge the liberty of conscientious opting-out from collaboration in procedures or practices that are in tension with the demands of particular religious groups*: the assumption, in rather misleading shorthand, that if a right or liberty is granted there is a corresponding duty upon every individual to 'activate' this whenever called upon. [emphasis added]

He argues that if it were possible to recognise religious conviction without interfering with, or blocking access to, the liberties guaranteed by wider society, due consideration should be given to doing just that:

> It would be a pity if the immense advances in the recognition of human rights led, because of a misconception about legal universality, to a situation where a person was defined primarily as the possessor of a set of abstract liberties and the law's function was

accordingly seen as nothing but the securing of those liberties irrespective of the custom and conscience of those groups which concretely compose a plural modern society.

When it comes to 'aspects of shariʻa' and following a model sketched by the Jewish legal theorist Ayelet Shachar, Williams makes a suggestion:

> It might be possible to think in terms of what Shachar calls 'transformative accommodation': a scheme in which individuals retain the liberty to choose the jurisdiction under which they will seek to resolve certain carefully specified matters, so that [to quote Shachar] 'power-holders are forced to compete for the loyalty of their shared constituents.' This may include aspects of marital law, the regulation of financial transactions and authorised structures of mediation and conflict resolution.

A Universalistic Response to Rowan Williams's Argument

Well, I did call it a fine piece of philosophical deliberation. Unfortunately, it was also an eloquent appeal to return to the application of religious laws in the name of religious 'group rights'. Ironically, this appeal was based on individual choice – with the choice situated within a group framework. Hence, he defends individuals' rights to opt out of universal state law in the name of religious groups' claims to difference.

Eloquent or not, Williams was clearly seeking a way out for religious groups, including his, from an increasingly secular society and its laws. Hence he called for a rule of law that could bypass the priority placed on a universal dimension of social existence and instead establish a space that 'affirms and defends a commitment to human dignity.' The problem is, if human dignity is not protected by a *secular single legal order* and connected to *human rights*, the situation will revert to what he was warning us about in the first place: the tyranny of religious dogma.

Let me explain by carefully evaluating what he described as solutions to his three objections.

First solution. In order to avoid a misuse of 'conscience-related claims', Williams suggests identifying or creating a recognised authority that would act for the religious group to help the state determine 'the relative seriousness of conscience-related claims.' And when the group is Muslims, he already has such a body in mind: none other than the much-criticised Islamic Shari'a Council.

This solution is problematic in two ways, one theoretical and one practical. Both show that the solution is not in fact a solution.

From a theoretical perspective, instituting such a 'recognised' authority will lead to a situation similar to the millet system of Ottoman times. The Ottoman authorities decided who would represent the religious minority, and then sanctioned that authority's control over the minority – and that control was both theocratic and authoritarian. Likewise, we are justified in asking who will choose or create this authority in Britain. And according to which criteria will it be decided that it does indeed represent the religious minority?

I think we are justified in having some qualms here, given that the British authorities have not exactly been well-informed in their cultural and minorities policies thus far. In fact, until the London terrorist attacks of 7 July 2005, the British authorities, following their plural monocultural policies, worked exclusively with Islamist groups, who follow an ideology of political Islamism. At that time they considered such groups the sole representatives of the Muslims, ignoring in the process the diversity of British Muslim communities, most of which did not even subscribe to the Islamists' worldviews. After 2005, the Blair government decided to work with 'non-violent fundamentalists' in its fight against home-grown terrorism, thinking that these would be the best antidotes to the ideology of 'violent fundamentalists'.[7] Apparently they were unaware that the boundaries between the two are often superficial. They are stages of extremism, both with totalitarian subtexts.

Given such blunders and ignorance, we can be excused for being suspicious when Dr Williams suggests establishing a 'recognised authority that speaks for the religious minority.'

Along the same lines, we are also entitled to ask the next question: Who will define this 'minority' in the first place?

This question was critically discussed by the authors of the ground-breaking report from the International Human Council on Rights, a Geneva-based NGO, entitled 'When Legal Worlds Overlap: Human Rights, State and Non-State Law'. They argued as follows:

A demand to recognise a 'community's' legal autonomy begins with defining the community, what has been called the 'dirty work of boundary maintenance.' Who draws these boundaries – individuals, communities, the culture, the Executive, the Judiciary or a combination of them all? Deciding who belongs and who does not is a political process communities engage in internally and states engage in vis-à-vis communities they recognise.[8]

The report argued that both state and non-state laws give substance to 'boundary maintenance' in several ways. First, they *construct* legal identities: they classify the population into different categories, such as class, caste, ethnicity, gender, citizenship, alien status, etc. Second, they prescribe the norms for, and structure of, relationships between these categories. Third, they stipulate the rights and duties of those falling into the categories in question. In fact, the report's authors see the irony in this process: different legal orders construct the identity of the population differently and thus the same group of people may be categorised differently by different legal orders and have different statuses, rights and obligations.[9] For example, in Nepal the Hindu law classifies some groups as untouchable castes and consequently prohibits them from entering some temples or drawing water from wells used by those of higher castes. On the other hand, the state law classifies them as citizens with equal rights, even as Dalits with special rights, for example giving them quotas in educational institutions.[10]

In fact, this could also be the case in Britain. If you doubt that, I suggest you consider the very 'authority' that Williams suggests as 'representative' of the Muslims: the Islamic Shari'a Council (ISC). And then consider what would follow recognition of its authority. This brings us to the practical critical aspect of Dr Williams's problematic solutions.

When we start to be specific, the gravity of the problem becomes clear. The ISC was created in 1982 after a meeting attended by imams representing a number of mosques in the UK. It describes itself as a welfare and non-profit-making registered charity (No. 1003855). It states that it was created to solve the matrimonial problems of Muslims living in the United Kingdom in light of Islamic family law. These problems include marriages, divorces and inheritance issues. According to its website, the council is 'made up of members from all of the major schools of Islamic legal thought (*mad'hab*) and is widely accepted as an authoritative body with regards to Islamic law.'[11] This is how it describes itself.

If this body was to be the much enhanced and recognised body speaking in the name of the Muslims, as Williams suggested, then we should take its opinions on the minimum age for marriage at face value. We should accept such rulings. Right?

Consider the position of Sheikh Haitham al-Haddad, a famous and controversial figure on the ISC. Of Palestinian origin, Al-Haddad was born and raised in Saudi Arabia. He studied Islamic shari‘a in Saudi Arabia and Sudan and sits on the ISC as one of its judges. On a video, which was later removed from YouTube, he stated his position on the minimum age for marriage, in response to someone asking for his opinion. His answer was straightforward: there is no minimum age in Islamic law and the younger the girl is the better. Here is my transcription of the conversation:

Interviewer: At what age should a teenage girl get married?
Haddad: Get what?
Interviewer: Married. Is it a family decision?
Haddad: Yes, it is a family decision.
Interviewer: Is there a particular age from an Islamic perspective?
Haddad: No particular age for the marriage of the girl; no particular age from an Islamic perspective. But as you know the earlier the better, especially for girls; but you have to be careful of the legal *yanni* [meaning] issues.
Interviewer: Legal issue? Is it from the rule of the land?
Haddad: Not necessarily. There are many *yanni* laws in the country here that are anti-Islamic, not Muslims, not Islamic laws, so if there is a way to live and avoid those anti-Islamic laws, then – and provided that you do not get yourself into trouble, yeah? – then you should go for that choice. What can you do? Yep.
Interviewer: The preference would be?
Haddad: Normally the younger the better.[12]

Simple. The younger the better and when you marry off your young girl do try and avoid getting arrested in the process. The law of Britain, which sets the minimum age for marriage at 16 (the UN's standard is 18), is un-Islamic; find a way to circumvent it.

So if we were to act on Rowan Williams's suggestion and recognise the ISC as the authority to speak for Muslims and determine what is Islamic and what is not, should we then take Al-Haddad's position as an Islamic principle? Should we then apply it to girls within the Muslim minority? In fact, the position that Islam has no minimum age for marriage 'and the earlier the better' has often meant accepting the marriages of nine-year-old girls. Should we then accept child marriage (which international standards also define as forced marriage) as a perfectly acceptable 'Islamic' principle? I will show in a later section that the general practice in Islamic countries is to set a minimum age, often at 18. But those that Williams sees as representatives of British Islam do not seem to subscribe to such modern ideas.

Al-Haddad does not stand alone in the ISC in the way he interprets of Islamic law. Another prominent figure on the council is Sheikh Dr Suhaib Hasan. Born in India, and raised and educated in Pakistan, he studied shari'a in Saudi Arabia, just like Al-Haddad. He completed his studies in Birmingham, England, and sits as a judge in the council.

When I met him in January 2013, the work of the ISC was under scrutiny after Baroness Caroline Cox submitted an Arbitration and Mediation Services (Equality) Bill calling for changes in the arbitration law in a way that would ensure gender equality. Baroness Cox warned of the danger of a parallel legal system and of the work of such shari'a councils. In one article, she wrote about an undercover investigation; the reporter revealed that a number of imams were willing to arrange marriages for underage girls. Two of them were imams from Islamic centres, one based in Peterborough, the other in East London. The two 'expressed their willingness to marry an under-age Muslim girl – aged just 12 – to a man in his 20s under the aegis of Shari'a law.'[13] Alluding to her article, I asked him what age of marriage was accepted at the ISC.

Compared to al-Haddad, Sheikh Hasan has a more qualified position on this issue. He told me that from an Islamic perspective there is no specific age for marriage. However, the age can be set and defined by a sultan. Hence one can accept the law of Britain as having been set by such an authority. He then argued that from an Islamic law perspective, if he were asked about a girl who was married at 13 or 14, and whether or not her marriage was valid, his answer would be yes, the marriage is valid:[14]

> Hasan: You see the age of marriage is something that is not binding in Islam that it should be a certain age. It is a matter which can be limited. The *mahr* [mandatory payment by the groom, in the form of money or possessions], is not limited, but the prophet said that [. . .] the lower the costs of marriage, the more blessed they are. So this is why you must make the *mahr* as low as possible, to make it *baraka* [blessed], not a very expensive *mahr*. But there is no limit here. There is no limit here. In certain cases, if the Khalifa Al Sultan, [if] he sets a limit, then he is allowed to do that. In the same way as far as the age is concerned, we can say if the regulation in this country, they have decided on 16 for example, yes this is acceptable to us. The only question is, we are not to marry a person under 16, because we know this is the law of the land, but when it comes to fatwa, if someone asked me that this woman was wed as a minor by her *wali* (guardian), by her father, at the age of 13 for example or 14, is it a valid marriage or not? The fatwa would be: yes it is valid, in regard to Islam it is valid, in regard to Islam it is valid. You cannot nullify it.
>
> Manea: But do you not think by issuing such a fatwa, indirectly, you are encouraging people to do that?
>
> Hasan: This is why I used the word fatwa, because in a certain situation you get a question and you have to answer it. Because you are responsible before Allah when you are answering it. So we can add to this here, but we will say 'Muslims should try to abide by the law of the land,' so we can add something to it here.

As I said before, the moment we start to be specific and look more closely at the content of what the essentialists are calling for, the gravity of their call becomes clear. So, going back to Williams's solution, if we were to recognise the ISC, which opinion should we accept here? Both Al-Haddad and Hasan are considered pillars within the ISC. Should we opt for Al-Haddad's direct no-nonsense response? That is, marry her off as a child and avoid the law. Or do we accept the more nuanced qualified opinion of Sheikh Hasan? Yes, we abide by British law, but if someone performs child marriage, then it is 'Islamically' valid.

By the same token, should we also take their positions on beating a wife as 'Islamically valid'?

Al-Haddad considers it a bad idea to question a husband who hits his wife. In a speech entitled 'Why Marriages Fail', he said:[15]

A man should not be questioned why he hit his wife because this is something between them. Leave them alone. They can sort out their matters among themselves. And even the father of the daughter, who is married to the man, he should not ask his daughter why you have been beaten or hit by your husband. Why? Because Islam is looking at the bigger picture in order to keep the relationship between the husband and wife together.

On the other hand, Sheikh Hasan, whom I quoted above, considers a 'one-time beating' to be 'not a very serious matter'. In 2011, employees of the *Guardian* newspaper produced a short film entitled *Inside a Shari'a Divorce Court*, and recorded the deliberations of two sessions. In one session, Sheikh Hasan was listening to a woman demanding a divorce. The following is part of a transcript of that conversation:[16]

Hasan: So you did ask for divorce?

Woman: Yes, I asked him, I asked him nicely. I said because there are children, we have to part on good terms. I asked him nicely.

Hasan: What does he say?

Woman: He gets offensive and he says 'oh you want money; you want money.' But he has never given me money. So I do not really... [he interrupts her]

Hasan: Do you want to marry someone?

Woman: No.

Hasan: Was he aggressive to you?

Woman: He can be, if he gets... [he interrupts her again]

Hasan: But he was not!

Woman [sound of her swallowing]: In terms of what? Physical?

Hasan: Hitting you?

Woman: He has hit me in the past, yes, he has hit me, he has hit
            me once.

Hasan: Hmm?

Woman: Once.

Hasan: Only once? [He laughs.] So it means it is not a very
            serious matter.

Woman: It is not serious in that way, but if you push him, he
            can crack.

Which of their opinions should be the standardised Islamic principles
for the Muslim minority in Britain?

It is not sarcasm that makes me repeat these questions. It is utter
dismay. For I have seen the consequences of such religious 'opinions' in
various Arab and Islamic contexts, and recently in British Islam. This is
never theoretical. It shapes girls' and women's lives. The fatwas and
opinions of these men have consequences − grave consequences. A child
will be raped in the name of religion. Raped. And it will be legal.
A woman will be beaten in the name of religion. Beaten. And it will be
legal. And Rowan Williams would like us to consider making the
organisations where these men are working the authority to determine
what is Islamic and not Islamic?

Is it far-fetched then to say that gradually we are seeing a situation
in Britain similar to that in Nepal, where the same group of people
may be categorised differently by different legal orders and have
different statuses, rights and obligations? A British Muslim woman
would be treated as an equal citizen before British law, but according
to the Islamic law practised within shari'a legal enclaves, she could
be treated as a minor, who could be married off as a child, and
beaten by her husband, and that would be considered acceptable.
Is it far-fetched to suggest that we are gradually seeing the
development of a modern millet system with consequences similar to
those we saw in Chapter 4: a stratified citizenry and the double-
discrimination syndrome?

***

Second solution. Let us move to Williams's second solution.
He suggested that two measures could be taken to avoid reinforcing

among the minority some of the most repressive elements of religious family law. These are:

(a) No 'supplementary' jurisdiction could have the power to deny access to the rights granted to other citizens or to punish its members for claiming those rights.

(b) Basic ground rules might be set to organise the relationship between jurisdictions, making sure that we do not collude with unexamined systems that have oppressive effects or allow shared public liberties to be decisively taken away by a supplementary jurisdiction.

The first measure does not provide a solid guarantee that human rights will not be violated and the second makes his call for supplementary jurisdiction obsolete.

Williams's first suggestion here is not a new one. In fact, proponents of legal pluralism have often argued that the availability of an 'exit option' – defined as the right to exit from the jurisdiction of a legal order – is a crucial guarantee of individual rights in the context of states that legally recognise cultural diversity.[17] The problem here is twofold.

First, an exit option is not a sufficient guarantee that people's rights will not be violated in a plural legal order. In fact, as the report I cited above, from the International Human Council on Rights, argued so accurately, the question is how far the 'free option' is a real one. It identifies three problems with an exit option and exercise of choice. It (a) requires the presence of a welcoming community outside; (b) presumes autonomy and access to other resources which many individuals lack; and (c) ignores the fact that pressure to conform to 'tradition' is usually strong and may also block one's exit. Ultimately, assessing the extent of individuals' 'free choice' in such cases can be next to impossible.[18]

The exit option and the ability to claim one's rights are even less likely to work within the closed communities of British Islam. A British women's rights activist with South Asian roots, who asked to remain anonymous, told me that in order to work with, and have access to, women in some closed Muslim areas, she has to wear the veil to avoid being intimidated and harassed.[19] If an activist feels the need to veil herself, how would a vulnerable woman inside the closed community feel?

This is not just an impression I had; it was a concern repeatedly stressed by women working within closed communities. In fact, this state of affairs was described in the House of Lords during the second reading of Baroness Cox's bill. Lord Stanley Kalms put it bluntly: Voluntary is not voluntary after all, considering how ghettoised the closed communities have become and British authorities' tip-toeing and fear of offending cultural sensitivities.[20] He said more:

> The second issue, which cannot be stressed enough, is raised by the concept of 'voluntary'. It is extremely easy for Members of this House to presume what those outside this place do is 'voluntary' or otherwise. But around this country, as numerous experts in this field can attest, the question of what is and is not 'voluntary' is highly contestable. We may, for instance, say in this place that no woman should submit to a ruling by a Shari'a court unless she has volunteered to do so. But how on earth are people here to know whether such acts are voluntary? What protection does the state provide when the police and social services, where they are not drawn from the same community as the girl in question, are too timid or fearful of anything which runs counter to the community's professed traditions or beliefs? There are many accounts of women who have found themselves trapped in precisely those situations. Whole groups and organisations have begun to be set up to support such women.
>
> Many of these areas are distinctly cut-off, ethnic and religious enclaves. How do people in this House suppose that a young girl born in such a town, and brought up to defer to religious leaders should behave when those same religious leaders hold themselves out also as legal authorities, when such authorities are in a position not merely to give religious advice but to lay down legal judgments? There is now substantial evidence that far from volunteering themselves up to judgment by Shari'a courts, many women in Britain at this time are in fact forced to do so.

Given this highly contested context, it is legitimate to assume that the greater the margin of legal order given to community authorities to govern the private lives of individual members, the smaller the possibility that individuals can invoke a broad set of citizenship rights.[21]

Second, Williams's subsequent suggestion – setting ground rules to organise the relationship between jurisdictions as a means to protect shared public liberties – will make the introduction of an Islamic supplementary jurisdiction redundant.

Let me put it this way. In order to make sure that Islamic law will not violate women's rights, that law must be reformed, a long and contentious if not torturous process. And until that happens, it would be bizarre to introduce a bad law, like William's second suggestion, and then hope it will evolve and reform in the process. I will explain later why I consider Islamic law to be bad from both a human and a gender perspective.

It would be equally peculiar to introduce a bad law and then argue, 'but we have set up an appeals system for women who wish to have an exit option.' What use is that for women who are trapped in closed societies? States have a duty to protect their citizens and therefore they should not experiment with the rights of their citizens, especially the most vulnerable ones.

Gita Sahgal, former head of Amnesty International's Gender Unit, Director of the Centre for Secular Space, and the founder of Women against Fundamentalism, articulated the argument above and captured the essence of its absurdity:

> It is a bad human rights argument to put in place bad law and then say 'it is ok, because you can then appeal it to the human rights committee or you can appeal somewhere else.' [. . .] It is only an argument of a human rights lawyer, who does not live in the real world [. . .] So you put people under tremendous pressure at the local level, you create this parallel system, and then you say 'it is ok, you can go and appeal'![22]

***

Third solution. Looked at from this perspective, Williams's third solution is also unrealistic. He would introduce a 'scheme in which individuals retain the liberty to choose the jurisdiction under which they will seek to resolve certain carefully specified matters, so that [. . .] power-holders are forced to compete for the loyalty of their shared constituents.' This so-called solution looks to me like it was envisioned by someone who does not live in the real world – someone like Dr Williams.

Again, it is absurd to suggest introducing a legal order based on bad law for a constructed minority, sealing the control of the most reactionary elements within the minority, and then expect the 'constituencies' to be in a position to react to the competition of the power holders and choose between them.

Williams's focus is *religious laws*; he wants to reintroduce them in society. Please pay attention to this: religious laws. He is not talking here about religion as a spiritual relationship between individual and God – something that I myself cherish and enjoy. His focus is the legal dimension of a religion – and we have yet to see a legal dimension of a religion that does not discriminate on the basis of gender. The Enlightenment did not spring out of nothing. It came as a reaction to the tyranny of religious dogmas. The Enlightenment had to tame the religion in question; in the European case it was Christianity. It had to separate religion from politics in order to establish a state that could guarantee civil and human rights *for all*. It was an accomplishment that took centuries to develop. It was not a God-given gift. It was a struggle to confine God to the private sphere and free the public sphere from the tyranny of religious laws.

We have yet to see this development in many Islamic states, especially as Islam has yet to be tamed. So why would anyone expect us to give up this cherished quality and accomplishment in the name of 'the liberty of conscientious opting-out from collaboration in procedures or practices that are in tension with the demands of a particular religious group'? In my opinion that is one more attempt by religious forces to bring religious laws back into the public sphere. And in my opinion that was Rowan Williams's real intention behind his sophisticated lecture. He used Islam as a vessel and he knew plenty, as the lecture indicates, about what is problematic on the legal side of Islam. Given what he knows, his action is utterly irresponsible.

Dignity AND Human Rights: The Two Come Together

I found one point very telling. Williams suggested that the role of rule of law is not to enshrine a 'priority for the universal/abstract dimension of social existence' but rather to establish 'a space accessible to everyone.'

When he said that he was concerned with the ability to affirm and defend a commitment to *human dignity*. I found this revealing for two reasons: human dignity is a vague term, and he deliberately disconnected it from *human rights*.

This point is significant. In a paper entitled 'Human dignity and Islam: A consequence-based approach to human dignity and rights', published in a volume on *Human Dignity and Human Rights*,[23] I discussed the vagueness of the concept of human dignity, and how it may be used to undermine the universality of human rights. I also said that dignity should be connected to rights if we are to defend the individual. In defending the individual, we will be in a position to guarantee the rights and equality of individual members of ethnic, religious and gender groups. This process works in only one direction: respecting the rights of the individual guarantees the overall protection of the group, and not the other way around.

Williams's emphasis on dignity and his omission of rights are significant because we cannot really define what human dignity is. Is it a fundamental human right? Or is it the basis upon which human rights depend? Or perhaps it is both? Human dignity remains vague and has yet to be defined. Most human rights documents use the concept of human dignity, meaning the dignity of the human person, and the essential worth of the human person, when they call for the protection and implementation of human rights. Many also use it as the ultimate justification for the universality of human rights. And while it can be used rhetorically, Brian Orend explains the problem involved: 'the appeal to human dignity is itself the resting point and the foundation for the justification of human rights'; hence, 'the difficulty with dignity has to do with what it refers to, with what it itself rests on.'[24] The key problem is the 'substantial vagueness surrounding the concept of human dignity.'[25]

Human dignity is a vague term. And that vagueness was very clear when the authors of the 1948 Universal Declaration of Human Rights justified the inclusion of dignity in the first article of the declaration: *All human beings are born free and equal in dignity and rights*. When the South African representative objected to the inclusion of the word dignity, insisting that there was no universal standard of dignity, the other authors responded by including it 'in order to emphasise that every human being is worthy of respect [. . .] and it was meant to explain why human beings have rights to begin with.'[26] In other words, dignity here refers to nothing but itself. Because it is so ambiguous, there is 'no universal agreement on the meaning of the term' – and that paves the way for its misuse.[27]

In fact, just as defenders of human rights used dignity as a basis to stress that these rights are universal, others, who are less convinced that these rights exist or that they are universal, have used it as a means to justify curtailing them. One example of this trend is the way some countries have used the term 'respect for human dignity' as a means to curtail people's fundamental right of freedom of expression. Remember the controversy in 2005 over the Danish cartoon including a drawing of Muhammed? In response to that controversy, on 26 March 2009, the United Nations Human Rights Council, led by Arab and Islamic states in addition to Russia, China and South Africa, adopted a non-binding resolution that says: 'defamation of religions is a serious affront to human dignity leading to a restriction on the freedom of religion of their adherents and incitement to religious hatred and violence.'[28]

My human dignity was not violated by some Danish cartoons depicting the Prophet of Islam in a disrespectful manner – even though I am a Muslim. In fact, I think we need more of these cartoons so that we in Islamic countries can learn to grow up and behave in a mature way when we see such things – instead of, like teenagers, letting loose another of our hot-headed outbursts.

Aside from my personal position here, does it come as a surprise that the countries spearheading this resolution are known for their grave violations of human rights, human liberties and freedom of expression?

Freedom of expression is crucial in order to reform religions, including Islam. It is fundamental for any critical discourse over government actions and policies. It is the bedrock of any functioning democracy. Its absence paves the way for the Pakistani apostasy laws that punish members of the Ahmadiyya community for using Muslims' greeting 'peace be upon you.' Some Pakistani members of Ahmadiyya minorities have been imprisoned for five years for doing just that. Its absence paves the way for Meriam Yahia Ibrahim to be sentenced to death in Sudan for choosing to be a Christian. It paves the way for Raif Badawi to be imprisoned and flogged because he criticised the conduct of religious police in Saudi Arabia. And without it, Russia, South Africa, China and other countries feel free to pass laws that curtail the freedom of the press and to imprison journalists who expose misuses of power and corruption.

By the same token, the two Islamic charters on human rights – the 1981 Universal Islamic Declaration of Human Rights (UDHR) issued by the Muslim World League, and the 1990 Cairo Declaration on Human Rights in Islam (CDHRI) issued by the Organisation of the Islamic Conference – make reference to human dignity, tie it to a divine source, and ignore rights as a basis for protecting citizens within an Islamic society.[29] The outcome is the stratified structure of the citizenry that privileges male Muslims.

Both charters disregard the secular nature of the universal human rights that the United Nations suggests; instead they assert that *God* is the main source of the rights they mention. In fact, according to this perception of human rights, in order to enjoy the rights the charters declare, the person must first fulfil his or her duties towards God. This automatically means that any person who has not performed those religious duties ceases to enjoy those rights.[30]

Both charters used the term dignity in justifying their religious perception of human rights, attaching this dignity to a divine force. The UIDHR states in its preamble that 'the human rights decreed by the Divine Law aim at conferring dignity and honour on mankind and are designed to eliminate oppression and injustice.' And the CDHRI asserts in Article 1, Clause A that 'all men are equal in terms of basic human dignity and basic obligations and responsibilities, without any discrimination on the grounds of race, colour, language, sex, religious belief, political affiliation, social status or other considerations.' It then affirms that 'true faith is the guarantee for enhancing such dignity along the path to human perfection.'[31]

Because both charters attach dignity to faith and to the divine law/ shari-a, they effectively reflect a perception of human rights that defines a human to be a man and of Islamic faith.

For example, in dealing with the Rights of Minorities in its Article X, the UDHR simply reiterates a principle used in Islamic law: non-Muslim minorities are to keep their religion and they have 'the choice to be governed in respect of their civil and personal matters by Islamic Law, or by their own laws.'[32]

This limited scope of rights fails to acknowledge the rights of non-Muslims in that state to be *equal citizens before the law*. In other words, it fails to acknowledge the equality between citizens regardless of religion or confession. The limits become glaring when we read Article XI, about the right and obligation to participate in the conduct and management of public affairs: this right is restricted by the term law/sharia. Thus Clause A says: 'Subject to the Law, every individual in the Community (*ummah*) is entitled to assume public office.' Given that Islamic law, as interpreted and practised over the centuries, has long imposed restrictions on the rights of non-Muslims to assume public office, the fact that this convention conditions this right through the Islamic law only further undermines any equality it presumes.[33]

It is ironic how these charters, in their vision of a theocratic state, invoke dignity and God to violate human rights and equality before the law, and also create a citizenship pyramid, at the top of which male Muslims stand supreme. On the other hand, Rowan Williams, while earnestly seeking to avoid the tyranny of religious dogmas, invokes dignity and the rights of religious groups to difference. In doing so he inadvertently does almost the same thing as the charters: he creates religious legal enclaves that produce stratified citizenship and the double-discrimination syndrome.

Dignity is vague. If dignity is not linked to rights and protected by a *secular single legal order*, it leaves the door open to interpretations that eventually violate the very individuals we are trying to protect. Again, once the state starts to situate rights within a group's frame rather than within the individual, the likely outcome will be segregation, inequality and discrimination.

Shari'a Law in Britain: An Anthropological Version of Law

When Rowan Williams talks about shari'a in his lecture, he does so in a way that reflects his sense of the white man's burden. He is apologetic, tiptoeing, pointing out his good intentions: the type of good intentions that pave a road to hell. He tells us that 'what most people think they know of Shari'a is that it is repressive towards women and wedded to archaic and brutal physical punishments.'

He quotes Tariq Ramadan, a traditionalist, propagating a political form of Islam, and hailed as an Islamic reformer, known for his ability to touch the guilt trigger of post-colonial and post-modern Westerners:

> The idea of Shari'a calls up all the darkest images of Islam [. . .] It has reached the extent that many Muslim intellectuals do not dare

even to refer to the concept for fear of frightening people or arousing suspicion of all their work by the mere mention of the word.[34]

Williams then insists that we must make a distinction between two types of shari'a. One, again using Ramadan's words, is shari'a as the 'expression of the universal principles of Islam' and 'the framework and the thinking that makes for their actualisation in human history.' The second is shari'a as 'some particular concretisation of it at the hands of a tradition of jurists.' Williams cautioned about what happens when contemporary legal traditionalists use the second type: 'the application of shari'a must be governed by the judgements of representatives of the classical schools of legal interpretation.' But, he says, 'a good many voices' are 'arguing for an extension of the liberty of ijtihad – basically reasoning from first principles rather than simply the collation of traditional judgements.'[35]

The fact that Williams makes this distinction between the two indicates that what he was seeking to introduce as a supplementary jurisprudence for the Muslims is the one guided by the first type of shari'a, a reformed type.

The problem is not only that this distinction is theoretical and rhetorical, lacking real substance. By introducing it within the context of a 'supplementary Islamic jurisdiction', he has also made it very misleading, with potentially grave consequences. The reason is straightforward: what we will end up with in reality, as I explained in the last section, is a jurists' reading of shari'a of the worst type.

We can philosophise as much as we want about shari'a as general principles that seek to bring justice. The fact remains that the religious laws governing family affairs and the lives of women and children are none other than the rigid conservative religious laws of medieval jurists.

When people advocate for introducing Islamic law into any legal system, Islamic or Western, they are not talking about an 'expression of the universal principles of Islam.' What they seek are concrete religious laws and rules – *fiqh* – which can violate human dignity and human rights. The countries that have introduced shari'a laws – including Iran, Saudi Arabia, Sudan and Afghanistan, and the jihadists in parts of Syria and Iraq – are notorious for violating rights: human rights, citizenship rights, and the rights of women, minorities and LGBT people. The

Islamists, who aim to implement Islamic law, never talk about shari'a in an abstract theoretical form. They immediately translate their calls into measures that will segregate the sexes and refer to laws that establish religion (being a Muslim) and gender (being male) as the markers for citizenship; in the process they violate their people's rights of equality and citizenship, and their human rights. In all of these cases what is being applied are rigid conservative religious laws developed by medieval jurists.

So if we accept at face value Williams's suggestion that shari'a is evolutionary and can be introduced in a 'reformed manner', we must remember that in fact it has a very 'long way to evolve.'[36] And until that happens, it is irresponsible to make such a suggestion, since we know well that what will be introduced are the laws of medieval jurists.

Tiptoeing over the problem, ignoring both the *actual practice* of Islamic law in modern history and the *discourse of political Islamism* that has hijacked any recent evolution of the law, is hypocrisy of the worst kind. This is not a theoretical debate confined to the words and ideas presented in closed seminars. It has consequences. Grave consequences.

Notwithstanding its consequences, this theoretical debate reveals the essentialists' worldview. When they speak about Muslims' rights to their religious laws, they often mean an anthropological version of Islamic law. By that I mean a version that remains isolated from its social, political or historical contexts; this version reinforces the essentialists' expectation that Muslims actually need this type of discriminatory law to regulate their affairs, and therefore we should leave them alone.

I first heard the term *anthropological version of law* in an interview with Tahmina Saleem, a co-founder of Inspire, the British Muslim women's organisation. Based on that interview and further interviews and reading, I define the term as a version of law void of any connection to its historical, political or even legal contexts. It is an essentialist version of law that is taken for granted by British authorities and promoted by conservative Muslim groups and Islamists.

In fact, what is being promoted are shari'a courts which function almost as a modern expression of the jirga system, the traditional tribal system of justice I discussed in Chapter 4. The British authorities ended up informally allowing non-state actors to function according to rules from the home countries of British South Asians, some of which are no longer applied there. In so doing, they accept an essentialist approach to law, they homogenise Islam, they overlook statutory laws and they depend on the opinions of 'experts' who promote this essentialist reading of Islam and of Muslims.

I know it is tricky to make an analogy, describing British shari'a courts as a modern expression of the jirga system. Certainly the similarity does not cover the type of laws applied within the two systems. The jirga system applies tribal customary law and the shari'a courts are implementing a conservative corpus of Islamic rulings in family affairs, although sometimes the two types of laws may overlap.

This aspect aside, one cannot help but be struck by the similarity in their form and perceptions. The jirga, as I explained in Chapter 4, is a council composed of two or more persons who sit together in a circle and arbitrate. They are often family elders and are dominated by the powerful tribal and feudal leaders in their area. Likewise, the shari'a courts are often composed of two or more persons who sit together and arbitrate. They are dominated by self-appointed community leaders, and self appointed 'judges', some of whom do not even have degrees in law and Islamic law.

Both systems are male-dominated, patriarchal and permeated with parochial and misogynous perceptions of women. Both use types of law that are discriminatory.

Women who have experienced the shari'a courts express the analogy in a different way. Some felt the context they were entering resembled rural areas in Pakistan or Bangladesh. One example is a woman I will call Shabnam, a British Muslim of Pakistani roots, who had a civil divorce but also needed a religious divorce because her husband refused to recognise the civil one. He bullied her, insisting he still had rights over her. The civil divorce granted her custody of her children and child support from him. After she contacted a shari'a council in London, the council summoned her to a meeting with one of its religious judges, and instructed her to bring along a male family member.[37]

Just as would happen at a jirga in rural Pakistan, at the meeting, the sheikh simply ignored her, speaking only to her brother in Urdu. She was stunned:

I felt like I'd gone to a rural court in a village in Pakistan, that I was a woman behind some kind of a partition and I cannot speak

my mind [. . .] I was aghast. I am independent, I am an educated
woman, I feel I can represent myself.[38]

Just like her husband, the sheikh seemed to see the civil divorce as being
of no consequence; he recommended that she try to reconcile with her ex-
husband. She refused and asked her divorce lawyer to intervene; he did
eventually get her the religious divorce.

Complaints like Shabnam's are often cited as being common today.
Suddenly a woman is snatched from her British context and brought into
another social context, a rural context with a system similar to a jirga
system, one where men make the decisions and are given the floor to
speak, rather than the women whose futures are at stake in the case.

Notice that Shabnam complained about being in rural Pakistan. She
did not say urban Pakistan. I hope the reason is as obvious to you as to
me. Urban Pakistan has a sophisticated court system. As Tahmina
Saleem put it, 'Pakistan has a legal system. It has some very bad law but
it also has some good legal judgments and jurisprudence. It has a legal
system, not some fatwa given by a cleric somewhere.'[39]

But what is being promoted in Britain is not this sophisticated
modern system, but the *anthropological version of Islamic law*, the one
Shabnam described.

Consider that the Pakistani Family Law Ordinance of 1961 made it
compulsory to register all marriages and divorces.[40] Other Islamic
countries, in South Asia, the Middle East, Southeast Asia and Africa,
insist on this registration and have long had this provision in place to
protect women from manipulation and loss of rights. For example, under
Malaysia's Islamic Family Law Act 1984, couples have to apply for
permission to marry and then go through a registration procedure.
Under Indonesia's Marriage Act 1974 and Compilation of Islamic Law
1991 a marriage can only be proven through a marriage certificate, and
an unregistered marriage has no legal standing.[41] Thus, the great
majority of British Muslims come from countries where registration is
required by law.

But in Britain, many Muslim couples do not register their religious
marriage, despite a provision in the Marriage Act 1949 requiring that
they do so. If the marriage ends in divorce, the woman is left in legal
limbo because the marriage is not valid in the eyes of British law.
In Chapter 6, I will discuss the reasons for this state of affairs.

Suffice to say at this point that one reason for this problem is British authorities' reluctance to force the Muslim minority to abide by the law of the land. Instead of protecting women by insisting that the law applies to everyone, and reminding people that similar laws exist in their, or their families', countries of origin, the British authorities are tiptoeing around the problem, unable to tackle it because of a bizarre cultural sensitivity.

Likewise, a civil divorce involving Muslims that is issued in Britain is valid and recognised in Pakistani courts. With some important exceptions, many British shari'a courts do not issue a religious divorce automatically when a woman approaches them with a British civil divorce. For many of them, it is a whole separate and complicated process.

This was the case in the Islamic Shari'a Council in Leyton, the Muslim Arbitration Tribunal in Nuneaton, and the Muslim Welfare House in East London. The Birmingham Islamic Shari'a Council was the only exception among the four where I spent time and conducted interviews.

The implications of such procedures are significant. Before I explain, let me first present the procedures of these Islamic councils or tribunals.

The procedures in a case where a civil divorce was obtained are similar in the Islamic Shari'a Council (ISC) in Leyton, the Muslim Arbitration Tribunal (MAT) in Nuneaton, and the Muslim Welfare House (MWH) in East London.

At the ISC, as Sheikh Hasan explained to me, if the husband entered the petition for the civil divorce, this means that he 'has deputised the court to give divorce on his behalf [. . .] and [has] given his consent.' In this case, 'there is no reason to stop this [Islamic] divorce.' If the petitioner is the wife, however, the treatment changes. She is required to bring a form on which the husband states that he has consented to the civil divorce. If he refuses and says that he wants to defend the marriage, the process starts over:

> Then we will start afresh. We will hold the meeting and we will try to help to persuade the man and the woman to reconcile. If she does not want to reconcile, eventually she will get [the divorce].[42]

On the other hand, the judges at the MAT consider a civil divorce to corroborate the 'fact that there has been a breakdown of the marriage,' as its director, Sheikh Faizul Aqtab Siddiqi, told me in an interview. However, because of 'the Islamic tradition', MAT is 'obligated to indulge in mediation first':[43]

> So if the judge is satisfied that the reasons that are being given are strong reasons and there is no scope for mediation, then he will give *faskh* [an annulment of the marriage]. But if he realises that there is scope for mediation, then he will not give *faskh*. He will try to mediate first.

When I asked him how he would deal with the case where the husband disputed the civil divorce, he described a procedure similar to that at the ISC:

> We will again deal with the case on its merits, and we will ask the woman why she wants the *faskh*, and we will ask the man why he does not want to grant the divorce, and if there is unreasonableness in the point of view of the man, and there is reasonableness in the point of view of the woman, and that is what she wants, and she has no other choice, then we will assist her.

Along similar lines, Dr Mohammad Shahoot Kharfan, the imam at MWH in East London, stated that if the couple has a religious marriage and they want a divorce, the procedure is to mediate first, whether or not they already have a civil divorce.[44]

Hence, in the three cases above, the procedure for couples who have already obtained a civil divorce is to start a *new* process of divorce that involves mediation.

But not in the Birmingham Islamic Shari'a Council of the Central Mosque. I asked Sheikh Mohammad Talha Bokhari, the coordinator of the council, about the procedure used when a woman came to him with a civil divorce, and whether he accepts civil divorce as grounds for a religious divorce. His answer was clear:

Bokhari: There is no need for her to come. Because when the [civil] divorce has come, issued from the civil court, then she is done. That is a divorce.

Manea: From a religious point of view?

Bokhari: Yes, it is not needed. But if they come, ok, then the procedure, we consider it easy. Because based on those things, and the shariʿa, we find also a shariʿa ground there, and we dissolve the matter.[45]

Amra Bone, the only female member of the panel of the Birmingham council, explained this position further:[46]

> We work within the law of the land as British citizens [. . .] Many of
> the women who approach us at the Shariah Council [. . .] only have
> an Islamic marriage contract. For one reason or another they do not
> have a civil marriage contract. When it comes to divorce these
> women or men do not have any recourse or access to civil courts,
> hence they come to the Council for dissolving their marriage.
> We stress on the fact that they need to register their marriage, as the
> law protects rights of women and children, which is in line with the
> Islamic principles. Those whose marriages were registered and are
> divorced within the civil courts are also recognised by our Shariah
> Council as legitimate, since it does not contradict the understanding
> of the principles of Islamic divorce.

So the Birmingham council adheres to the common legal practice in many Muslim countries, including Pakistan: if a woman has been granted a civil divorce, she does not need a religious divorce, because her civil divorce is considered valid from a religious point of view.

Why is this important?

Most of the women coming to these councils seek a religious divorce. They do not want mediation or arbitration. All they want is to be released from their religious marriage. Because of the Islamisation that took place in the British Muslim communities over the past three decades, many women truly believe that a civil divorce does not suffice from a religious point of view. The shariʿa councils and the Muslim Arbitration Tribunal have an interest in reinforcing this assumption to justify their own existence.

Now imagine if the British authorities did their duty and enforced the law by registering Muslim marriages, and launched an awareness campaign informing Muslim women of the fact that a civil divorce is religiously valid. Then would there be a need for these 'courts'? And what if they created an office that would issue religious divorces automatically after the release of the civil divorce? Would that not be a better solution than letting these councils proliferate and control the lives of women? Yet no one is tackling the problem through procedures that apply to everyone. Instead, we end up with calls to introduce an anthropological version of Islamic law in the name of protecting the group right of Muslims to apply their 'own laws'.

But there is a political reason for this negligence: the urge to control.

Sohail Akbar Warraich and Cassandra Balchin wrote a ground-breaking report, *Recognizing the Un-recognized: Inter-Country Cases and Muslim Marriages and Divorces in Britain.*

They asked why shari'a councils asked to confirm a civil divorce do not automatically issue a certificate that the marriage is also dissolved under Muslim laws, and why they instead insist upon a lengthy process. They also asked why no researchers have looked into this. Their answer illuminates the political aspect of the issue:

> The answer cannot be merely that the Shariah council process provides more appropriate opportunities for reconciliation or greater 'cultural sensitivity' because in a majority of cases the husband simply refuses to attend any such reconciliation meetings; if reconciliation were the issue, the period between the decree nisi and decree absolute in civil divorce allows for this. A more political reading would argue that by insisting on a separate and complex process rather than appearing to rubber stamp the civil proceedings, the Shariah councils given themselves an opportunity to demonstrate and retain their social and political influence over the community.[47]

Again, we see that what matters is the political function.

An Essentialist Academic Argument for Islamic Law

One last remark is warranted here before I move to the next section and discuss the nature of the Islamic law that has been suggested to regulate family affairs. The anthropological version of Islam is propagated and reinforced by essentialist scholars and experts, who provide an argument for Islamic law in the West by essentialising and homogenising Islam and Muslims.

Consider how a Turkish scholar, Ihsan Yilmaz, tried to justify the need for shari'a courts in the UK:

> It is a wide known fact that Islam 'demands full allegiance from a person, once he has chosen freely to embrace it.' If the Muslim law conflicts with the secular laws of nation-states, it is divine law that must prevail. This general principle that God's law must prevail appears in specific directives to Muslims not only in the West but also in their nation-states 'to contest, defend and protect themselves against rational and secular authority.' Indeed, the impact of the juristic discourse can be seen in Muslim law's 'potential of being a powerful resource for a reassertion of Islamic identity.'[48]

Such sweeping generalisations, while playing on the ignorance of the wider public, are extremely inaccurate and misleading.

First, they bring in an essentialist argument of political Islamism, which insists that Islam should control every aspect of a Muslim's life. Then they claim that it is representative of how Muslims think and behave. This argument, as I will discuss in Chapter 5, can be traced back to writings by leaders of political Islamism: Hassan Al Banna, Abul A'la Maududi, and Ruhollah Khomeini.

Second, they homogenise more than one and a half billion people and consider them one block with identical traits, features and perspectives on law and society. Such generalisations disregard their nationalities, races, political and ideological orientations, denominations and religious practices, traditions and culture, insisting that all those are irrelevant. Because, after all, these people are Muslims. Hence, an Egyptian is a Yemeni is an Omani is a Chinese is an Indonesian is a Tunisian is a Nigerian is a South African is a Tajik. How simple.

Finally, these generalisations disregard the fact that Muslims are indeed members of diverse groups with different ideologies and orientations to religion and life. They seem to think they can simply cut and paste and place the label of Muslim on everyone, and by doing so remove all the diversity expected in a Western context, along with the possibility that different Muslims might be non-religious, agnostic, atheist, liberal, conservative, etc. Somehow, in their thinking, diversity is not possible when we talk about Muslims, for after all, these are *Muslims*. And if they are Muslims, they must be religious or Islamists.

I find it perplexing to read such sweeping generalisations by a Turkish scholar. He should know better, given Turkish society's refreshing mosaic diversity and the current contested discourse on the role of religion and political Islamism in society and politics. One could be excused for assuming that his argument might be part of that very contested discourse on religion and politics, providing a political argument to return Islamic law to the larger society. In that he would be just like Rowan Williams, who used shari'a in his attempt to bring religious laws to the public sphere.

Islamic Law and Universal Human and Women's Rights

Every time the essentialists suggest introducing Islamic law into the Western legal system they temper their argument by saying things like 'it will only affect family affairs,' and 'it will be restricted to issues of divorce, marriage, etc.' It is as if those statements will make those issues minor, insignificant, of no consequence. But precisely because the suggestion deals with this sphere, it should be rejected. Again, I repeat, the essentialists are asking for nothing other than legally sanctioned discrimination.

In fact, if we examine the type of Islamic law that the essentialists are considering and suggesting, it will become clear that it has very little to do with Rowan Williams's wishful abstract type of shari'a as the 'expression of the universal principles of Islam.' Meanwhile it has everything to do with the medieval jurisprudence tradition, which freely violates human rights and the concept of gender equality.

Before I delve into this point, let me offer my own definition of shari'a. I tend to avoid using expressions like divine law or God's law to describe shari'a. There are different approaches to defining it. One approach would be similar to the way Ramadan and with him Williams tried to distinguish between shari'a as the 'expression of the universal principles of Islam' and shari'a as *fiqh*: the 'doctrinal traditions developed by jurists over centuries.' This definition by distinction has a particular purpose: to make space for new interpretations of Islamic law by emphasising the limited authority of the *fiqh* and to create space for others to contribute to developing norms for *fiqh* in a changing world.[49]

Another approach would avoid defining shari'a in legally philosophical terms and would focus more on studying the sources[50] that are understood to constitute the corpus of shari'a, especially on the work of pre-modern jurists, work which is so central to the study of Islamic law in the twentieth century.[51]

The first approach, while it deserves our applause, ignores how Islamic law is being implemented in reality. It also reinforces the constructed perception that shari'a is indeed God's law, and has thus far failed to acknowledge the limits of religious interpretations. Put simply, trying to avoid acknowledging the human nature of religious texts, including the Qur'an, makes any attempts at reform futile and holds those texts captive within specific religious boundaries. In addition, we must recognise the historical nature of many Quranic verses, like those that see wife-beating as a disciplinary action, or that allow a man to have female slaves in addition to four wives, or to kill 'unbelievers', or to engage in corporal punishment. And we must also state clearly that these interpretations can no longer be seen as appropriate in a modern society. Unless the advocates of this approach recognise these differences, such an approach will be both superficial and ad hoc – and will fail to address the problems inherent in the legal side of Islam.

The approach I adopt here, which is closer to the second one mentioned above, defines shari'a by the way it is being implemented in Islamic states and within Muslim family laws. I see it as a selection from the corpus of legal opinions of jurists developed over the course of Islamic history, especially between the seventh and tenth centuries.

Looking at shari'a from this perspective will highlight its problematic nature, for we are not considering its theoretical potential to provide justice. What we are in fact looking at is its actual implementation and hence its obvious limitations and how it contravenes *modern* concepts of human rights. What matters is how it is being interpreted and used today, not how it could be used a century from now.

I deliberately used the word modern above, because – let me repeat – the jurisprudence suggested and under consideration was developed between the seventh and tenth centuries. This historical period, early in the development of Islam as a whole, shaped its content and its perception of women's role in society, and is reflected in its worldview of what constitutes a human and who can enjoy human rights.

In fact, if we look at the actual corpus of Islamic law, human rights can be defined as the privilege 'only of persons of full legal capacity.'

A person of full legal capacity is 'a living human being of mature age, free [not a slave], and of Moslem faith.' Under this definition, others who lived in the Islamic state, including non-Moslems and slaves, were 'only partially protected by law or had no legal capacity at all.'[52] This definition was formulated in 1946 by Majid Khadurri, an Iraqi-born American academic recognised as a leading authority on Islamic law and the modern political history of the Middle East.

More than 50 years later, that definition was qualified by Abdullahi Ahmed An-Na'im, a leading Sudan-born American authority on Islamic law and human rights. In 1990, he accepted Khadurri's statement as 'substantially accurate' and added a qualification concerning the status of Muslim women. He acknowledged that Muslim women 'have full legal capacity under Shari'a in relation to civil and commercial law matters,' but they 'do not enjoy human rights on an equal footing with Muslim men under Shari'a.'[53]

What does that mean?

It means that in addition to creating a stratified citizenry dominated by free male Muslims, the way shari'a dealt with the status of women was often contradictory, offering women some rights but withholding many others, while maintaining the notion that the Muslim man is the keeper and guardian of the Muslim woman.

In general, one can discern two levels of statements in the Qur'an regarding women's status. The first level treats women and men as equal before God – that is, in the afterlife. For example, one verse states 'Whoso does evil will be requited only with the like of it; but whoso does good, whether male or female, and is a believer – these will enter the paradise; they will be provided therein without measure' (Qur'an 40:41).

Qur'anic verses at the second level place women at a legal disadvantage. These are the statements on issues of family and sexual relations, rules of marriage, divorce, custody, maintenance, inheritance and testimony – that is, rights within this life. On these issues, Qur'anic verses reflect the social tribal patriarchal context of the seventh-century Arabian Peninsula, specifically the city of Medina. They favoured men and accorded women a lower and dependent legal status. From this we see the clear inconsistencies on the status of women between the Qur'anic provisions and the modern statements on human rights, such as the 1948 Universal Declaration of Human Rights (UDHR) and the

Convention on the Elimination of All Forms of Discrimination against Women (CEDAW).

Let us start with the first part of An-Na'im's qualification. He says that under shari'a, a Muslim woman has full legal capacity in relation to matters of civil and commercial law. This means that she can own property as a separate person and that when she marries she can keep her name. Hence when I married, I kept my family name, Manea, and did not take my husband's name. Nor did he take over whatever property I had. It remained in my possession. From this perspective, a Muslim woman is treated as an individual.

Yet An-Na'im is also correct to state that, under shari'a, Muslim women do not enjoy human rights on an equal footing with Muslim men. In fact shari'a laws contravene various provisions of human rights conventions, specifically the UDHR and the CEDAW mentioned above.

Human rights conventions are clear in their statements about the equality of man and woman. The essence of their worldview is expressed by Article One of the 1948 UDHR: that all human beings are born free and equal in dignity and rights. This principle paved the ground for Article 16 of the same declaration and Article 16 of CEDAW. Both articles envisioned marriage and family relations as an equal partnership that would be entered, shared and dissolved by both man and woman on an equal footing. Marriage should be entered into by two persons of full age, with their free and full consent, without any limitation due to race, nationality or religion. The spouses should have the same rights and responsibilities with regard to guardianship of children, and the same personal rights as husband and wife, including the right to choose a family name, a profession and an occupation. And both spouses should have the same rights in respect of the ownership, acquisition, management, administration, enjoyment and disposition of property, whether free of charge or for a valuable consideration.

This is not the case in the world view of classical Islamic law: the woman is part of a hierarchical social structure dominated by the man at the top; and as a legal person the woman is controlled before her marriage by her male guardian and after marriage by her husband.

The rules regarding marriageable age and guardianship make child marriages and forced marriages possible, and rules on divorce and maintenance rights discriminate against the wife.

In fact, the Islamic law's view towards the position of the wife within marriage can be easily discerned by considering the legal term used for marriage – a term, remember, that was developed in the Middle Ages.

In Islamic law, the term for marriage is *nikah*, which literally means carnal union. Jurists describe *nikah* as 'an agreement, which results in the lawful enjoyment of a woman.'[54] The reference to enjoyment applies only to the husband, because that right belongs especially and pre-eminently to him. In fact, the husband is entitled to intercourse with his wife at his pleasure. On the other hand, two realities restrict the wife's right to enjoyment. First, she has no right to claim intercourse with her husband, except for one time after marriage, and second, she may have to share him with other wives.[55]

This perception of marriage is not theoretical. In fact it has been used repeatedly in various Islamic and Arab family laws, such as those in Yemen, Kuwait and Syria. All of them state in their first article that marriage is a legal union or a contract that gives the man the legal permission to access his wife sexually. The only time this definition has changed has been in genuine attempts to reform the classic Islamic law on family relations. For example, the Moroccan Family Code of 2004 states, 'Marriage is a legal contract by which a man and a woman mutually consent to unite in a common and enduring conjugal life.'[56]

Aside from the legal definition of marriage, classical Islamic law does not envision marriage and family relations as an equal partnership between man and woman. In the paragraphs below I summarise the common provisions regarding marriage and divorce.

Marriage

- **Age of marriage:** A Muslim man or a woman must be of sound mind and must have attained puberty to be considered legally eligible for marriage. In classical Islamic law, puberty occurs with the physical signs of maturity such as the emission of semen for boys and menstruation for girls.[57]
- **Guardianship:** In contracting a marriage, male guardianship is necessary. The established interpretations of Islamic jurisprudence schools insist that a woman cannot marry without the consent of her male guardian. A guardian handles all kinds of affairs for both his male and female wards, including contracting marriage. When the ward is a male, the guardianship ceases when the boy reaches puberty.

For a girl, however, a guardian has the power to impose a marriage on a virgin girl without her knowledge or consent.[58] If she contracts a marriage without her guardian's consent, the marriage is not valid. If she was divorced, her consent, in addition to that of the guardian, is necessary to contract the marriage.

The one crucial exception to this rule in Sunni Islam occurs in the Hanafite school of jurisprudence; it is also present in Shi'a jurisprudence. Guardianship is required when the girl is not of age, that is, has not yet reached puberty. But once she reaches puberty, she is allowed to contract her marriage without her guardian's consent.[59] However, under Hanafite jurisprudence, if the guardian is not satisfied with her choice of husband, he has the right to demand that marriage be annulled on the basis of lack of *kafaa:* social equality. As I explained in Chapter 3, the concept of *kafaa*, literally suitability, gives the guardian the right to dissolve and annul a marriage, if he considers the groom/husband not to be fit or suitable.

- **Polygamy:** A Muslim man may be married up to four wives at the same time but a Muslim woman can only be married to one man at a time. A Muslim man may marry a Christian or a Jewish woman, but a Muslim woman may not marry a non-Muslim man.

Divorce

- A Muslim man may divorce his wife, or any of his wives, by unilateral repudiation, *talaq*, without having to give any reasons or justify his action to any person or authority. When he divorces his wife by uttering the word three times, the divorce is considered irrevocable: *bain.* In order to return to him, she must first marry a different man and get a divorce from the new husband.

- A Muslim woman can obtain a divorce in three ways: (a) by gaining the consent of her husband; (b) by getting a judicial decree for limited specific grounds/harms; or (c) by *khula*. This means a divorce sanctioned by a judge, but she must give up her financial rights to gain it.

- A woman divorced by her husband must observe a waiting period (*iddah*), normally lasting three months. During this period she cannot marry another man.

- A divorce in which the word is uttered fewer than three times is revocable (*raji'i*). So even if a woman gets a divorce, her husband may change his mind. During the waiting period, he has the right to return her to his household against her will and he need not sign another marriage contract. One reference on *fiqh* explained this rule this way: 'until the period of *iddah* has elapsed, the repudiation is revocable (*raji'i*), and the husband may resume conjugal relations with his wife, if he be so inclined, by a revocation of the repudiation. This he can do whether she be willing or not.'[60]

Obedience, Maintenance, and Beating

• Obedience is considered a duty of the wife. A wife should be obedient to her husband insofar as his commands are legally allowed and are ordained as duties of marriage. If a wife is disobedient, she loses her right to maintenance. According to Hanafi jurisprudence, a wife is considered disobedient if she leaves their home without the consent of her husband or without a lawful excuse. Other schools of jurisprudence, however, say that even if she stays at home, she will not be entitled to maintenance if she refuses sexual intercourse.[61] A husband may beat his wife if she is disobedient. The husband can resort to several measures when his wife disobeys him, the last of which is the most severe: beating her. If the woman obeys him, then he should stop using these measures.[62]

Maintenance after Divorce

• Maintenance for a divorced wife ceases after the *iddah* period, the three-month waiting period after the divorce.
• After a divorce, the wife is only entitled to the sum of money set in the marriage contract: the *muakhar*.

Inheritance

• A Muslim woman receives less than the share of a Muslim man when both parties have an equal degree of relationship to the deceased person. Hence, a sister inherits from her father half of what her brother inherits. A Muslim husband inherits half of what his wife leaves, provided that she did not have a son. If she does, then the husband inherits a quarter. A Muslim wife inherits a quarter of her husband's estate if he has no son. If he has a son, then she inherits an eighth.[63]
• Being of a different religion is a total bar to inheritance. Thus a Muslim may neither inherit from, nor leave an inheritance to, a non-Muslim.[64]

Custody of Children

- After a divorce, the custody of a child is entrusted to either the mother or father, depending on the child's age and sex. Younger children tend to be placed in the mother's care and the father takes over custody when the child reaches a given age. However, shari'a makes a distinction between custody and guardianship: the father is the guardian of the child after separation even if the mother is granted the right to custody up to a certain age, after which custody reverts to the father.[65]
- If the mother decides to remarry she automatically loses her right to custody.

Testimony

The testimony of two women equals that of one man. Originally this rule was meant for financial affairs; but the jurists expanded the rule and made it a general rule.

***

These clearly discriminatory provisions are not theoretical. They shape the perception of women's rights in Islamic charters on human rights. In fact Article 6 of the Cairo Declaration on Human Rights in Islam reflects the classical Islamic view of law in a literal sense. A woman is equal to a man in *human dignity* but not in *human rights*. She has her own civil entity and financial independence and the husband is responsible for her maintenance. Yet this financial responsibility of the husband is inherently connected to the wife's obedience.

By the same token, the practice of letting theological interpretations influence decisions on family affairs takes two forms in the Arab MENA region. First, some countries, including Egypt, Bahrain, Lebanon, Qatar and Saudi Arabia, have no unified personal status code, so the issue is left entirely to the judiciary, 'which is heavily influenced by the conservative nature of classical Islamic jurisprudence.'[66]

In Egypt, for example, several personal status laws exist, some dating back to the 1920s. However, in cases where the law contains no textual provision, recourse is made to the established views of the Sunni Hanafi school of jurisprudence. Rulings made in accordance with those views could contradict the spirit of the current era and human rights. One famous example is the 1995 ruling, upheld by the Court of Cassation or Supreme Court, ordering the Egyptian scholar Nasr Hamid Abu Zaid to divorce his wife, against his will or hers, on the ground that he committed apostasy in some of his books. The court based its ruling on the Hanafi opinion that a heretic must be divorced from his wife.[67]

Second, other Arab states, including Jordan, Algeria, Kuwait, Yemen and Syria, have codified provisions of Islamic jurisprudence into a unified law that applies to Muslims.

Family laws may be less discriminatory in some Arab countries than in others. As a rule, personal status laws in North Africa are more progressive than those in the Arab Middle East. In fact, Tunisia, and to a lesser extent Morocco, stand as examples of how such laws can be reformed in a way that mostly reflects the concept of gender equality.

Notwithstanding the above, certain characteristics are common to family law in all Arab states, with Tunisia and Morocco again the exceptions. These include the notion that men are women's keepers and have a degree of command over their lives. This notion has been translated into several laws that are relevant here: laws obliging husbands to support their wives financially while commanding their wives to obey them, laws that grant men alone the right to unilaterally divorce their wives and the right to require their return in the event of revocable divorce, and laws restricting women's ability to marry, move, work or travel freely without the consent of their male relatives or husbands.[68]

Hence, a woman may have the right to be elected to parliament or be chosen as a minister in a Arab government cabinet, yet this very parliamentarian or minister may not be allowed to travel outside the country with a government delegation if her husband withholds his permission. If you think this situation is only theoretically possible, think again. A female Arab minister mentioned it to me during an interview.

It should be mentioned at this point that the family laws of Islamic states differ in the minimum age of marriage. Some countries with codified systems legislate minimum ages for marriage and set restrictions on child marriage.[69] For example, in Bangladesh, Tunisia, Algeria and Morocco the minimum age for girls is set at 18. Other countries set a very low minimum age or none at all. In Syria, that age is 15, in Iran 13, in Sudan 10. And in Yemen and Saudi Arabia there is no minimum age for marriage.

In addition, some of the laws that set a minimum age of 18 are full of loopholes and the provisions are rarely accessed. The weaknesses in the law and its implementation often result in a wide gap between the legal minimum age of marriage and the minimum age practised in communities. Hence, some families take advantage of the loopholes that give judges leeway to allow underage girls to marry at the request of their guardians. And other families bypass the law by arranging a religious marriage ceremony for their underage daughter and then wait until she is 18 to officially register the marriage. If the marriage is not registered and the husband decides to leave, the child bride is left without any legal protection for herself and her children.[70] This situation does not only occur in Egypt or Jordan. It happens in Britain as well.

***

Which brings me to the question: What type of Islamic law is being implemented within Britain's shari'a courts? The short answer is: the classical Islamic law with all its contradictions and discrimination.

The five 'judges' I interviewed who are involved with these tribunals stated that they rely on one of the four classical types of Sunni jurisprudence. The Muslim Arbitration Tribunal uses the Hanafi jurisprudence by default, but does refer to the others at times. When a person of Shi'a background comes to them, they apply the Shi'a jurisprudence on her/his case.

To them, what they are applying is not only *fiqh*, the jurists' traditions. They are applying what they think of literally as God's Law, the law of Allah. Hence, depending on the type of shari'a court applying this law, it can either seek a fundamentalist interpretation of *fiqh*, or it can try to make the lives of women easier by seeking the most lenient interpretation. But the mindset is framed by the perception that shari'a is God's law and therefore better than any other secular law. The mindset is also shaped by the acceptance of the rules I mentioned above, that regulate marriage, divorce, polygamy, guardianship, inheritance, etc., anything related to family affairs and women's position within the family. They accept these rules and do not question them. Hence during my interviews with the five 'judges', including the female judge, they reflected their perception that this *is what Islam commands, this is what God commands, and we are following God's law.*

Those interviewed are not interested in considering modern *ijtihad*, rational independent juristic reasoning. If you bring up examples of it,

like Abdullahi Ahmed An-Na'im, the well-known Muslim scholar
who studies human rights and Islamic law, or the Moroccan Family
Code of 2004, which used *ijtihad* as a means to reform family law in a
way that would integrate gender equality, or if you allude to the
evolutionary nature of *fiqh*, the doctrinal traditions developed by
jurists over centuries, their reaction would be a polite rebuff. Or it
might be a clear-cut answer like this one from Sheikh Faizul Aqtab
Siddiqi, the director of the Muslim Arbitration Council:

Sheikh Siddiqi: I do not disagree with the idea of *ijtihad* and
                 qiyas [independent juristic reasoning and one of
                 its techniques and analogies]. This is our forte.
                 We have to do *ijtihad*. But no *ijtihad* can cancel
                 the direct rule of God, the *hukum of Allah*. This
                 is not possible. There cannot be any evolution of
                 the direct rules, *ahkam*. For example, the rule of
                 corporal punishment – cutting off the hands –
                 hukum of *had* – can be suspended due to certain
                 social circumstances, but cannot be terminated
                 as barbaric or irrelevant to modern society. I do
                 not think so. I am a firm believer in corporal
                 punishment, *hudud*, but in the right social
                 environment.
Manea: And what is the right social environment?
Sheikh Siddiqi: Equal distribution of wealth, there is full
                 education within the community, there are the
                 people who are believers, *momeneen,* people who
                 are living according to true belief in Allah and
                 they are leading their lives to please Allah.
                 In those circumstances, where they have no
                 excuse whatsoever but to accept the rules of
                 Shari'a, *hukum al shariah*, then in those
                 circumstances, if there is a transgression then
                 I believe the corporal punishments, *hudud*,
                 should be implemented.

Within this mindset, the jurists' traditions somehow seem to become
sacred in these judges' minds; they reflect a 'divine wisdom' that

transcends our understanding. Naturally this leads them to apply the classical Islamic law to the letter, picking and choosing as they want from within that pool of traditions.

Consider the issue of the proper age for marriage. Sheikh Siddiqi of the Muslim Arbitration Tribunal is clear regarding this issue:

Sheikh Siddiqi: In my view, puberty is the right age. But puberty is the minimum age; then the next criterion is the decision of the guardian, he has to make the decision. Because in some societies, 12- or 13-year-old women, girls, they are more or less fully fledged women, they are fully functional, and you in Western societies, [...] are having babies, they are having sex, so they are fully grown and fully mature; there are some 12-year-olds that are not in that condition, they are very weak, they are not fully functional as women, and they do not want to get married. So it is the job of the *wali,* the guardian, to ensure that the girl is protected and the girl is not subjected to a marriage in this situation where her personal circumstances do not allow this marriage to take place.

Again, we see classical Islamic jurisprudence being used as a point of reference in these courts.

The guardianship issue clearly illustrates this point. As we saw above, Sheikh Siddiqi considers that the guardian knows best for his ward. Dr Mohammad Shahoot Kharfan, of the Muslim Welfare House, demands that the bride and the groom and the guardian be present at the wedding ceremony. But to contract the marriage, the guardian has to approve. One example he gave me was of a woman in her thirties who wanted to marry. Dr Kharfan asked for her guardian to contract the marriage. When she told him he lives in another country, he called him to get his approval and to ask him to delegate his right of guardianship to another person, a male of course. When I asked Dr Kharfan if her voice was not enough, his answer was matter-of-fact: 'the guardian is present, the guardian is present', meaning, we have a guardian here, and he will decide.

By the same token, Hanafi jurisprudence allows the guardian to annul the marriage of his female ward if he is not satisfied with her choice of groom, and the people I interviewed consider this provision valid. In fact, it has been used and applied in the Islamic Shari'a Council, Leyton, and the Birmingham Islamic Shari'a Council of the Central Mosque. As I said before, the latter is considered to be supportive of women's needs.

The following transcript of the interview I conducted with Sheikh Suhaib Hasan, of the ISC in Leyton, exemplifies what I mean about a mindset that leads people to apply the classical Islamic law to the letter, picking and choosing as one likes from within a pool of outdated traditions.

I asked whether he requires the permission of the guardian for a marriage, and he answered this way:

Sheikh Hasan: You see this is the beauty of this council that you have all forms of ideas [schools of jurisprudence], and we try to pick the idea which is more acceptable and more appropriate for the Muslim masses living in this country [...] When it comes to the guardian, *wali*, we know that most of the people here come from India and Pakistan and most of the Muslim community is from a Hanafi background. And in Hanafi jurisprudence, they allow an adult woman to conduct her marriage without the knowledge of her *wali* [the guardian]. But one thing [...] that people do not know [is] that the guardian, the *wali*, is allowed to ask for *faskh*, the invalidation [dissolution] of the marriage on two grounds: one, that this woman has married someone who is not equal to her status, that is *kuuf*, suitable, [*kafaa*] [...] The second [is if] she has accepted a dower amount which is far less than the dower amount accepted in her house. For example, her sister got 500 pounds, her cousin got 500 pounds, and she only accepted 10 pounds, so the guardian has the right to go to the judge – *qadi* – and say, 'I challenge

	this marriage on one of these two grounds.' So he can invalidate this marriage.
Manea:	But have you encountered such cases?
Sheikh Hasan:	Many.
Manea:	Really?
Sheikh Hasan:	Yes, yes. But [suppose] the man is coming from a Shafii [jurisprudence] background, [then] there is no problem, because the Shafii, they say, there is no *nikah* [marriage contract] without a guardian, *wali*, and a witness, the Shafii believe in that, the Hanbali and Maliki [jurisprudences] believe in that. [Then,] if they are coming from this background and they are saying this marriage was conducted without a guardian, *wali*, then there is no problem to invalidate it, easy. So we can invalidate it easily.
Manea:	But have you really had a case where the father said, I don't accept the marriage of my daughter?
Sheikh Hasan:	Yes. We had [such a] case. And [the father] strongly contested [his daughter choosing her own husband] [. . .] If the woman is also ready to invalidate the marriage, then it is no problem. You [just] say your father is asking and you are willing. The problem is that [this woman] does not want to invalidate [her marriage] and she is attached to this boy and the father is asking for the invalidation of this marriage. We told the father, you have these two grounds; if you can prove to us that she is married to someone [not] equal to her, [. . .] or she has accepted a very low dower amount, then we can invalidate it, and we did invalidate some marriages on this ground.

Sheikh Mohammad Talha Bokhari of the Birmingham council does not question the validity of this provision: he says the guardian has the right to invalidate a marriage if the groom is considered unfit. Nonetheless, he says they try to implement this rule in a more 'sensitive' manner – if one can use that adjective. He explained to me:

Sheikh Bokhari: [...] the Hanafi jurisprudence gives the right – the *haq* – to the guardian – the *wali* – to object to the marriage, *haq al Kafaa*, [...] because she has married a man who was a source of shame for their family. But [this role is only valid] up to [a point]. As a rule, if the girl is not pregnant, *kafaa* is possible. If the girl has become pregnant then his guardianship has [expired]. This is the Hanafi ideology for this matter. And mostly it is suitable in this situation in this world.

Manea: And have you had cases like this?

Bokhari: Yes.

Manea: Really? Could you give me an example?

Sheikh Bokhari: For example, a lady came; she was nearly 29 and she found someone and that person has become Muslim. The husband was not born Muslim. She was from Somalia and the husband was from Ghana. The father was not happy with that [because the husband was from Ghana] and objected to this marriage. And [we asked him] why have you objected. Because he is Muslim, thank God, and according to Islam he has all the rights that a Muslim has. He [the father] said 'but he is from Ghana, I do not like it.' I said this not legal; [the father's position] is not a matter of Islam, because Islam says all [Muslims] are equal. He is a Muslim. Because he is doing a very good job as a bank manager and she was very happy, the father said ok. [...] And she has become pregnant. And we said your objection is annulled. You have lost your right to *kafaa* and guardianship [because of her pregnancy].

***

It is a mindset – a mindset that does not belong to the twenty-first century. A mindset that does not see harm in beating a wife. It is *how one is beating his wife* that seems to be under question: one should not harm the woman by hitting her on the face, nor should he leave marks on her body. In fact, if one follows the 'correct' example of the Prophet, one should use toothpicks to hit her: 'How much will she get hurt from the toothpick (*miswak*)?' Or 'you can make a knot in her scarf' and hit her with it: 'How much can a person feel from that?' For the main purpose of *beating* is to *hurt her feelings, not her body*.[71] Of course, if the husband beats her 'savagely' then that is a ground for divorce.

Consistency in logic is not a feature of this mindset or these outdated laws.

When a law tells us that the rights of a child or a woman are irrelevant, that it is 'ok' to force a child or woman to marry, or to simply ignore her choice and wish to remain married and annul her marriage because her guardian has a *legal right* to do so, when a law tells us that man and woman are not equal in dignity *and* rights, when a law makes it possible to violate a woman's dignity and strip her of her equal rights, then it is incumbent on us to take a difficult step and make a judgement: these are *bad laws* by today's standards. They have no place in a modern society. It is our duty to make that judgement.

Cultural relativism cannot justify a child marriage, cannot justify forcing a woman to marry and cannot justify beating a wife. Doing so is a matter of domestic violence in any language. Using Islamic jargon will not make it tolerable. Using a culturally relativist argument about group rights or religious rights to justify the application of such rules is not only shameful. It is outrageous.

Women and men in Islamic countries have been fighting to change and modernise these laws. Yet, to the essentialists, their struggle seems irrelevant, inconsequential. The essentialists would prefer to bring in a religious law, snatched out of its medieval social and historical and geographical contexts, and apply it today in the middle of Britain. They think they are protecting 'Muslims' rights'. After all, that is what the 'Muslims' want. Well, perhaps it is time to ask this question: Who is speaking in the name of Muslims, and whose rights will be protected here? This brings me to the political dimension of the call to apply Islamic law within a Western context.

CHAPTER 5

ISLAMISM AND ISLAMIC LAW IN THE WEST: STATING THE OBVIOUS? BRITAIN AS AN EXAMPLE

'There is a disconnect!' Gita Sahgal told me. She is the Indian-born British director of the Centre for Secular Space in London and the founder of Women against Fundamentalism. People in Britain working on security issues, and fighting extremism, are not concerned about shariʿa courts. But, she explained, the two issues are connected.

Yes, the two issues are connected.

Her statement confirmed what other interviewees emphasised repeatedly. In fact, looking back at the beginning of my research, I too tended to look at the two issues as separate. My aim was to look at the issue from a gender perspective: to investigate the human rights consequences of applying Islamic law in family affairs within a Western legal context. It was only during the course of my interviews that I realised how often the connection was highlighted and emphasised. Given that these interviewees had different ideological backgrounds, I started to see a pattern in what they were describing.

Moreover, when I began to develop a list of people to interview for my research, asking for possible names from well-informed intellectuals and lawyers working on the issue in the UK and Brussels, I was surprised when they suggested experts on extremism. And I still remember asking myself: 'Extremism? Why extremism?'

Extremism in shari'a councils was specifically mentioned in the 2012 response of the Quilliam Foundation to Baroness Cox's Arbitration and Mediation Services (Equality) Bill. The foundation is run by British Muslims, some of them former Islamists, who are dedicated to fighting extremism in the UK. The response written by Dr Usama Hasan – a senior researcher and the son of Sheikh Suhaib Hasan of the Islamic Shari'a Council, Leyton – was treading a fine line.

It welcomed the bill, and acknowledged its aim of protecting Muslim women. It warned that it might be mis-construed as an attack on Islam and shari'a if not framed carefully and then pointed out that traditional Islamic jurisprudence was developed for male-dominated societies and needs to be rethought for modern contexts. Then it talked about extremist clerics:

> There remains the problem of extremist clerics sitting on UK shari'a councils and publishing extremist fatwas that make life difficult for Muslims, especially women. For shari'a councils to evolve into mainstream, civic bodies that specialise in mediation, counselling and appropriate arbitration, such extremism must be curbed.[1]

The more I researched this issue, talking with experts and activists from within the Muslim communities, the more it transpired that the issue is not only about extremist clerics sitting in UK shari'a courts. It is about a reactionary worldview held by religious leaders, who belong to specific South Asian religious movements, a perspective that seeks to separate 'Muslims' from the outside world. This worldview in turn set the stage for a strategy promoted by supporters of political Islamism to essentialise Islam and Muslims, to insist on the homogeneity of Islam and Muslims, and to present their own Islamist demands as the demands of all Muslims and of Islam.

The two groups of societal and political Islamism share a similar worldview about creating an Islamist state and implementing shari'a law, and about the supremacy of Muslims and Islam. The two groups also share a narration of history that portrays Muslims and Islam as perpetual victims subject to hegemonic attacks and persecution. Historical facts and self-criticism are conspicuously absent in such recollections. According to this narrative, the world is divided into two camps: 'us' and 'them'. The West, which is considered as 'them' – the other – is presented as homogenous, and certainly the enemy, intent on destroying Islam and Islamic values and cultures.

British authorities, regardless of which governments we are talking about, share the responsibility for naively constructing the Muslim community, reducing its diverse migrant communities of people from Islamic countries to their religious identity, and promoting unelected Muslim/Islamist leaders as speakers for the community. This policy has started to change recently as extremism has become more of a problem in the UK.

Not surprisingly, when the essentialists promote the idea of legal pluralism and aim to introduce Islamic law for Muslims within Western legal systems, it is the narrative of these Islamists and conservative/reactionary religious groups that is considered authentic and worth defending. They take the narrative of victimhood for granted and believe that defending these groups and their agenda of separation is part of fighting Western hegemony. Women's voices, and voices fighting extremism, fundamentalism and Islamism in their own communities, are often disregarded as less authentic. The facts that Islam is multifaceted, and that the Muslim community is a construct that conceals a complex diversity, are given only lip service.

If you think that this story only concerns Britain, think again. Just pause for a moment and observe who speaks for Muslim minorities in Western countries and you will be surprised.

The British case, while extreme, is therefore important because it reveals a pattern that seems to repeat itself in different forms within the different contexts of Western countries. The pattern is constructing a minority, and reducing it to its religious identity. It constructs Muslims, Islam, and of course Muslim women, in separation from their historical, national, social and religious contexts. Indeed, it is an essentialists' construct.

This brings me to the point where all this started in Britain: when identity politics and group rights were introduced in the name of multiculturalism.

Constructing Muslim Community: Establishing the Landscape

In Chapter 2 I described how British authorities started a multicultural project within a context of increased racism. I mentioned how Roy Jenkins, Labour politician and Home Secretary, gave a speech in 1966 in which he discarded the option of a British melting pot and opted instead for cultural diversity, coupled with equal opportunity in an atmosphere of mutual tolerance. Instead of this multiculturalism being implemented as a living experience, the exercise promoted the idea of group rights and ended up with segregated communities and what Amartya Sen later called plural monoculturalism.

In the 1960s the discourse was of multiculturalism, which was considered a magic tool to fight the racist demon lurking within British society. Today, instead, the discussion is of a crisis of multiculturalism. In fact, the very same Roy Jenkins who promoted multiculturalism came to regret his policies during the Salman Rushdie affair of 1989, saying that perhaps they should have been 'more cautious about allowing the creation in the 1950s of substantial Muslim communities here.'[2]

His remark annoyed, and still annoys, the lobby for multiculturalism in the UK. Yet, what interests me in his statement is his choice of the word 'creation'. I know he did not mean it that way, but that is exactly what British authorities did: they created the Muslim community.

The creation, and with it the construction, of a Muslim identity involved a process of concurrent developments initiated by different actors and groups. The process did not start with the publication of Salman Rushdie's book *Satanic Verses,* although many seem to think of it that way. It did not take shape out of the blue. In fact, it started just as Jenkins said, in the 1950s. It became a field for power struggles among different Islamist and Islamic groups, was instrumentalised by cynical politicians and took a clear shape in the late 1980s. The Rushdie affair only decided the outcome of the power struggle within the Muslim communities, and made it clear whom the British authorities considered as speaking for the Muslim community: Islamists! Indeed, it chose none other than a group that advocates the ideology of political Islamism represented by Jamaat-e-Islami and the Muslim Brotherhood.

Before I discuss this history, let me first briefly summarise the landscape of British Islam.

The Landscape of British Islam

The 2001 census estimated that the Muslim population in the UK is 1.6 million, or 2.7 per cent of the total population. Between 2004 and 2008, according to the Office of National Statistics, the number grew by more than 500,000 to 2.4 million, a growth rate ten times that of the rest of British society. In 2011 the number rose to more than 2.7 million. Nearly half of those people were born in the UK.

The Muslim population is divided into 14 nationalities. The majority, about two thirds, have South Asian roots: they are from Pakistan or Bangladesh, followed by India.[3] The rest come from Afghanistan, Algeria, Bangladesh, Egypt, Iran, Iraq, Morocco, Nigeria, Pakistan, Saudi Arabia, Somalia and Turkey.[4] Heterogeneity in their denomination, languages and ethnicities is a key characteristic, as is clear from Table 5.1.

The table was published in 2009, by the Department for Communities and Local Government in a summary report about the Muslim communities in the UK.[5] It highlights in no uncertain term how diverse this so-called 'Muslim community' is and identifies three characteristics of differentiation within the Muslim communities: denomination, language and ethnicity.

Another feature is the regional and linguistic diversity within these nationalities. For example, British Pakistanis include a number of distinct regional and linguistic groups. A study commissioned by the Department for Communities and Local Government published in 2009 has showed that most British Pakistanis put an emphasis on their distinct language, culture and way of life as a means of differentiating their regional identity as a separate ethnic group.

Hence, Pathans distinguish themselves from Punjabis, while many Mirpuris choose to describe themselves as Kashmiris in order to distinguish themselves from other Pakistanis. While accurate figures are absent, it is estimated that 60 per cent to 70 per cent of Pakistanis in the UK are from the Kashmir Mirpur region, and are settled mostly in Birmingham, Bradford, Oldham and surrounding towns. In London, however, the communities are more mixed and include equivalent numbers of Punjabis, Pathans and Kashmiris. Moreover, there are also small communities of Sindhis and Balochis in London; these are two distinct regions with complicated and difficult relationships with the Pakistani state.[6]

Table 5.1 Key characteristics of Muslim ethnic communities in England: religion, language and ethnicity

Community	% of total country-born population Muslim	Main religious denominations	Other religious denominations	Main Languages other than English	Main Ethnic Groups
Afghan	77%	Sunni (Hanafi, sub-groups incl. Deobandi)	Shi'a (particularly those from the Hazara ethnic group)	Pashto, Dari	Pashtun, Tajik, Uzbek, Hazara, Turkmen, Aimaq, Baluchi, Nuristani, Farsiwan
Algerian	86%	Sunni (Maliki)	Sunni (Salafi)	Arabic, French, Berber languages (incl. Tamazight)	Arab, Berber
Bangladeshi	92%	Sunni (Hanafi, subgroups incl. Barelwi, Deobandi, Tablighi Jamaat)	Sunni (Shafi)	Bengali, Sylheti	Bengali
Egyptian	56%	Sunni (Hanafi)	Sunni (Shafi, Salafi)	Arabic	Arab, Coptic
Indian	12%	Sunni (Hanafi subgroups incl. Deobandi, Barelwi)	Shi'a (Ismaili) Khalifa Jamat	Gujarati	Gujarati, Khalifa, Tamil, North Indian
Iranian	68%	Shi'a (Twelver)		Farsi	Persian, Azeri, Kurdish, Lur, Arab, Baluchi, Turkmen, Qashqai, Armenian, Assyrian and Georgian
Iraqi	74%	Shi'a (Twelver)	Sunni (Hanafi, Maliki)	Arabic	Arab, Assyrian, Kurdish

	%			Language	Ethnic groups
Moroccan	77%	Sunni (Maliki)	Sunni (Shafi, Salafi, Sufi orders)	Arabic, French	Arab, Berber
Nigerian	9%	Sunni (Maliki)	Shi'a, Sufi orders (Tijaniyah, Qadriiyah)	Yoruba, Hausa, English, Arabic, Ishan, Edo, Efik, and Igbo	Hausa, Yoruba, Ibo
Pakistani	92%	Sunni (Hanafi, various sub-groups incl. Deobandi, Barelwi, Tablighi Jamaat)	Sunni (Ahl-e Hadith/Salafi)	Urdu, Punjabi	Kashmiri, Pathan, Punjabi, Sindhi, Baluchi
Saudi Arabian	64%	Sunni (Hanbali/Wahabbi)		Arabic	Arab
Somali	89%	Sunni (Shafi)	Sunni (Salafi)	Somali, Chiwmini	Clans: Darod, Isaq, Hawiye, Dir, Digil, Mirifle, Bajuni, Benadiri and Bravanese
Turkish-Cypriot	26%[7]	Sunni (Hanafi) Shi'a (Alevis, Ismailis, Jafaris)	Various Sufi orders	Turkish	Turkish Cypriot
Turkish	83%	Sunni (Hanafi) Shi'a (Alevis, Ismailis, Jafaris)	Sunni (Shafi particularly Kurds), various Sufi orders.	Turkish	Turkish, Kurdish

'Percentage of total country-born population Muslim' is based on religion and country-of-birth data from the 2001 census (Commissioned table, C0644, C1013). The percentage Muslim figures for Turkish Cypriot Muslims and Egyptian Muslims should be treated with care. The figure for Turkish Cypriots is for the Cyprus-born population in England, not 'Turkish Cypriots', the number of which is not recorded in the census. The figure for the Egyptian born population excludes 'White British'.

Societal and Political Islamism(s) in the British Context

Thus it is obvious that we cannot speak of a British 'Muslim community' in the singular form. We are talking about communities, in the plural, and these are diverse and heterogeneous with multiple national, denominational, linguistic and regional lines of differentiation.

Individual members of these communities are often aware of this diversity, of the complex layers of their identities, and they often flinch when they are reduced to their religious identity, lumped together under the label 'Muslim'.

Just imagine encountering a group that includes a Somali, an Iranian, a Saudi, a Pakistani, a Tunisian, an Egyptian and an Indian — and tell me why you think they should be considered 'one'. If you met an Italian, a Pole, and an Irish person would you say they are one homogenous cultural group because they are all Catholics?

This tendency to reduce national groups to their Islamic religious identities has become the norm in Europe and North America, especially after the Rushdie affair in the UK and the terrorist attacks of 9/11 in the United States.

Interestingly, however, advocates of two types of Islamism have been working systematically since the 1950s to cement this homogenising of the Muslim identity, insisting that Islam is one and that identity is religious. The British plural monocultural policies have facilitated their mission.

The first type of Islamism is societal and the second is political.

I begin with *societal Islamism*. I first used this expression in my book *The Arab State and Women's Rights: The Trap of Authoritarian Government*. It refers to these puritanical religious movements, which concern themselves with changing social behaviours based on their rigid worldviews, call for an Islamic mode of life, separate their followers from the wider society, and refrain from political engagement.[8]

Olivier Roy calls them 'neo-fundamentalists'[9] while Barbara D. Metcalf[10] refers to them as 'traditionalists'. Still, Roy and Metcalf and I agree that the societal type of movement is a category distinguishable from the category of political Islamist movement. This type focuses on behaviour, insisting on strict adherence to a range of ritual and personal behavioural practices, especially worship, dress and everyday conduct. In short they insist on implementing the shari'a in a strict and literal manner. But unlike political Islamist movements, they lack a systematic political ideology and are not concerned with state building, at least not at this phase.[11] I understand that this distinction is theoretical and sometimes the two types intertwine in a way that makes them indistinguishable. Yet it is necessary to clarify our terminology – especially as this clarification does have implications for the war against terrorism. Put simply, there is no point in tackling the ideological jihadist message of political Islamism without confronting the religious message of societal Islamism.

In making this distinction I do not imply that societal Islamist movements do not share the agenda of political Islamism. They do share it. Their worldview embraces the ultimate objective of creating an Islamist state that implements what they consider the laws of God and they actively promote concepts of military and missionary jihad. In fact, Roy argues, and quite correctly, that these groups have even superseded the political Islamic movements as the proponents of jihad against the Western world.[12] The West is an enemy: one that should be fought, if not always by violence, then by separating oneself from its influence.

But the approach of societal Islamism is quiet and bottom-up; it prefers to work with the masses silently. Ghaffar Hussain, an expert on extremism and Islamism in Britain, described the approach of one branch of Societal Islamism, the Deobandi movement, in the UK:

> They are powerful as well, but they were very very quiet, they did not want to make a noise or be noticed by the mainstream society; they wanted to do their work in the mosques, hidden away in mosques. So when we speak to them as [political] Islamists, they would say: you guys are trying to change the system from the top, but we are like lots and lots of ants, which are eating away at the system slowly. What they think they are doing is slowly converting everybody, and they will automatically be Islamists. So they are not opposed to the idea of enforcing Islam through the state, but they just do not believe in political revolution and political engagement.[13]

Another important element brings the two types of Islamism together: they both start with woman and control of her behaviour and body in their preaching about an ideal Islamist world, a point I will return to later.

Within the British context, the societal Islamist movements include the Deobandi, the Tablighi, the Ahl Al Hadith and the Salafi, but also, for reasons I will explain in the following section, the Barlevi movement.

What these movements have in common is their message of separation and intolerance. They call on their supporters to separate themselves from those surrounding them (Muslims and non-Muslims alike) and to adhere to their puritanical teachings to the letter.

I will focus on five main societal Islamist movements working within Britain. These are the Deobandi, the Barelwi Sufis, the Tablighi Jama'at, the Ahl Al Hadith, and the Salafis.

The Deobandi movement is often described as the Wahhabi branch of the movement on the subcontinent, despite its distinct origins.[14] It advocates for a strict Sunni orthodoxy, frowns upon the Sufi tradition of Islam, considering it a form of polytheism, and insists on a separate Muslim identity and application of shari'a law. The Taliban in Afghanistan bases its religious interpretation on Deobandi teachings. It is within the Deobandi mosques and shari'a councils in the UK that the practice of shari'a councils started. The Deobandi movement has a strong influence in the Birmingham Shari'a Council I described in the last chapter.

Just like Wahhabi (Salafi) Islam, this school of thought goes back to a puritanical reformist movement of the eighteenth century, led by Shah Waliullah (1703–62) and then by his offspring. The movement, based on Sunni Hanafi jurisprudence, advocated that Islam must be purified of all alien influences. It is named after Deoband, a town in northern India, where the seminary of Deobandi (Dar al-ulum) was established in 1867, consolidating the movement. The seminary aimed to ensure scriptural orthodoxy, assert the Islamic identity of its students, and preach the strict literal application of the holy texts of Islam as the only solution to the problems of daily life.[15]

Two factors explain the fundamentalist nature and isolationist tendencies of the Deobandi movement. The first factor is often neglected: the influence of the thirteenth-century Salafi theologian, Ibn Taymiyyah. Shah Waliullah lived long before the British took over India; he studied in Mecca and Medina for eight years and was taught by religious scholars known for supporting the theology of Ibn Taymiyyah. The latter's writings were also crucial in shaping the ideology of the Wahhabi movement.[16]

On the other hand, the factor most often cited is the end of the Islamic Moghul Dynasty, based in Delhi (1526–1857). Its end marked the transfer of the rule of British East India to the British Crown. Muslims, who represented a minority within India as a whole, did not merely lose political power. They also lost their earlier privileges, which were now contested by the Hindu majority. Now they faced a new situation where their fellow citizens, Hindus and citizens of other faiths, had complete freedom to use the public space to practice their own rites, even when, in their own view, these violated Islam.[17]

This second factor, along with the transformation of Muslims' status within British India, generated two strategies, which would both have a profound impact on the situation of South Asian minorities in Britain. The first strategy sought to rebuild and defend a community identity in the face of the Hindu majority and non-Muslim rule. In other words, Deobandis started to emphasise that Islam was its own unique religion, radically separate from the non-Muslim world. The second strategy, communalism, aimed to reassert Islam by establishing separate electoral colleges for Muslims and Hindus, a step that eventually led to Pakistan separating from India. The two strategies reinforced each other: the first provided the rules and laws that propagated belief in the new political order; and the second embraced the concept of a 'Muslim' population that would lay claim in its own name to a separate space, Pakistan.[18]

The Deobandi movement was and still is instrumental in mainstreaming the first measure by emphasising orthodox Islamic behaviour and engendering a separate communal identity within India. Though the Deobandis did not support the separation of Pakistan after India became independent, they insisted on a parallel legal system that allows them to implement shari'a law, something that British colonial authorities and then post-colonial India readily granted.

Hence, within non-Muslim India the Deobandis sought to achieve a form of what Gilles Kepel called 'jurisprudential apartheid' between them and the Hindus. This strategy, Kepel argues, would later become essential, after individual Deobandis moved to Europe and Britain. In fact, their autonomy vis-à-vis the state prepared them especially well for the task of decreeing rules that would form the base of a closed community identity in the UK.[19]

Indeed, the approach has been implemented to the letter within Britain. Innes Bowen described today's Deobandi movement and its segregationist approach in her book *Medina in Birmingham, Najaf in Brent: Inside British Islam* using the example of the Muslim community in Leicester, where the movement has a strong presence. She cited a cable leaked via Wikileaks that described the community's lack of integration as 'striking' and the 'most conservative in Europe.' These were the observations of the US State Department's senior adviser for Muslim engagement, Farah Pandith, who visited the city in 2007. In a local bookshop, she had seen texts in English which seemed designed to 'segregate Muslims from their wider community [...] playing up the differences between Islam and other religions [...] and feeding hate of Jews to the young.'[20]

Leicester is not unique in this regard. Visiting Alum Rock Road and Coventry Road in Birmingham, I entered several bookshops. Regardless of which shop I entered, I found a plethora of books promoting a fundamentalist interpretation of Islam. These books give guidance on how to 'separate Muslims from the polytheists.' They describe the 'Land of War' as 'any land in which the laws of the disbelievers are superior.'[21] And they insist that jihad is an obligation. Books that promote a prototype of an Islamist woman are abundant, mainly focusing on how a 'good Muslim wife' should behave. Obedience to her husband is a given and covering her body is portrayed as an obligation she cannot question. These bookshops are part of a global chain of publishing houses that promote not only the Deobandi version of Islam but its Arab counterpart, Salafi Islam.

Back to Leicester. Innes Bowen stated that many among its Deobandi population will 'voluntarily submit themselves to the authority of the Deobandi ulema [Sheikhs]. A local shari'a council helps to settle disputes between adherents.'[22] She also observed a new phenomenon that is increasing not only in Leicester but also in many areas with a Muslim minority: women veiling their faces. Although it was once unusual among Muslim women, now it is the practice of a substantial minority.[23]

The Deobandi movement in the UK controls almost half of the mosques in the country, together with the Tablighi. In the UK over the last 30 years it has established 25 *dar al-ulums*, seminaries responsible for training the imams for their mosques. The annual output of graduates from these highly conservative literalist Deobandi seminaries does meet the British government's demand for English-speaking imams, but fails to support the British values of equality, tolerance, liberty and religious pluralism.[24]

The second group is the *Barelwi Sufism movement*. I said when describing societal Islamism that I tend to include the Barelwi movement within this category. I do that despite its Sufi orientation, an orientation often associated with political moderation. Sufism constitutes one branch of Islamic tradition; associated with both Sunni and Shi'i Islam, it manifests the mystical side of Islam. This religious movement, with its different groupings, is widespread in South Asia, Central Asia, North Africa, and parts of Turkey, Saudi Arabia, Yemen, Syria and Egypt. Adherents to some of its currents emphasise personal responsibility and accountability, and stress the possibility of merging the human's entire being, both physical and mental, in God. Others emphasise membership in a Sufi order and obedience to the order's sheikh (male) or sheikha (female).[25]

Followers of Sufism are known in general for their strong devotion to the personality of Mohammad, the Prophet of Islam, and they often make pilgrimages to the shrines of Sufi saints. In general its ethos has been egalitarian, charitable and friendly. One of its main features was blending local cultures and cementing Islam's place in the local culture, from North Africa to the Indian subcontinent.[26]

Perhaps because of this background some Western scholars thought of Sufism as a natural ally in the fight against violent extremism. This was at least the opinion of the Rand think tank in a 2007 report entitled *Building Moderate Muslim Networks*. Its authors argued that the West could find partners in the effort to combat Islamist extremism; the Sufis were one example. They based their argument on the fact that Salafis and Wahhabis are relentless enemies of Sufis. Whenever the latter gained power they have sought to suppress the practice of Sufi Islam, destroying its shrines in the process. Because of this victimisation, 'Sufis are natural allies of the West to the extent that common ground can be found with them.'[27] The authors were aware of the diversity within this tradition and appreciate that some of its currents may be less moderate than one would expect.

The latter point is important for our discussion here. There is diversity within the Sufi tradition. Though this diversity is fairly moderate, it does not preclude the possibility that the tradition may have experienced changes that led individuals to form different currents, based on their own circumstances.

The Barlevi movement is one such tradition. Radicalisation breeds counter-radicalisation. This is a phenomenon I observed in Egypt, where the rise of both societal Islamism and political Islamism led to individuals rediscovering their Christian Coptic identity and then to an emphasis on strictly practicing Coptic teachings. The same can be said in Yemen about the Zaydi tradition, which is part of the Shi'a denomination, but perceived as being closest to the Sunnis. This traditionally moderate strand of Islam was radicalised as the Wahhabi Salafi groups steadily encroached on their stronghold region, Sada'a, and constantly demonised its teachings.

The Barelwi movement appeared towards the end of the nineteenth century in the north Indian town of Bareilly as a reaction to the ideological attacks of the Deobandis. The writings of its founder Ahmed Riza Khan (1856–1921) were an impassioned defence of the superhuman nature of the Prophet of Islam and of the Sufi tradition of worshipping all kinds of saints and holy men. And just as the Deobandis publicly condemned the Barelwis religious practices, saying its adherents were heretics and shrine-worshippers who were not true to the original teachings of Islam, so Ahmed Riza Khan pronounced the leading Deobandis of his time to be *kaffirs*, unbelievers.[28]

Though no one has specific statistics on these groups, experts argue that the majority of South Asian Muslims follow this line of Islamic interpretation and that they control 39 per cent of Britain's mosque capacity. Yet, just like the Deobandis, and perhaps because of the Deobandis, as some interviewees told me, this type of Sufism has created a mental and cultural separation from the surrounding world. Gilles Kepel asserts that while this separation is at least as intense as the closed identity built by the Deobandis, the Barelwis have other criteria for defining community boundaries. 'They construct a strictly defined Islamic identity: the intercession of saints and the prophet allows the faithful to live according to Islam in its traditional form, without thinking about the attitude of the state or dominant social norms.'[29]

Innes Bowen confirms this perception; she says that when it comes to creating an Islamic state that applies shari'a law the emphasis within this group takes a mental form. She quotes Sheikh Faizul Aqtab Siddiqi, a fellow Barelwi and the leading sheikh in the Muslim Arbitration Tribunal I mentioned in the last chapter. He said that the movement is a spiritual centre of guidance and the 'circles of politics are not for us';

still, 'an Islamic state of the mind among the majority would ultimately result in an Islamic state. Because a political state is a manifestation of the state of the mind of the people essentially.'[30]

In our interview, Sheikj Siddiqi indicated a desire for separation, albeit not only a mental one. It takes the shape of a legal separation that allows 'Muslims' to 'live' their religious identity:

I am now a citizen of this country [Britain]. This is my home. But the point is, I should not have to go to a Muslim country to get Islamic services. All my Islamic services should be provided here. Halal food, halal this, [halal that], including Islamic shari'a.[31]

Sheikh Siddiqi insists that living according to a different law is not a sign of separation. Rather, he says, it is a means to help him and his 'community' to follow their own tradition and be good Muslims. He thinks of his tribunal as a 'service provider, one that should deal with all aspects of the community's problems, including inheritance, custody of children, sexual abuse and domestic violence.'[32]

It is a 'parallel mind-set about religious and legal dealings,' says Rashad Ali, an expert on British Islam and extremism, whom I interviewed twice. In a follow-up email exchange, he stated that 'despite the absence of a radical political outlook,' the Barelwis 'had created some separatist ideas.' They did this through 'conceptualising the sovereignty of God and the Shari'a versus the existent legal system.'[33]

The strict devotion of the Barelwi to the cult of Prophet Mohammad's personality may explain why this movement was an active and passionate part of the angry uproar that ensued after the publication of the *Satanic Verses* in 1988 and the Danish cartoons in 2005 – and why they often support anti-blasphemy legislation in Pakistan and elsewhere.

Before concluding this part, it is worth mentioning that the fierce rivalry between the two revivalist/isolationist movements – Deobandi and Barelwi – has marked their relationship in South Asia as well as in the UK. In India, for example, in 2009 the Barelwi mufti, the highest Barelwi expounder of Islamic law in India, issued a fatwa decreeing that 200 followers should marry their wives again because they had participated in a funeral prayer led by a Deobandi imam. The fatwa stated that since they do not regard the Deobandis as being sufficiently Muslim, all those who said their *namaz* (prayer) under that imam ceased to be Muslims. In the UK, on the other hand, the work to create community cohesion may end up in a deadlock because of the rivalry and animosity between the two groups. In fact, both engage in disputes over control of mosques and each group refuses to pray after an imam of the other group.[34]

The third group is the *Tablighi Jama'at,* often referred to as Tabligh. This group formed in 1927, under the influence of the Muslim scholar Muhammad Ilyas. This fundamentalist movement pushes the desire for autonomy to the extreme. It defines the community on the basis of strict religious observance. It propagates as widely as possible, but especially among the uneducated, a rigorous Islam cut from the literalism of religious scholars and purged of Sufi practices.[35]

Ilyas said Muslims were politically weak because they did not practice their faith sufficiently. His promise to those following him was simple: 'if they became better Muslims in their daily lives, they would 'dominate over non-believers,' and would be 'destined to be the masters of each and everything on earth.'[36]

In other words, just like other societal Islamist movements, the Tabligh share the aim of creating an Islamic state. They believe, however, that this aim will be accomplished through God, who will give political power to the Muslim 'nation' as a reward for its strict piety.

Kepel argues that through its proselytising, the Tabligh has become one of the most important re-Islamising movements in the world. Like the Deobandis, it separates its followers from the surrounding society, isolates them culturally from the 'ungodly environment', and re-socialises them within an Islamic community, one that is characterised by strong pietism. This same model, Kepel contends, would be adapted to the new conditions of immigration in the UK and Europe, isolating its followers from the potential attraction of Western societies.[37] The Tabligh is the group involved in the mega-mosque controversy in East London.

The fourth group is *Ahl Al Hadith.* Literally the people of the prophetic narrations, this is another revivalist movement that grew out of India in the nineteenth century (1870s). They are Salafis but are known as Ahl Al Hadith in South Asia and since the 1960s have maintained close ties with the Saudi religious establishment. They recognise only the Qur'an and the Hadith (the sayings and doings of the Prophet of Islam); they claim not to follow any jurisprudence, and are puritanical in matters of faith and in their practice. They criticise Sufism as a wrongful innovation and are hostile to the practices of most South Asian Muslims, especially the Barlewis, whom they consider to be practising a form of polytheism. They oppose all those whose beliefs differ from theirs, including the Deobandis, and are convinced that they alone embody the authentic faith.[38] Sheikh Suhaib Hasan of the Muslim Shari'a Council, Leyton, along with some other members of the council, follows this line of interpretation of Islam.[39]

Just like the Deobandis and other societal Islamist movements, this line of teaching emphasises that Muslims are superior by virtue of their belief – a concept that borders on fascism. Followers of other religions are considered kuffar, the plural of kaffir: infidels or non-believers.

According to Dr Taj Hargey, of the Muslim Educational Centre of Oxford, 'The word kaffir is a very pejorative, negative, disparaging term. When you call someone a kaffir, they are not worthy to be associated with. This kind of intolerance is something that gives rise to extremists.'[40]

This perception shows clearly in Ahl Al Hadith's religious teachings, jurisprudence and speeches. For instance, when Sheikh Suhaib Hasan wrote about eligibility for inheritance according to the Sunnah (the sayings and doings of the prophet of Islam) he put it this way: 'The Prophet explained that the Muslim child of a Kaffir [disbeliever], the Kaffir child of a Muslim, and the murderer of his/her own father, none of these can inherit.'[41]

More to the point, Sheikh Hasan was secretly filmed by Channel 4's *Undercover Mosque* programme, aired in January 2007. He was quoted in a speech proclaiming the supremacy of Muslims in encounters with non-believers. And in other speeches he predicts the coming of the Islamic state: 'Allah has decreed this thing that I am going to be dominant, the dominance of course is a political dominance.' He continues, saying this dominance will lead to the application of shari'a law, which will include 'the chopping of the hands of the thieves, the flogging of the adulterers and flogging of the drunkards.' Jihad is part of this mindset and it will be launched by this Islamic state: 'Then jihad against the non-Muslims, against those people who are the oppressors.'[42]

The fifth group is the Salafis, or Wahhabis. Salafism is an orthodox Sunni movement founded in the eighteenth century by Mohammed ibn Abd al-Wahhab who was convinced that the Muslims had deviated from the 'pure Islam' of the Prophet Mohammad. It advocates the strict practice of and absolute obedience to Islam as decreed (according to their interpretation) by the Prophet and the early generations of his followers. These are known as the Salaf, or the forefathers – hence the adjective Salafi. It rejects any form of mediation between God and the individual believer and strictly forbids the use of shrines or sculptures – a position that often led to their destruction wherever the Salafis came to power. It takes an intolerant fundamentalist stance towards non-Muslims and non-Salafis and obliges Muslims to distance themselves from them. It considers it an obligation of Muslims to respond to the call for holy war/jihad and defines the conditions for such a response.[43]

Saudi Arabia was established based on an alliance made in 1744 between Mohammed ibn Saud, the founder of the Saudi dynasty, and ibn ibn Abd al-Wahhab, the founder of the movement. They pledged to create a state according to Wahhabi principles. The same pledge was reinstated by Ibn Saud a century and a half later and provided the foundation of today's modern Saudi Arabia.[44]

Salafism draws a fine line between two completely contrasting positions. One the one hand, Salafis must remain politically quiet even before the most evil ruler as long as he is technically a Muslim. However, once the ruler, or the society at large, ceases to be Muslim, violent opposition is permitted. This explains why most Salafis in the Middle East have been politically quietist, in fact dogmatically so, while a minority of Salafis has turned to armed struggle.[45] The two positions share a key aspiration: to build an Islamic state and to apply shari'a, as they understand it. Jihadist Salafis, embodied by ISIS (Islamic State of Iraq and Syria) in its worst form, combine the teaching of violent Salafism and the ideology of political Islamism represented by the writings of radical Islamist thinkers such as Sayyid Qutb of the Muslim Brotherhood.

In Britain, Salafism is influenced by diverse sources in addition to the teachings of Mohammed ibn Abd al-Wahhab. The South Asian Salafi leader Ahl Al Hadith, whom I mentioned in the section above, is one source of influence. Another source is more recent popular but controversial Salafi personalities. Three key ones are:

- Haitham Al-Haddad, who sits on the Islamic Shari'a Council in Leyton;

- Abu Hamza, who was imprisoned in 2004 and sentenced to seven years for soliciting murder and inciting hatred; and
- Omar Bakri Mohammad, founder of the Muhajiroun, who was denied a re-entry visa to the UK after a visit to Lebanon.[46]

These preachers promote a list of beliefs and activities that will mostly seem familiar by now: the separation of Muslims, the hatred of non-Muslims and the West, the need for jihad and for an Islamic state, the necessity of applying shari'a, permission to take non-Muslims as slaves in time of war, and, yet again, the supremacy of Muslims and their ultimate domination over non-Muslims.

Sheik Al-Haddad articulated all of these views in a variety of videos, programmes and texts in both Arabic and English; they can be found, with their transcripts, on a website dedicated to countering what it describes as Far Right Islamists in Britain. Tellingly, Al-Haddad openly describes what 'co-existence' with 'non-Muslims' means and how, from his point of view, 'multiculturalism' is useful in paving the way for the supremacy of Muslims and their ultimate 'control over the world'. Here is part of a transcript from an interview he gave to the English-language Salafi Huda channel:

Haddad: Of course, as Muslims, we believe that this co-existence cannot take place unless they are living under the umbrella of al-Islam, under the system of al-Islam. But brother Jamil and brothers, we have to differentiate between a situation of a necessity that we are dealing with and the ultimate aim in an ideal situation. Now we are talking about minorities living in the West so we have to provide them with workable solutions in the short run. And as we said, these visions and strategies are meant to be for a short run, means within fifty years, something like this. It is not the far ultimate aim of Muslims because the far ultimate aim for Muslims is to have Islam governing the whole world, Islamisation of the whole globe. This is the ultimate aim of any Muslim and of all communities, Muslim communities. But we are not talking about that at the moment, we are talking about the immediate goals. So, in terms of immediate goals we need this peaceful co-existence and they claim that they are promoting it and we need to take it from there. And we need to tell them that this peaceful co-existence, in order to have real peaceful co-existence, then we have to talk about real multiculturalism, we have to talk about real pluralism. And you said, if you remember in the previous episode, the discussion that many people have, which is yes, you are calling for multiculturalism – [that] means Islam to be officially recognised as a religion in all these European countries and Muslim needs are fulfilled officially within these countries.

Jamil Rashid (programme anchor):

So, this is what I was going to return to, this is what [. . .] a lot of the so-called sceptics say [. . .] They say that what Shaykh Haitham, what you're saying is what the aims of this multiculturalism is, which is for Islam to take over. Because Islam now, you're asking now, you're saying that 'Look the problem is that we need to find out what's actually better for society as a whole.' So really you're calling to society to accept Islam, so really this is disguised as multiculturalism. Really it's not about multiculturalism, it's about getting Islam into the door. What do you say to that kind of. . .?

Haddad:

Even if we say that, what's wrong with that? Because this is our aim at the end of the day, and I don't want to react as so many Muslims reacted towards the issue of integration when they had this attack. They said 'No, no, no we are integrated.' I don't want to say 'No, no, no we are not going to take over.' Our ultimate aim is not a matter of taking over using this terminology, our ultimate aim as Muslims is to have, to see Islam spreading

all over the world and to see the word of Allah
dominant on the whole globe, because justice will
never be achieved unless the word of Allah is
dominant.[47]

Given the obviously totalitarian streaks of this ideology it is rather
worrying that this strand of Islamism is on the rise in the UK. Fewer
than 100 of the UK's 1,700 mosques were under Salafi control in 2013.
However, Innes Bowen observes that between 2009 and 2013 the
number of Salafi mosques in the UK increased by 50 per cent. This made
the movement the fastest growing of the UK's major Islamic trends.
According to figures gathered by Mehmood Naqshbandi, the webmaster
of MuslimInBritain.org and collector of the most comprehensive
publically available data on mosque affiliations, half of all new mosques
opening each year in the UK were Salafi controlled.[48]

The second type of Islamism is political.

Political Islamism is an ideology, a modern ideology that seeks to
use the state's political power as a means of changing and transforming
existing societies. Power is only a means to an end; its goal is
revolutionary change compelled by a vision of a puritanical society and
state, a society that is governed by God's law, not laws made by men and
women. It envisions a state where identity and citizenship are based on
and defined by religious affiliation and observance. Consequently,
universal human rights, citizenship rights, minorities, LGBT, and
women's rights are often violated.[49]

There are different versions of political Islamism. Some movements
seek to create this vision of society and state through outright violence.
Al-Qaeda and ISIS (which combines Salafi Islam and jihadi political
Islamism) are two examples of this type of movement.

There is, on the other hand, a non-violent version of political
Islamism, one that uses an incremental approach.

In this approach, violence is still Salonfähig especially if it concerns
Israel. But the overall strategy is gradual change: making society more
Islamic by using the education system, the mosque, religious teachings
and the media. It is no coincidence that every time Islamists enter a
government, whether Arabic or Islamic, the first ministry they insist on
controlling is the education ministry and the first measure they undertake
is changing the curriculum to mold it according to their ideology.

This strategy is not confined to Arab and Islamic states. It is also practiced in Western societies where Muslim minorities are living. For example, in Britain Islamist educational organisations associated with the Islamist Jamaat-e-Islami movement successfully campaigned to revise the content of the public school curriculum on Islam and to introduce texts written by Islamists propagating a political Islamism position, portraying it as a mainstream Islamic position. Writings by other Muslim and non-Muslim writers with different views were simply discarded as not 'authentic'.[50]

There are two main political movements that embody the ideology of political Islamism. From these two sprang other groups, both violent and non-violent. The two are:

- the Muslim Brotherhood, created in Egypt in 1928 by Hassan Al-Banna, a primary school teacher; and
- the Jamaat-e-Islami, created in British India in 1941 by Abul A'la Maududi, an Indian-born journalist who later moved to Pakistan.

The ideology of the two movements divides the world into two competing camps – Islam and the West – which are engaged in an existential confrontation.

Both movements insist that Islam is not only a religion. It is a political system and a social order. It governs every aspect of society including politics. And Muslims have to surrender their wills to its stipulations.

It was political Islamism that first articulated this 'concept' ideologically. Hassan al-Banna was the first who formulated it in his tracts[51] and all other major writers of political Islamism propagated the idea. They succeeded in mainstreaming this idea – that Islam is not only a religion but also a social order and a political system – to the extent that people today repeat this statement without reflecting on it.

Both movements share the aspiration of creating an Islamic state that applies Islamic law: shari'a. And both use a systematic strategy to achieve their goal: participation within the political process. And both use grassroots organisations to mobilise popular support. In addition to their general work in education, Islamists often establish youth centres and organise activities including religious education and physical education courses, which help them recruit youth to their ranks. Moreover, control of specific mosques has been a key asset in propagating their political message. Finally, they often engage in charitable activities, which provide badly needed relief, medical and educational services. The aim is to build a base of support and strengthen the loyalty of existing adherents while recruiting more.[52]

It is important to emphasise here that neither movement encourages political participation with the aim of following the rules of the democratic game. If they participate in the political system, they do so with the aim of changing it to their version of an Islamic state, even if that will take decades.

Given the importance of the two movements, I will discuss each of them briefly.

The Muslim Brotherhood is considered the cradle of the ideology of political Islamism. It was created in 1928 in Al-Ismailia in Egypt by Hassan Al-Banna (1906–1949). Just like Maududi, Al-Banna divided the word into two camps: 'us', the good Muslims, versus 'them', the morally corrupt but scientifically advanced West. The ideology of the Muslim Brothers has been clear, and simple: each Muslim has two alternatives to choose between. The first is Islam, with all its principles, rules, culture and civilisation. The second is the West, with its modes of life, its systems and styles. Which alternative is better? The Islamic way. Just like Maududi, Al-Banna insisted that Islam is not only a religion that regulates the spiritual relationship between God and the individual. Rather it is an all-encompassing system:

> Islam is a comprehensive system which deals with all spheres of life. It is a state and a homeland (or a government and a nation). It is morality and power (or mercy and justice); it is a culture and a law (or knowledge and jurisprudence). It is material and wealth (or gain and prosperity). It is an endeavor and a call (or an army and a cause). And finally, it is true belief and worship.[53]

Al-Banna's worldview provided the foundation upon which political Islamism has based its arguments ever since: Islam is a way of life. It governs every aspect of society including politics. And Muslims have to surrender their wills to its stipulations.

It also set the stage for an ideology that is clearly expansionist and imperial in its core. Listen to what Al-Banna has to say about the goal of his movement:

This means that the Noble Quran appoints the Muslims as guardians over humanity in its minority, and grants them the right of suzerainty and dominion over the world in order to carry out this sublime commission. Hence it is our concern, not that of the West, and it pertains to Islamic civilisation, not to materialistic civilisation.

We have come to the conclusion that it is our duty to establish sovereignty over the world and to guide all of humanity to the sound precepts of Islam and to its teachings, without which mankind cannot attain happiness.[54]

Abd Alqader Auda (1907–1954), the strategist who helped establish the ideological foundation of the Muslim Brothers, added another element to their conception of Islam: the application of shari'a:

The reason for our backwardness was that we did not apply the shari'a a full and just application. And if the reason for our backwardness is our negligence of shari'a, it will not help us to adopt positive law; no it would only further our backwardness. The effective remedy is to eliminate the reason of our backwardness – and get back to the provisions of shari'a.[55]

Mr Auda neglected to specify what he meant by shari'a. To him, it was simple, self-evident and cut out of its historical context, just like the Islam he and Al-Banna envisioned.

Islam is a way of life. Shari'a should govern society. And, Al-Banna says, 'Jihad is a religious duty obligatory on every Muslim.'[56] Thus, jihad is the third component of the ideology of the Muslim Brotherhood. Hassan Al-Banna was again clear about the jihad he meant, and it was not a peaceful one. He said:

God has imposed jihad as a religious duty on every Muslim, categorically and rigorously, from which there is neither evasion nor escape. He has rendered it a supreme object of desire, and has made the reward of martyrs and fighters in his way a splendid one, for he has conjoined with them in their reward only those who have acted as they did, and have modelled themselves upon them in their performance of jihad.[57]

Sayyid Qutb fostered this militant component of the ideology of political Islamism. Given his importance for the radicalisation of Muslim youths in Europe, I will elaborate more on his ideology. Tortured and imprisoned by Egyptian authorities in the 1950s and 1960s, Qutb wrote his book *Milestones*, which would later be considered the manual for violent jihadist Islamists.

Maududi had described societies which conferred power on parties or men who did not rule according to God's law as having fallen into a 'pre-Islamic ignorance and false belief' – or *jahiliyyah*. Building on Maududi's work, Qutb applied the term to those forces that worked against the implementation of the divine directives throughout history, which were especially prevalent in his own time. In his words, 'Today we are surrounded by Jahiliyyah. Its nature is the same as during the first period of Islam, and it is perhaps more deeply entrenched. Our whole environment, people's beliefs and ideals, habits and art, rules and laws – is Jahiliyyah.'[58]

According to Qutb, every society in today's world – without exception, and including Muslim societies – is to be classified as *jahili*, ignorant. Like Maududi, Qutb perceived sovereignty (*hakimiyya*) as the exclusive prerogative of God, who alone is qualified to fashion principles appropriate to the proper functioning of a social, political and economic order. God is the legal sovereign as well as the lord of nature. The human being is no less *makhluq* (created) than the rest of creation and has but to serve the Creator. In Qutb's view, the goal of humans is neither to know nor to love God, but to serve Him.[59]

Qutb provided clear guidelines on how to achieve the Islamist state he envisioned. First, God's *hakimiyya* is dependent on the formation of a vanguard (*tali'a*) of believers who will remove themselves from the corrupting influences of the surrounding *jahili* culture.

Second, the belief of this group must be pure and its members devoted to serving God alone. This, in turn, requires that they separate themselves from the corrupting influence of *jahiliyya*. Third, the believer has to remain aloof from society but will deal with polytheists for practical reasons only. Fourth, this group will constitute the only true and legitimate Muslim community. It will continue to preach, propagate, proselytise and persuade. Patience is the motto of this phase. Fifth, it will engage in confrontation: 'Preaching is not enough.' Violence is necessary to achieve power.[60]

The Muslim Welfare House, whose judge I described in the last chapter, is considered an offshoot of the Muslim Brotherhood.

Jamaat-e-Islami, the second group, is the only re-Islamising movement originating in the subcontinent with clear political objectives and mission. It is also based on the same premise as the Tabligh: the demand for strict religious observance. But instead it campaigns to immediately construct this ideal Islamic state. Created in 1941 by Maududi, an Indian-born journalist who later moved to Pakistan, the Jamaat-e-Islami became one of the indispensable parts of the Islamist movement worldwide, comparable to the Muslim Brotherhood. Maududi and the Jamaat-e-Islami set themselves the immediate aim of restoring a state, which would apply shari'a. According to this political ideology, *hakimiyya* belongs not to the people, but to Allah alone and power is only legitimate if it governs according to the commands of god. Hence, the only legitimate state is an Islamic state with the sole aim of applying shari'a.[61]

Maududi's vision of an Islamic state is clear: an 'Islamic state with the Quran as the constitution; legislation would be limited to the interpretation of shari'a; and its president would be a devout Muslim surrounded by an all-Muslim council. Non-Muslims would return to *dhimmi* status' – a category of group protected but not granted equality nor full citizenship. And Muslims who do not conform to the Maududi worldview are cast away altogether.[62]

The original embryo of the Maududist network in Britain was the UK Islamic Mission, established in 1962 and headquartered in Islington in North London. According to Lorenzo Divino, a leading expert on political Islamism in the West, the mission declared its political agenda from the beginning and defined itself as an 'ideological organisation' grounded in the belief that 'Islam is a comprehensive way of life which must be translated into actions in all spheres of human life.' It declared in its official mission statement that the organisation sought to 'establish the social orders of Islam for the Muslims and non-Muslims living in Britain.'[63]

While the UK Islamic Mission was engaged in charitable and missionary work to establish that order in the UK, another offshoot of Madudi's Jamaat-e-Islami succeeded in molding the British education system on issues regarding Islam and Muslim pupils according to its own worldview.

For example, in 1980, the Leicester Islamic Foundation arranged to introduce the Muslim Guide, which was aimed at 'teachers, employers, community workers and social administrators in Britain.' Kepel remarked, not without some due sarcasm, that the guide had a glowing introduction from 'the head of the Commission for Racial Equality' and that it 'presents the Jamaat-e-Islami's radical Islamist stances as the norm accepted by all Muslims.' Indeed, in addition to the teaching of the sacred texts, the guide puts forward as 'recommended reading' the writings of Maududi and various authors closely associated with the Muslim Brotherhood. It omits any reference to publications which present an alternative view of Islam, even those written by Muslims. Even Barelwi Sufist writers are absent from the list of recommended texts, despite the importance of their movement in Britain. Starting from the 1970s, the UK Islamic Mission established a network of mosques. Concurrently, another Jamaat-e-Islami inspired organisation, the Islamic Foundation, became the primary publisher of Maududist literature.[64]

The ultimate 'Maududists' political coup', as Innes Bowen put it, was its control of the Muslim Council of Britain (MCB), created in 1997. The British government recognised it as the representative body of Muslims in the UK.[65]

The government's designation of the MCB as the spokesperson for the 'Muslim community' was a political decision and was not based on the organisation's real representation. In fact, in 2007, Policy Exchange, an influential centre-right think tank, conducted a survey among British Muslims. When asked to name an organisation that represented their views as Muslims, only 6 per cent named the Muslim Council of Britain.[66] Only 6 per cent!

And yet, until 2005 British authorities continued to treat the MCB as the sole speaker for the Muslim community in Britain. The year is significant because it witnessed the 7 July London terrorist attacks and was a wake-up call about the home-grown terrorism in Britain. It was also a wake-up call for the British authorities, who recognised for the first time the Islamist political nature of the organisation they considered to be a representative of a faith group.[67]

Which brings me back to the point where I started this chapter. How and why did Britain come to this point?

Constructing the British Muslim Community

Three factors played roles in the construction of the British Muslim Community; together they succeeded in concealing the diversity of South Asian communities and instead lumping them together in the so-called British Muslim community. These were: (1) two specific features of the British context; (2) concurrent measures taken by movements for societal and political Islamism; and (3) British policies and the need for intermediaries to speak for and get the 'Asian vote'.

The British Context

Two specific features of the British context facilitated the process of bringing Muslims into one community and constructing their religious identity. These were former colonial policies towards colonies/protectorates; and the British understanding of nationality.

As colonial Britain ruled and administered its colonies and protectorates it established specific policy measures, which continued as Britain became a post-colonial nation. First, within its various colonies and protectorates Britain often used intermediaries to establish indirect control. Second, it often refrained from interfering in the social customs of its colonies and protectorates, at the same time fostering systems of legal pluralism.[68]

In the Arabian Peninsula, these intermediaries could have been sheikhs, sultans or emirs. Within British India, more relevant to our discussion are the political leaders who attained power by presenting themselves as the exclusive representatives of what they wished to define as a 'religious community'. Through this process, heterogeneous populations were combined and homogenised on the basis of a sociological definition of what Kepel calls their 'Muslimness'.[69]

These leaders were promoting a political agenda: they wanted to carve their own state, Pakistan, out of India. Meanwhile, colonial Britain had an interest in weakening Indians' nationalist aspirations using the strategy of divide and rule.

This worked, as the historian David Page explains:

By treating the Muslims as a separate group, [the colonial government] divided them from other Indians. By granting them separate electorates, it institutionalised that division. This was one of the most crucial factors in the development of communal politics. Muslim politicians did not have to appeal to non-Muslims; non-Muslims did not have to appeal to Muslims. This made it difficult for a genuine Indian nationalism to emerge.[70]

Thus we see that the colonial British frequently used the policies of governing through intermediaries and developing a communalism that combined diverse groups into one for political reasons.

Likewise, legal pluralism was not foreign to colonial British policies. In fact, the system had a political function: it facilitated the fragmentation of the colonial societies.

For example, in British India the legal system resolved family disputes according to the Warren Hastings Act II of 1772, adopted as the Regulation of 17 April, 1780 and enacted in section 27. The act stated that 'in all suits regarding inheritance, succession, marriage, caste, and other religious usages or institutions, the laws of the Qur'an with respect to Mohammadans [Muslims] and those of the Shastras with respect to Gentoos [Hindus], shall be invariably adhered to.'[71]

Similarly, Aden – under British rule since 1839 and granted the status of colony in 1937 – was to follow in the footsteps of the legal system in India, which was similar in its essentials to those that existed in other British colonies. The colonial legal and judicial system tried all cases of legal infringement and heard them in English. But in matters pertaining to marriage, divorce and inheritance, religious and customary stipulations remained in force. Starting in 1840, the General Government of Bombay decided that laws, which were 'purely social or religious', should continue to be the concern of the Muslim *qadis* (judges). Religious minorities in Aden, such as Jews and Hindus, were allowed to have their separate religious courts to resolve their family disputes.[72]

While communalism, the use of intermediaries, and legal pluralism were established policies in colonial Britain, the British understanding of nationality and citizenship further paved the way for what was to come in the post-colonial UK.

Britain does not understand nationality and citizenship as a homogeneous concept. Instead, political identity is expressed by various national identities existing side by side: English, Scottish, Welsh and Irish. Citizenship as such is the sum of various different nationalities. Kepel was quick to see how this concept of citizenship created the conditions within which the political system received the immigrant populations coming into Britain after their former colonial territories became independent. These immigrants were not required to assimilate into the dominant society. Instead they were granted a parallel status, similar to that of the Welsh and Scottish nations, which already existed at the time.[73]

These two specific features of the British context created the setting within which new immigrants coming from former colonies moved to the UK in the 1950s.

Measures Taken by Islamist Movements, Societal or Political

The parallel status that the British government gave to South Asian migrants was cemented by actions and measures taken by members of the two types of Islamist movements I have described: societal and political Islamism.

The main strands of societal Islamism had worked persistently since the 1950s to create a Muslim identity among south Asian communities – an identity that ultimately separated 'Muslims' from the general British society. Concurrently, different foundations and organisations following the ideology of political Islamism were created in the early 1960s, primarily to promote and mainstream the concepts of political Islamism. Though they pleaded for Muslims to participate actively in British society, they did so by making demands for Islamist exceptionalism.

The ghettoising of Muslims that began in the 1950s and 1960s was facilitated by the xenophobic reactions of landlords who refused to rent to 'Pakis'. Mosques representing the different strands of societal Islamism, specifically the Deobandi and Barelwi, were erected. At the same time, scholars began to see a communalism expressed in what they called 'market segmentation'. Religious taboos were enacted, necessitating the need for halal food and Islamic financing. Supermarkets selling halal food and employing Muslim youth, whose assistants and cashiers wear a uniform with a veil, were also created around these mosques. Kepel researched this development since its inception, and observed it accurately:

The organisation of communal networks around the first mosques thus allowed the immigrant Muslim communities to set in train a process of identity differentiation affecting all aspects of daily life.[74]

Differentiation took on a further dimension when associations connected to the Jamaat-e-Islami started to campaign actively for an Islamic, or rather Islamist, education, asking for revisions of the curriculum, and special conditions for Muslim students in public schools: halal food; permission for girls to wear trousers, tunics and veils; and separate prayer rooms for Muslims. They were most successful where they organised themselves to lobby local authorities.[75]

This lobbying succeeded in establishing a close working relationship with British authorities.

For example, the Muslim Education Trust, created in 1966 by members of the Maududi movement and Jamaat-e-Islami, was instrumental in pushing for an Islamic/Islamist educational agenda. According to its website, the trust was created to cater 'for the Islamic educational needs of the British Muslim children and advising their parents on how to bring up their children in a un-Islamic materialistic society.'[76]

The trust was successful in providing what it describes as 'practical help and advice to British education authorities, schools, educational bodies, Muslim parents and non-Muslim teachers, and a host of other people involved in education about the general and Islamic needs of Muslim pupils in British schools.'[77]

One achievement it boasts about is the preparation of the GCSE religious education (ISLAM) syllabus as a fully fledged examination subject. The syllabus was approved by the then SEAC (Secondary Examinations and Assessment Council) and introduced by the erstwhile University of London Examinations and Assessment Council (ULEAC, now EDEXCEL). According to the trust, so far more than 25,000 pupils have taken the exam using this syllabus.[78]

Though the trust has a close working relationship with the British educational authorities, it is important to emphasise that the 'Islamic education' it has been promoting was designed to perpetuate a specific Islamic cultural identity and to prevent the assimilation of Muslim children into British society.[79] Significantly, it clearly propagates the political ideology of Islamism, especially Maududi Islamism.

For example, one the most popular books the trust promotes on its website is *Islam: Beliefs and Teachings*, written by the trust's founder

Ghulam Sarwar, a member of the Jamaat-e-Islami. In the introduction to its eighth edition (2006), the book boasts that it is widely used in the English-speaking world and is also increasingly used in 'maintained schools in England to teach Islam as part of the Religious studies curriculum.'[80]

Ed Husain, a senior fellow for Middle Eastern Studies at the Council on Foreign Relations in New York, and a one-time Islamic fundamentalist, confirmed this assertion; in his memoir he wrote that Sarwar's book was the main textbook for those studying religion in his school.[81] Rashad Ali, an expert on Islamism and also a one-time fundamentalist, confirmed this, saying that the book was very popular and used in the school he attended.[82]

These standard readings about Islam used in British schools promote the ideology of political Islamism, not an understanding of a faith.

In fact, they emphasise that in Islam there is no separation between religion and politics: 'the separation of religion and politics is meaningless in Islam. We have already learnt that Islam is a complete system of life, and politics is very much a part of our collective life.'[83]

It insists that Allah alone exercises sovereignty:

> Allah is the source of all powers and laws. It is Allah who knows what is good and what is bad for His servants. His say is final. Human beings should not and must not change. There are many laws in the Quran concerning our life, and those laws must be put into practice by an Islamic state for the greater good of all human beings.[84]

It praises the work of the Muslim Brotherhood and Jamaat-e-Islami and other Islamist organisations in the world to establish the Islamic state on earth:

> There is not a perfect Islamic state in the world today. There are many Muslim countries. An Islamic state is based on the model of the Prophet's state in Madinah while a Muslim state is one which has a majority Muslim population and some Islamic features. However, organised efforts are being made in many parts of the world to establish an Islamic system of government to implement the laws of the Qur'an and Suunah. Notable among the

organisations which have been working for an Islamic society are the Muslim Brotherhood in the Middle East, and Jamaat-e-Islami in Pakistan and Bangladesh.[85]

And it insists that jihad is an obligation and that 'when the needs arise', Muslims 'have to give' their lives 'for Allah's sake':

> We would like to see truth prevail and falsehood vanish, but we are aware that this cannot happen on its own; we have to do our utmost to achieve it. The performance of other Islamic duties will be meaningless if they do not motivate us to engage in jihad.[86]

And this is the book that has been used continuously in religion classes in British schools and is promoted in mosques and Muslim homes across Britain as an introductory text for young Muslims.[87] This fact alone highlights how successful political Islamists were in their campaign to promote their own agenda as one that represents the Islamic religion and the 'whole of Muslims'.

One can detect a similar pattern the guidelines issued in 2007 by the Muslim Council of Britain to British educational authorities on how to meet the needs of Muslim pupils in state schools. In addition to the 'Islamic dress code', halal food, and accommodation for Muslim prayers, another practice is withdrawing pupils from collective worship (which was introduced to bridge the divide between faith groups) unless it is done in an 'Islamic way'.

Muslim children are also exempted from classes in dance, music, drama, figurative drawing, sex education, relationship education and mixed swimming.[88] Staff members are warned that 'most Muslims do not usually shake hands with a member of the opposite sex,' and that they 'need to be aware that some pupils and parents may exhibit reluctance or even refuse to do this, for example, at prize-giving ceremonies.'[89]

Please notice that the MCB demands regarding music, drama, drawing and hand-shaking in fact represent the most fundamentalist reading of Islam; these subjects are taught in many Arab and Islamic states and hand-shaking is also customary between the sexes in many Arab and Islamic states.

The question therefore arises: why did the British authorities take at face value the claim of these Islamist organisations and with them societal Islamists? This brings me to the third factor that facilitated the construction of the Muslim community.

British Policies and the use of Intermediaries to get the 'Asian Vote'

Slowly but steadily, across the later decades of the 1900s, a certain reality started to take shape. Consider the elements of the context: Citizenship was and is perceived as the sum of different nationalities, and the policies and conduct of post-colonial Britain were shaped by a colonial legacy of communalism and the need for intermediaries. In this context, the efforts of the societal and political Islamists to create a separate religious 'community' were bound to find a receptive audience in the British political establishment.

The parallel status that was given to what would be called the 'Muslim community' took its full shape in the 1980s. Government policies, regardless of their ideological orientation, played a large role in the process that constructed and homogenised the diverse South Asian communities.

First, the conservatives, headed by Margaret Thatcher, created the policy of 'rolling back the state', and outsourcing public services to civil society actors. This process fostered partnerships between the state and civil society actors, especially faith organisations.[90]

Thatcher strongly believed in 'individual freedom and individual prosperity [...] in diversity of choice, [and] in the preservation of local rights in local communities.' But her concept of neo-liberalism and a limited role for the state was founded in her Christian beliefs and her conviction that the Church should take on strong functions in civil society.[91] Almost by default, this role was extended to other 'faith groups'.

Religion was also seen as a tool for facing social maladies within the British context.[92] In fact, in the 1980s some argued that the 'Muslim community's religiosity should be encouraged because it helped maintain relatively low crime rates' among 'young Asian men compared to their Afro-Caribbean counterparts.'[93]

Second, while the conservatives were urging a larger role for faith organisations, the Labour Party also played its part in constructing the Muslim community. Here the issue was getting votes. Labour needed to recruit from the Asian communities to compensate for the erosion of its traditional working-class electorate.[94] But when it recruited these voters, it used those same British colonial techniques of communalism and intermediaries. Early on, for example, it would recruit 'clan elders who could deliver votes en masse.' The assumption was that 'the elder would simply tell everyone in the clan to vote for their candidate.'[95] Slowly the 'Asian vote', also dubbed the 'ethnic vote', started being labelled the 'Muslim vote'.

The need for intermediaries transcended the issue of votes. The racial tensions of the early 1980s highlighted what some local officials called the need for 'some new channel of communication' between local councils and the communities: 'something to compensate for the lack of political representation.'[96]

This new channel took the shape of religious intermediaries. For example, in 1981, to create this new channel, the Bradford local authority helped set up and fund the Bradford Council of Mosques, which would play later an important role in inciting resentment towards Salman Rushdie's *Satanic Verses*. Naturally, the council members belonged to the Deobandi, Barelwi and Jammat-e-Islami movements, the very advocates of societal and political Islamism that were pushing for a separate religious identity for the diverse south Asian communities.

Kenan Malik observes that the Council of Mosques was not primarily a religious organisation. Rather, it was set up to present itself as the true voice of the 'Muslim community' and to be the 'conduit between that community and the public bodies in the city.'[97]

A plethora of mosque-based social projects started to flourish: in the case of the Council of Mosques this included two centres for the elderly, a variety of workers offering advice, services for women in hospitals and clinics, and a series of centres for Muslim youth and the Muslim community. With these projects the council started to focus on demands for separate religious and cultural accommodations, such as separate Muslim schools, separate education for girls and serving of halal meat at schools. All these demands were met without much discussion.[98]

The newfound relationship between the local councils, the mosques and social service provision marginalised the more secular movements. Most importantly, it gave greater credibility to the conservative religious leadership within those communities. Likewise, this type of policy encouraged the emergence of a certain type of leader: one who has an interest in perpetuating the community boundary, since it makes him or her indispensable as an intermediary.[99]

Together, all of these factors and measures provided the backbone of the British policies of multiculturalism. Given that these measures focused on separation and even tribalism, it was not surprising that they led instead to the reality of plural monoculturalism. Multiculturalism was well intentioned but the efforts to develop it actually ingrained differences rather than celebrating what brings together different people from different backgrounds. It was focusing on what makes them separate and that separateness was promoted in policy measures. And when these efforts concerned South Asian communities, they were made in a political and Islamist context that homogenised people and reduced them to their religious identity.

Today, that separateness is seen and felt on a daily basis. I asked Tehmina Kazi, Director of British Muslims for Secular Democracy (BMSD), whether she agrees with the statement that multiculturalism led to a specific cultural separation between communities. Her answer reminded me of the closed communities of the Millet System of the Ottoman Empire:

A separation of communities? Well if you go to places like Bradford and Oldham, even parts of East London, you will see a lot of communities that sort of rub together side by side. They are kind at best, they tolerate each other, and at worst there is sort of very little interaction and very little mixing. [There are . . .] lower rates of what I consider markers of integration such as interfaith marriages and [cross-cultural] relationships. For example, in whole swathes of Bradford you have Asian schools and Asian areas, and white schools and white areas and it is sad that these communities are disparate. They do not feel that there is anything bringing them together.[100]

Plural monoculturalism led to another outcome: a new generation of Muslims who identify themselves first as 'Muslim'. According to a 2009 study commissioned by the Department for Communities and Local Government on 'Muslim communities', the significance of ethnicity and faith in relation to identity has changed over the generations:

For older generations in particular, affiliations relating to nation, clan, tribe, location of origin can all play as significant a part as faith identity and links with countries of origin remain strong. For younger respondents there are indications of a growing religiosity and a more pan-Muslim sense of identity that rejects other ethnic boundaries and practices seen as specific to a cultural group rather than to Islam, though this qualitative finding needs further substantive research.[101]

Within this new generation some individuals developed 'Islamist fundamentalist tendencies'. Dr Usama Hasan, a senior researcher at the Quilliam Foundation and a one-time fundamentalist, put it in these words:

And so that experience [of the British idea of multiculturalism] started from the 60s and 70s of the last century and continued until recently, and that is when the Islamic resurgence happened. I have grown up with that and saw it firsthand in the late 70s, but the 80s and 90s especially, at least two or three decades. Two or three generations of Muslims, who were affected by this resurgence, they developed very strong Islamist fundamentalist tendencies and all this just happened under the radar really of British society, who did not really notice until 9/11. Well, the Rushdie Affair was one wake-up call in the late 80s, so people realised that there is some kind of a problem here, but they did not really think that it is widespread and that it is so bad.[102]

The Salman Rushdie affair[103] was described as a watershed, a historical event and a turning point in the relationship between British society and its 'Muslim communities'. In fact, it only decided the outcome of a power struggle between representatives of political and societal Islamism and determined whom the British authorities considered to be the official spokespersons of the 'Muslim community'. It was the culmination of four decades of communalism and identity politics.

While representatives of the Deobandi, Barlevi and Jamaat-e-Islami movements organised the demonstrations and burnings of Rushdie's book, what really made the Jamaat stand out as speaking for the Muslim community was the establishment of the United Kingdom Action

Committee on Islamic Affairs (UKACIA) out of a number of Jamaat-influenced organisations in Britain to coordinate the campaign against the book. Saudi Arabia encouraged this move, which institutionalised the influence of political Islamism within the British political system.[104] The Muslim Council of Britain was born in 1997 out of the womb of UKACIA.

Therefore the Rushdie Affair was a different sort of wake-up call. Ghaffar Hussain, whom I mentioned earlier, put it this way:

> The government for the first time woke up to the reality that actually you have got Muslims, who are behaving politically as Muslims rather as Pakistanis or Arabs, they are behaving as Muslims and that was very convenient for the British.[105]

It was convenient because the British political establishment, as Hussain reminds us, was used to this approach in British India, where they 'treated the Muslims as a political block.'[106]

Those Muslims behaving politically were Islamists working through the Muslim Council of Britain and this organisation 'became *the* default organisation that any British government, official, or media went to on any issue' related to Islam. So, he continued,

> if it is halal meat, or hijab, anything, they went straight to the Muslim Council of Britain. So what actually happened was that Islamists, who were kind of small in number, were essentially the most powerful organisation, the Muslim Council of Britain and in fact, the only gateway to the Muslim community for the mainstream society.[107]

Since the bombing attacks of 7 June 2005 in the London Underground, the relationship between the British political establishment and the Muslim Council of Britain has been constantly changing. People began to recognise the diversity of the Muslim communities and the media began more assertive coverage that still plays a critical role in exposing the fundamentalist and radical messages promoted by both societal and political Islamism.

It took a while for the government to adjust its strategy to fight terrorism and frame it around the concept that non-violent Islamism may indeed pave the way for violent Islamism. This was articulated clearly in a March 2015 speech by Theresa May, Home Secretary, with the title 'A stronger Britain, built on our values: A new partnership to defeat extremism.'[108]

May acknowledged that the 'most serious and widespread form of extremism we need to confront is Islamist extremism.' She also argued that 'extremism can take many forms. It can be ideological, or it can be driven by social and cultural norms.'[109] While 'not all extremism leads to violence and not all extremists are violent,' there is a 'thread that binds the kind of extremism that promotes hatred and a sense of superiority over others to the actions of those who want to impose their beliefs on us through violence.'[110]

This recognition made it clear that shari'a councils may also be part of this social and cultural extremism. In fact, for the first time since the practice was introduced in the 1980s, the British government connected the dots and specifically mentioned the application of 'Shari'a law being used to discriminate against women' as an example of this type of extremism.[111]

Connecting the Dots: The Significance of these Connections

How does all of this relate to our discussion of weak legal pluralism and the introduction of shari'a law in the family affairs of Muslim communities in the UK and the West in general? There is a political dimension here that we tend to ignore when discussing the issue: those 'Muslims' in the West who call for the introduction of legal pluralism and the use of Islamic law are often affiliated with either forms of Islamism, societal or/and political. The essentialists take their calls at face value, in the process ignoring the political agenda of Islamism and its totalitarian nature.

Remember what I quoted Gita Saghal as saying at the beginning of this chapter? 'There is a disconnect!' People working on security issues, people fighting extremism: they are not concerned about shari'a courts in Britain. But the two issues are connected, she explained.

The two are connected in three ways: through membership, ideology and co-optation.

First, consider membership. I alluded to this point while discussing types of Islamism. The key is that many members of the shari'a courts belong to the various movements promoting societal and political Islamism.

Maryeam Namazi, Director of One Law for All, is an Iranian-born human rights activist and one of the leading voices lobbying for the end of shari'a courts in Britain. She described the programmatic nature of this connection to Islamism:

> It is not [that] a group of Muslims came together and said 'oh, we want to have shari'a courts as a form of mediation.' If you look at the shari'a courts themselves, the people who are running the courts, they have links with the Islamic movement [...]. But also a lot of them are linked with the Muslim Brotherhood and Jamaat-e-Islami; they have this link.[112]

Rashad Ali, the expert on extremism I quoted earlier, also mentioned this aspect, in a matter of fact way. Just like Gita Saghal and Maryam Namazie, he highlighted the link and gave the following example:

> I think in some respects you will find that the shari'a Council in Birmingham, in the Central Mosque in Birmingham, is a mixture of Jamaat-e-Islami, Maududis and Deobandi scholars who run it. The central mosque is an affiliation of the two groups [...] So I think you do get trends [... and] find transnational [Islamist] movements like the Muslim brotherhood and Jamaat-e-Islami being involved with such movements.[113]

My research supports this observation. Members of the two types of Islamism, societal and political, often control British shari'a courts. For example, according to its website, the Islamic Shari'a Council in Leyton was founded by several organisations that have known affiliations with political and societal Islamism: Jamaat-e-Islami (UK Islamic Mission), Muslim Brotherhood (Muslim Welfare House), and global Wahhabi Islam (Muslim World League).[114] Some of those working in the council as 'judges' belong to Salafi Islam (such as Haitham Al Haddad) and to Ahl Al Hadith, the Salafis of South Asia (such as Dr Suhaib Hasan). According to the 1995 Channel 4 Dispatches documentary *War Crimes File*, the head of this council, Sheikh Maulana Abu Sayeed, was a senior member of the Al-Badr

Squad – a paramilitary offshoot of the Jamaat-e-Islami – which allegedly served as Pakistan's death squad in 1971 during Bangladesh's War of Independence.[115]

Second, consider ideology. Those working in the shari'a courts often display the ideological and political features of Islamism, an aspect I illustrated earlier in this chapter when I discussed the two forms of Islamism. These features include the emphasis on creating an Islamic state through incremental steps, on implementing shari'a, on jihad against enemies of Islam, and on the division of the world into two camps, believers and non-believers. Controlling women and their behaviour through a patriarchal and archaic interpretation of Islam is another common feature.

Dr Usama Hasan, who in 2012 authored the Quilliam Foundation's response to the Baroness Cox Arbitration and Mediation Services (Equality) Bill, specifically mentioned the problem of extremism in relation to the shari'a councils: he referred to the ways that extremist clerics sitting in the UK shari'a councils make women's lives hard. He commented on this aspect in a follow-up interview:

> Yes, there are certainly people with strong Islamist ideas [sitting in the shari'a councils], but you know Islamist ideas have infected Muslims worldwide, so that is no surprise. So, yes, there will be people who have these vague notions of the Islamic state, shari'a and the caliphate and jihad and all this stuff.[116]

This ideological feature, which he described as fundamentalist in nature, affects the way 'they look at certain issues in terms of resistance to reform,' specifically in relation to gender relations. It explains why it will be difficult to reform the shari'a councils. Indeed the attitude is of a literalist adherence to the strict, restrictive parochial worldview of women and insistence on their treatment as minors:

> [These extremist clerics] will say, a woman can never marry on her own accord, she can never divorce on her own accord, she can never have equal inheritance with men, let alone more than men. And they are all basing this on a literalist interpretation of the Qur'an, which is one characteristic of fundamentalism in my understanding.[117]

Third, consider co-optation. Islamists have co-opted the idea of weak legal pluralism to suit their own political agenda. I heard this message repeatedly, from a range of sources. People clearly see the political significance of introducing Islamic law into Western legal systems. But many are afraid to mention it, lest they be accused of being Islamophobic.

The shari'a courts 'certainly grew out of an ideological' Islamist agenda:[118] the first council, created in the UK in 1982, was the Islamic Shari'a Council in Leyton and it has clear connections with transnational Islamist groups, both societal and political.

Over time, however, and because of the Islamisation in British Muslim communities, as Rashid Ali explains, some of these courts have become a venue for resolving 'practical issues' for some individuals with specific religious beliefs who need 'to have issues resolved' in ways that fit their dogma, and so 'councils sometimes serve as a place for fatwa, serve as a place to help them fulfil their own religious needs.'[119]

Given the problems and discrimination women face in the shari'a courts, some Muslim religious scholars, such as Dr Usama Hasan, try to extend help to women and assist them in getting what they need: a religious divorce.

That said, the Islamist co-optation of shari'a courts takes several shapes. One is what Tahmina Saleem, co-founder of Inspire, the British Muslim women's organisation, describes as framing the use of these shari'a councils as obligatory and presenting a de-contextualised patriarchal interpretation of Islamic law as the standard that should be used:

I do see a relationship between Islam being used for political purposes and shari'a councils within the UK. I would describe the relationship being presented as 'obligatory', meaning that the existence of these councils is presented as fulfilling fundamental religious needs within Muslim communities that are not being met elsewhere within the British context. Many of these shari'a councils are supported by conservative bodies, such as affiliates of Jamaat-e-Islam and the Muslim Brothers, both of which promote patriarchal, narrowly defined, roles for women. These roles are based on de-contextualised interpretations of shari'a that are irrelevant to the UK today. Yet these interpretations are promoted as the defining standard by which all other standards are secondary including Western legal notions of women's human rights.[120]

Co-optation takes the form of defending shari'a courts regardless of their shortcomings, and arguing that for Muslim communities, 'implementation of shari'a' is a 'religious necessity'. This presentation precludes any mention that the necessity is linked to the political agenda of Islamism, and that such courts do not meet the general needs of diverse communities of Islamic heritage. Dr Usama Hasan put it this way:

> But it is also true that the Islamists co-opt this whole project as part of their own, and that is also why the Islamist groups in this country have tended to defend the shari'a councils no matter what whenever there have been criticisms. They rallied around the shari'a councils because [of] this desire to implement shari'a [...] And the wider society can see that, they can see the Islamists active and talking about shari'a a lot, and they see the shari'a councils trying to implement a kind of form of shari'a within family law and family situation, and they often put the two together because in their mind they are linked. And yes, there is that link.[121]

The Islamists co-opt weak legal pluralism on two levels.

The first level is the transnational institutional arms of political Islamism. The global institutional arms of societal and/or political Islamism often propagate the idea of a separate legal system based on shari'a for the 'Muslim minority'. The issue is often framed in a way that portrays it as a religious demand that should be respected under the banner of freedom of religion.

This example illustrates my point. The European Council for Fatwa and Research (ECFR) is an influential, private institution based in Dublin, Ireland. It was founded in March 1997 in London on the initiative of the Federation of Islamic Organisations in Europe (FIOE). It is often introduced by English-language Islamist websites as 'one of the most representative bodies within this area'; the area is supplying interpretations 'of Islamic law tailored to Muslim minorities.'[122]

Once the council was established, the first recommendations of its two inaugural regular sessions fostered an Islamist worldview that defines identity by religious affiliation and observance. It also ignores the nationalities of migrants of Islamic heritage, and calls on them to follow Islamic law in their lifestyle and seek to recognise Islamic law in their family matters.

Hence, it called on Muslims 'to preserve their Islamic identity and religious personality, follow what the Lord has commanded in what he allowed and forbade' in their 'worship and dealings'. It also demanded that they 'work hard' to get the states where they live to recognise 'Islam as a religion, and [...] Muslims as a religious minority like other religious minorities.' This recognition would include 'full enjoyment of their rights, and ability to regulate their personal status such as marriage, divorce and inheritance' according to Islamic law.[123]

A key fact is often missing in the presentation of these recommendations: this council and the federation that created it are all international arms of the Muslim Brotherhood.

The ECFR is headed by Sheikh Yusuf al-Qaradawi, the Chairman of the International Union of Muslim Scholars, and a well-known global spiritual leader of the Muslim Brotherhood movement. He has often used his television show on the Aljazeera and Qatar TV channels to support and spread Islamist causes worldwide. He has also fostered the idea of Islam, or more accurately Islamism, conquering Europe gradually without resorting to the sword. For example, he said this on one TV show:

> The peaceful conquest has foundations in this religion, and therefore I expect that Islam will conquer Europe without resorting to the sword or fighting. It will do so by means of *da'wa* [proselytising] and ideology. Europe is miserable with materialism, with the philosophy of promiscuity, and with the immoral considerations that rule the world, considerations of self-interest and self-indulgence. It is high time Europe woke up and found a way out from this. Europe will find no lifesaver or lifeboat other than Islam. Islam will save Europe from the raging materialism from which it suffers. The promiscuity, which permits men to marry men and women to marry women, is horrifying. All religions condemn this. [Islam] is capable of granting Europe and the entire West the world to come, without denying them this world. It can grant them faith without denying them science. It can grant them truth, without denying

them power. It can connect them to the heavens, without tearing them away from the earth. It can grant them spirit, without denying them matter. The message of Islam is a message of global balance, and therefore, I believe the next conquest will be conducted through *da'wa*. But, of course, the Muslims must start acting in order to conquer this world.[124]

Moreover, the *Online Muslim Brothers Encyclopaedia*, published in Arabic, identifies the FIOE, the council's parent organisation, as 'the European wing of the global Muslim Brothers movement.'[125]

This political affiliation is simply absent from the English website of the FIOE. Instead, it defines itself as a 'cultural organisation' – one with hundreds of member organisations spread across 28 European States.' It also portrays itself as the 'largest Islamic organisation on the European level.' Whether this reflects reality is open to discussion; it is certainly well funded and highly organised. What is important, though, is that this organisation is a political organisation, one that works as an arm of the global political Islamism movement.[126]

In pluralistic Western democracies the two organisations are certainly entitled to their opinions regarding Islamic law in the West. The problem I see is with the way they present their demands as Islamic, ordained by Islam, and hence religious demands of the Muslim minority. In fact, what they call for are political demands of a political ideology: Islamism. They never openly acknowledge this link.

The second level at which they co-opt weak legal pluralism is through the national-level organisations of political Islamism. These organisations and associations working at the national level in Europe and North America often endorse the application of weak legal pluralism for the Muslim community.

For example, in the UK, the Muslim Council of Britain (MCB), with its clear links to Jamaat-e-Islami, has been at the forefront in attempts to 'mainstream' shari'a courts and to introduce Islamic law in family affairs, as 'religiously mandated arbitration panels'. It reiterated this point in its latest paper, on the 2015 general election.[127] Again, similar to the strategy of the transnational institutional arms of political Islamism, the MCB presents its Islamist perspective as 'British Muslims' perspectives at the 2015 General Election' – the title of its paper. It fosters the separation of Muslims by promoting the notion that British Muslims have specific needs that can only be fulfilled via special treatment for them, including sanctioning the work of the shari'a councils.[128]

Most importantly, it politicises any critique of these courts as a 'critique of Islam' and an expression of 'Islamophobia'. Baroness Cox is one target of such accusations.

Baroness Cox was one of the first members of Parliament to alert the public to the problem of the quasi-legal systems working in the UK and how they affect women negatively. When she first published her 2011 bill, mentioned earlier, which seeks to amend the arbitration law of 1996 and make 'criminal and family law matters not arbitrable,'[129] the MCB issued a statement criticising it and insisting that the shari'a councils operate under the concept of 'consent'. Khurshid Drabu, an adviser on constitutional affairs to the MCB, commented on the bill in an interview with the *Guardian*:

Bills of this kind don't help anybody. They don't appear to understand that we live in a free country where people can make free choices. Yet again, it appears to be a total misunderstanding of the concept that underpins these arbitration councils. Shari'a councils operate under consent. If there is a woman who suffers as a result of a decision by one of these councils a woman is free to go to the British courts.[130]

Never mind that 'consent' in a closed community is often framed by structures of power and patriarchy that render the 'freedom' to go to the British courts excruciatingly unrealistic. The MCB went on to pick on Baroness Cox and her personality in a tactic that Islamists often use in response to any critique of their agenda, or of extremism, or of the negative consequences of applying Islamic law. They simply brand the person or group and the government as 'Islamophobic'.

Dr Usama Hasan, known for being a pious scholar critical of extremism and Islamism, recalls what happened:

They brought separate grievances around baroness Cox's work itself. Because she has worked in Sudan for example on behalf of the Christian communities there, [. . .] she was painted as a caped crusader, who is attacking Islam and Muslims mainly because of her work in Sudan and [. . .] other areas on behalf of Christians. And they [. . .] turned that into a political issue.

They tend to label anybody who does raise these issues as Islamophobic. If you criticise anything Muslims do, or any interpretation of shari'a or Islam like that, the standard response 'oh this is Islamophobic and you cannot do this.' I have been accused of being Islamophobic for talking about extremism, so that is how it is.[131]

These three elements – membership, ideology and co-optation – highlight the political dimension of the issue. Ignoring it will not make it go away. It does have implications, not only for the fight against terrorism and extremism, but also for the cohesion of society and the successful integration into British society of diverse migrants of Muslim heritage. Islamists are making use of a theoretical discussion promoted by the essentialists' paradigm to achieve political goals in what one may call a 'cultural jihad': one that aims to Islamicise migrants of Muslim heritage according to tenets of societal and political Islamism, and to separate them from their wider societies and gradually 'conquer the West', to use the words of Sheikh Yusuf al-Qaradawi.

Many Western politicians and academics are hesitant to voice their concerns over this political dimension for fear of being labelled 'racist' or worse, 'Islamophobic'. The essentialists, on the other hand, either ignore this dimension of weak legal pluralism or do not consider it valid in the first place.

The same can be said about the perception regarding the consequences for human rights and women's rights of introducing this system in Western legal systems. Two attitudes prevail: either people belittle these concerns or they consider them part of a natural process, one that will ultimately lead to a moderation of the 'conservative reading of Islam'. Female scholars, activists, and organisations of Muslim heritage beg to differ. In fact, while the essentialists are pushing to introduce Islamic (religious) laws in Western legal systems, in Islamic countries the discourse is going in the other direction: moving away from family laws with a religious basis to laws that respect concepts of gender equality and justice. In the next chapter I address this dimension, contextualise the debate within women's daily reality and show how people are contesting the application of shari'a law.

CHAPTER 6

CONTEXTUALISING THE DEBATE IN WOMEN'S REALITY: SHARI'A LAW CONTESTED

When the Muslim Council of Britain defended the idea of shari'a councils, it argued that the issue was freedom of choice. It criticised the Baroness Cox Arbitration and Mediation Services (Equality) Bill, saying that it does not 'understand that we live in a free country where people can make free choices.' It added, 'Shari'a councils operate under consent. If there is a woman who suffers as a result of a decision by one of these councils a woman is free to go to the British courts.'[1]

Islamists frequently use this argument. On the one hand, they insist that application of Islamic law is paramount and mandatory – indeed, a religious obligation. On the other hand, when defending this application in a Western context, they insist that this is the essence of pluralism.[2] Accordingly, they say, Muslim women are allowed the freedom of choice, and they are using this freedom in turning to shari'a courts. If they suffer from that experience, they have the British courts. The choice is theirs.

Academics and scholars who subscribe to featuring the Essentialist Paradigm are often the first to support such arguments – and they have, unwittingly, become the strongest allies of Islamists. The essentialists sincerely believe the issue is about a plurality of legal options. A privatised market of legal orders is almost like a supermarket: one has only to choose the best product, the one that best fits one's individual need. I would be tempted to describe it as a form of neo-liberalism, where the state is only one producer of norms and other non-state actors are free to join the market and offer their 'services' if not their 'products'. But then, the essentialists are the first to criticise neo-liberalism in the forms introduced by Margaret Thatcher, Ronald Reagan and George W. Bush.

Again, all the features of the essentialists' paradigm are visible. They strongly support group rights and the white man's burden. By that I mean the idea that the colonial past has to be redeemed at any cost, even if that entails undermining the very democratic system, founded on concepts of equality in citizenship and rights, that they claim to protect. These claims are often made without context, in discussions that are purely theoretical. They do not acknowledge the role of Islamism, and often describe the social reality of women from a perspective of cultural relativism. The consequences for women of introducing Islamic law are often treated as trivial and minor: something that women should endure for the sake of such a social experiment.

Consider the argument of Tariq Modood, a British citizen of Pakistani origins, and Professor of Sociology, Politics and Public Policy at the University of Bristol. His argument has all the features mentioned above, of a theoretical discussion void of context.

In his chapter 'Multicultural citizenship and the Shari'a controversy in Britain' he introduces his concept of 'multicultural citizenship' – a citizenship formed through group identity. He says it is 'Based on the idea that citizens have individual rights.' But, he continues:

> [As] individuals are not uniform, their citizenship contours itself around the specific individuals that make up a citizenry of a particular time and space. Citizenship is not a monistic identity that is completely apart from or transcends other identities important to citizens. Their group identities are ever-present, and each group has a right to be part of the civic whole and to speak up for itself and for its vision of the whole.
> [. . .]
> Thus civic inclusion does not consist of an uncritical acceptance of an existing conception of citizenship of the 'rules of the game' and a one-sided 'fitting-in' of new entrants (or new equals'-mostly ex-subordinates of colonial experience). To be a citizen, no less than to have just become a citizen, is to have a double right: to be recognised, and to debate the terms of recognition.[3]

Despite the eloquence of his argument, the core of it is straightforward: each citizen is an individual with many identities, and group identity is the one that transcends all the others. Therefore people have to renegotiate the rules of the game to accommodate this paramount identity. It is another version of Charles Taylor's politics of recognition, which I described in Chapter 2, just more sophisticated.

As Taylor's does, Modood's argument assumes that a group has fundamental unchangeable traits and is homogenous. It disregards the fact that a group does not represent one cultural block with similar and standardised features and traits or homogeneous demands. The power structures within minority groups further complicate matters, especially when some claim to be representatives of a certain cultural group and with it assume the right to define what is the authentic identity of their group and what is not.

In the last chapters, I have shown how this minority group – in our case Muslims – is constructed by different actors, and I have highlighted the political context of this construction process. Significantly, the one group that has benefited from this process in the UK is a minority of Islamists, who have a clear political goal: to propagate a totalitarian ideology.

Modood considers this political dimension – Islamism in its two forms – and the Islamists' political agenda to be 'scaremongering on a large scale.' He believes people mention this aspect as a tactic 'to avoid discussing and conceding what is reasonable because someone else might later demand something unreasonable is irrational.' Further, he says, 'to associate a whole group, in this case Muslims with their extremist elements is a kind of political demonisation that may appropriately be called anti-Muslim racism.'[4]

It is interesting that Islamists use the tactic of Islamophobia to stop any critique of Islamism or Islamic law, and the essentialists use 'anti-Muslim racism' as a tool to brand those who are sincerely worried about the consequences of integrating these councils and laws into the British legal system. Never mind that many of those branded as anti-Muslim racists are mostly female scholars or/and activists of Muslim heritage. It is this very language that seeks to stop the discussion before it even starts. But then there is a gender dimension to this whole discourse that we should not ignore.

I have also shown that the rules of the game that Modood suggests people must renegotiate are not trivial. If we translate them into down-to-earth language we will discover questions like these: Can a girl be married off? Does a male guardian have the right to impose a marriage on a young girl? Does a male guardian have the right to cancel the marriage of his daughter if he deems her groom to be 'unfit'? Does a husband have the right to beat his wife? Is a woman an individual equal before the law, capable of making her own choices? Or is she a perpetual minor, in need of a male guardian? And most significantly, can a constructed minority be separated from its wider society by ideological claims of superiority, hatred of non-believers and goals of domination?

These rules of the game go to the core of what constitutes democracy, equality before the law and gender equality, and the very way a society functions. They are not negotiable. One gets the impression that the type of liberalism Modood and other essentialists are calling for is one where anything goes.

In fact, Modood never mentions the type of Islamic law that is being used in the shari'a councils. Ignoring this issue will not make it go away. It is a bad law that is being used – and I believe once we talk about the content of this law (see Chapter 5), this claim is substantiated.

What Modood does acknowledge is the patriarchal nature of these councils. He refers to a thorough study by Samia Bano, who researched women's use of shari'a councils in Britain; her results suggest that the 'actual practice of the arbitration services reflects patriarchal assumptions and power relations.'[5]

Modood uses reassuring language reminiscent of that used by Christian Giordano, Charles Taylor and former Archbishop Rowan Williams:

> As I originally argued, the vulnerability of women (and children) in the process must be highlighted and their rights safeguarded. So I would fully support the involvement of women at every level of consultation and institutional design. I would perhaps hesitate to make that a necessary condition of approval of a Shari'a body. Requiring such bodies to publish their *fatawa* [religious edicts] would go some way to alerting women's organisations, professional advisers, and individual supplicants about the track record of a council and so enable women-friendly bodies to be selected and hopefully to proliferate over time. For me the bottom line is that if such bodies already exist and are growing in number

and scale then it is better to bring them into the system and regulate them.[6]

I find it peculiar to suggest introducing a system that establishes a bad law, knowing full well that women and children will be subjected to prejudiced and discriminatory treatment as a result, and then compensate for this problematic side by involving women in the process, and even then make their participation of no consequence. Clearly it is the law that is biased. The system will continue to violate women's rights. Unless Islamic law is reformed, the system will not correct itself over time. It is just as absurd to take the easy way out and recognise these abusive bodies using the argument 'but they already exist.' What Professor Modood suggests is institutionalising a discriminatory system – one born out of Islamist ideology – and arguing that over time councils more friendly to women will proliferate. In this scenario individual women clients will be in a position to choose from this supermarket of shari'a councils and state courts.

Choice again. Islamists are insisting that weak legal pluralism is a matter of choice and the essentialists emphasise pluralism and women's ability to choose – a choice formed by their own group identity.

Absent from this 'choice narrative' is the actual context of women's reality and the reason why women are turning to these councils. They go to them because they want a *religious divorce*. Unlike what many claim, women can satisfy this demand within the British legal system; they do not need the shari'a courts. Also absent from this 'choice discourse' are the counter-narratives presented by women's groups, scholars and/or activists, many of Muslim heritage, along with the way they perceive this system and its consequences and how they contest shari'a law. In the following sections I deal with these aspects.

Women's Context

The treatment of Muslim women in our society is bad; you have to be heartless.[7]

These were not the words of a British scholar or activist with South Asian roots or Islamic heritage. Rather, they are the words of

Dr Ghayasuddin Siddiqui, a British Muslim leader in the UK, and a founding trustee of the Muslim Institute and of British Muslims for Secular Democracy.

In the 1980s and 1990s Dr Siddiqui was a controversial figure, first as an active member and student of Jamaat-e-Islami, then as a supporter of Khomeini's fatwa against Salman Rushdie who had close relations with Iran, and finally as a president of the Muslim Parliament – a non-governmental organisation founded in London in 1992 that aimed to pursue a clearly separatist and Islamist agenda.

Today the Muslim Parliament has been transformed into a platform promoting secular democracy, and advocating against forced marriage, domestic violence, 'honour' killing, and radicalisation.[8] A transformation as astonishing as the one Dr Siddiqui himself went through.

When I asked him about the reasons for his change of ideology, he said it was a 'gradual thing', 'through trial and error'; he questioned the Islamist ideology of Maududi, then felt 'disappointed' in the Iranian revolution, witnessed a lot of 'miseries and problems taking place in Muslim societies,' and then finally recognised that the 'religious discourse is as [...] corrupt as [that on] the other side.'[9]

His gradual change of ideology and heart also led him to recognise the need for a change in women's situation. Having worked within Muslim communities for more than 30 years, he has first-hand experiences of women and their treatment. Hence his statement 'the treatment of Muslim women in our society is bad; you have to be heartless.'[10] He added that the 'women's issues were perhaps the main cause of my conversion. I became restless [...] the beginning will come when we recognize there is a problem. We do not recognize it; there is always some *kaffir* [unbeliever]'[11] to blame.

Tackling gender problems in the closed communities of Muslim heritage has been a very delicate issue in the UK. On the one hand, the government took a while before it acknowledged the need to address these issues without justifying them on cultural grounds. Interviewees working in the field, such as Sawsan Salim, Director of the Kurdish and Middle Eastern Women's Organisation in Britain, said that people really recognised the need for action only after the terrorist attacks of 11 September 2001. Before this date, the cultural sensitivity of the gender issue hindered any open discussion about forced marriage, domestic violence or honour-based violence.[12]

Jenan Al Jabiri, the chair of the same organisation, further qualified this observation:

> Before 9/11 they [the police and courts] used to be lenient with honour cases, considering the cultural factor a reason to give lighter sentences – five years in prison for killing a Turkish woman for example. But we as women activists working in different feminist movements from different communities – South Asian, Arab, Middle Eastern – we kept pressuring the authorities to treat honour crimes like any other crimes. It was only after 9/11 and then 7/7 [7 July 2005] that their language and treatment started to change.[13]

These women's accounts correspond to the developments in addressing gender issues of cultural dimensions in the UK. In fact, while the statutory agencies began to tackle gender violence in 1999, their approach was riddled with a culturally relativist approach; only in 2005 did this approach began to change.

For example, according to a report summarising the results of two conferences on gender equality from comparative European contexts, the UK public became aware of forced marriage in 1999 because of three high-profile cases that alerted them to this human rights violation:

1. The 1998 murder of 19-year-old Rukhsana Naz by her brother and mother. Ms Naz left an arranged marriage with a Pakistani husband, whom she had only seen twice since her marriage at age 15, and became pregnant by another man. She was killed when she refused to have an abortion.[14]
2. The case of 'Jack and Zena Briggs', who were forced into hiding for more than a decade when Zena's family employed bounty-hunters after she refused to marry a cousin in Pakistan and instead insisted on marrying a non-Muslim white British man.
3. The successful return to England of KR, a young Sikh girl of Indian origin, whose parents abducted her to India to marry her off. KR left home at 16 to live with her sister, who had earlier moved in with a man against her parents' wishes. The police returned her to the care of her father after he reported her missing. She was then sent to India.

After establishing that her stay in India was not voluntary, she was flown back to the UK and made a ward of the court.[15]

Although these cases led to the creation of a Working Group on Forced Marriage in 1999, women's groups criticised this very group for its relativist approach. The Southhall Black Sisters (SBS), a non-profit organisation of women from across Asia established in 1979, describes on its website how it had to resign from the working group because it insisted on offering mediation and reconciliation to women at risk of forced marriage:

> We argued that women usually come to organisations like ours as a last resort, having almost always attempted reconciliation through traditional community mechanisms involving meetings with family elders, relatives and community leaders. We argued that a woman's safety is paramount and that her safety could not be monitored or guaranteed when she was reconciled into the home.
>
> We were especially concerned by the reluctance of statutory agencies to intervene because forced marriage was seen as a cultural practice to be tolerated rather than challenged. We campaigned to gain widespread acceptance of the view that it is racist not to intervene to protect a young person from forced marriage and that forced marriage is an abuse of their human right to choice in marriage. We argued that all women should expect and be afforded state protection against violence, including forced marriage.[16]

The SBS account of how the statutory agencies were reluctant to intervene on cultural grounds was reiterated in 2007 by the Shadow Thematic Report on violence against women in the UK, written by Purna Sen and Liz Kelly for the Committee on the Elimination of all Forms of Discrimination against Women. As Sen and Kelly wrote:

> British policy commitment to multi-culturalism has fostered a reluctance to intervene in the private or cultural life of minority groups in the UK, resulting in a neglect of crimes in the name of honour. Only recent high profile cases and campaigning by NGOs have made it a policy concern within, for example, the Metropolitan Police.[17]

Therefore what alerted the authorities to honour based violence within closed communities was the combination of lobbying by women's organisations working in and coming from these communities, and the ramifications of the two high-profile terrorist attacks. Together, they finally had the necessary impact.

In January 2005 the government established the Forced Marriage Unit (FMU), a joint effort of the Foreign and Commonwealth Office and the Home Office. Today it stands at the forefront in the fight against forced marriage, providing confidential support and information for potential victims and concerned professionals. The assistance it provides ranges from simple safety advice, to helping a victim prevent her unwanted spouse from moving to the UK (in what is called a 'reluctant sponsor' case); in extreme circumstances, the unit has rescued victims held against their will overseas. In 2014, the UK government issued the Anti-social Behaviour, Crime and Policing Act 2014 making it a criminal offence to force someone to marry.[18]

Hence, on the one hand, it took a while, but the British statutory agencies are now acknowledging honour-based violence within minority communities and addressing it with the means and urgency it deserves. On the other hand, the communities of Muslim heritage have still not indicated that they recognise the problem. Dr Siddiqui did have a point when he criticised the common reaction, saying, 'We do not recognise [this violence]; there is always some *kaffir*, some unbeliever, to blame.'[19]

Several women activists working within their own communities expressed the same exasperation in interviews with me. For example, Tahmina Saleem, co-founder of Inspire, the British Muslim women's organisation, articulated her frustration this way:

> There is something dreadfully wrong [with the gender situation in the community], and with us as a community continuing with the 'we are an oppressed community, we are the victims, the wider society dislikes us, and we have got to battle Islamophobia.' [. . .] The very fact, that you don't even, if you even acknowledge there was a problem as a community, [if] the Muslim leaders stood up and said yes, we need to start thinking about gender equality within the Muslim community, we need to start bringing women's empowerment into the public agenda; [the wider] society would say 'all right, you may not be up [on all the issues] but at

least you have acknowledged the problem.' But the frustration is that they will not even acknowledge the problem.[20]

This type of 'deny the problem and blame the other' discourse is not confined to the British context. In fact, it is widespread in many communities of Muslim heritage in both Europe and North America. It is also common in the Arab context. I alluded to it in a previous book I wrote about Islam, on the West and human rights; I called it the 'turtle shield syndrome'.[21] Indeed, if you carefully follow the type of discourse taking place lately about Islam, integration problems and Islamism you will notice that some of the activists of Muslim heritage, who may otherwise be very critical of some of the traditions and norms practiced within their own community, have become very cautious in what they say. They have become more defensive, suspicious, wary, and quick to assume the worst in any attempt to talk about integration problems.

They feel sandwiched in. They hear voices that are growing louder in both European and North American societies, which portray their religion as synonymous with terrorism and reduce it to the most reactionary practices of its adherents. At the same time, they feel appalled by what some Islamic fundamentalists describe as their Islamic religion. And because they feel angry with both sides, they end up using what I call the 'turtle shield' line of argument: 'this has nothing to do with us, it has nothing to do with our religion.' Or they would start to use the 'blame the West' argument, which makes the West responsible for every historical mishap the Muslim world has experienced.[22] Taking responsibility for one's mistakes and one's future is not part of the turtle shield line of argument.

It is worth mentioning at this juncture that Islam is not always to blame for all the social problems women are facing in their closed communities. This is why I deliberately mentioned the case of the Sikh girl of Indian origin to remind us that problems of forced marriage and honour-based violence occur in different patriarchal contexts regardless of religion. In Switzerland forced marriage is practiced in different migrant communities with different nationalities and religions – including people from Sri Lanka (Hinduism), Kosovo (Islam and Catholicism), and Turkey (Islam).

Cultural norms are responsible for these violations and violence. I am afraid there is no politically correct way to say this: it is the culture of patriarchal structures common in rural and tribal areas of developing or transitional societies. This may explain why in the UK gender-based violence especially affects Pakistani and Bengali communities where the majority have origins in tribal regions.

I define patriarchy as 'a system of social relations privileging male seniors over juniors and women.'[23] In such a system women learn from their very early childhood to respect their male relatives. They learn to 'put others before themselves and to see their interests as embedded in those of others, especially familial others.'[24] Simply put, they learn that their interests are linked to those of their male kin. Men, on the other hand, learn to take responsibility for their female relatives and younger brothers.

While respect and responsibility are positive virtues, they may become tools for repressive behaviour.[25] The emphasis on respect can turn into a demand for obedience, which leaves little room for the girl's freedom of choice; meanwhile responsibility can easily be transformed into social control, where the older male relatives control the behaviour of the girl and make sure she will not engage in what they consider 'immoral conduct'. In extreme cases, this type of social control may result in 'crimes of honour': murdering the girl in the name of protecting the family's 'honour'.

Forced marriage occurs quite often in such patriarchal structures.

That said, two aspects of Islam contribute to the gender problems within closed communities. The first is the legal dimension of religion: insisting on applying Islamic jurisprudence in the regulation of family affairs may in fact facilitate forced and child marriage, as I explained in Chapter 4. Second, a re-Islamisation process can lead to the mainstreaming of fundamentalist interpretations of religion, especially the Salafi and Deobandi strands of Islamic fundamentalism, which treat women as a source of evil and as having less value and intellect than their male counterparts. Violence and forced marriage are sanctioned as these reactionary religious ideas operate together.

Notwithstanding the above, the turtle shield line of argument used by Muslim leaders in the UK does not hold today because, as Saleem rightly pointed out, 'the figures do not add up. People are seeing it with their own eyes.'[26]

Here is some of what they are seeing. Women in the UK with South Asian roots are more likely to live in poverty, to be unemployed, to be in poor health, and to inflict self-harm and attempt suicide, compared to their female counterparts of other ethnicities.

In general, people of Pakistani and Bengali backgrounds have around three times as much risk of being in poverty as white British people; they are also more likely to have a limiting long-term illness or disability and to live in more crowded conditions. In addition, Pakistani and Bengali women have extremely high poverty rates of around 50 per cent, and their children are more likely to be poor and stay poor. They have the lowest incomes, both household and individual incomes. This is because the other household members, usually the men, have relatively low individual incomes, and face relatively high demands on those incomes because of the relatively larger average family size. They also have very high levels of non-employment, both economic inactivity and unemployment: around 80 per cent, compared with around 30 per cent to 50 per cent for other women.[27]

The negative effects of poverty and unemployment or economic inactivity are compounded by the type of gender-based violence considered widespread within the communities.

Gender-based violence is a problem most prevalent among minorities. Asian women are most afflicted and suffer from mental illness as a result. Rashida Manjoo, the UN Special Rapporteur on Violence Against Women, reported on this among her findings after a mission to the UK in 2014:

> Black and minority ethnic (BME) and migrant women experience a disproportionate rate of domestic homicide, and [...] Asian women are up to three times more likely to commit suicide than other women. Young BME women, in particular, are also more likely to experience domestic violence from multiple perpetrators, such as extended family members.[28]

Her finding corresponds with the results of studies by women's groups and epidemiologists that have consistently correlated suicide mortality rates with ethnicity in the UK. According to the SBS report *Safe and Sane*, wider research shows a disproportionately high rate of suicide, attempted suicide, suicidal ideation and self-harm amongst South Asian women, especially young women. Very few of these women had any pre-existing history of psychiatric illness. Research spanning three decades confirms that South Asian women, particularly those aged 15 to 34, are up to three times more likely to kill themselves than women in the general population.[29]

Anita Bhardwaj, who reported on the findings of an important study on self-harm and suicide among South Asian women, explained that these behaviours were considered to be coping mechanisms for the unbearable distress women faced in their lives.[30] It helped them survive from day to day and manage their 'desolation, self-loathing and particularly their feelings towards others that they felt they were unable to articulate.'[31] One 18-year-old she interviewed put it this way:

> I don't know, at the time it looked like I was just messing up inside. If I hadn't done anything [self-harm], I think I would have just blown up. It's like your head was full of so much, you wanted something to calm you down and if I hadn't done that, I would have just gone mad.[32]

The factors that led to their emotional distress centered mainly on parental, family and community-related oppressions. The study, which spanned over two years of interviews and observations, showed that although generational conflicts do exist in most cultures, Asian women have to deal with additional social and religious pressures.[33]

The community and cultural oppressions described by these women include rigidly defined matrimonial roles and the duty of women to maintain the family *izzat* (honour). As a result, the inequalities between men and women go far beyond mere unequal treatment. Instead, the restrictions imposed on Asian women are intertwined with their role as 'bearers of community and family honour', who can single-handedly jeopardise the standing and honour of their family and extended kin. They can bring *sharam* (shame) on their families. This leads to a level of social control that borders on locking up girls and women – a treatment that stands at odds with the type of freedom and privileges their brothers enjoy. Consequently, violence and physical abuse towards young women continue to be a community-sanctioned method of controlling their independence.[34]

Many of the women Bhardwaj interviewed were burdened by the unrealistic expectations their families demanded of them. Women aged 25 to 30 in a focus group made this point:

[Asian women] have to be perfect – they have to be everything the
mother-in law wants, be everything the husband wants, be
everything their parents want, be everything.[35]

Social control is not only confined to pre-empting any potential disgrace.
In fact it extends to the gender roles expected from women – a message
that is constantly conveyed, latently, explicitly, or otherwise. Hence, as
one woman in that same focus group explained, her parents will be on
her side in her disputes with her husband, but they will not tolerate any
discussion about separation or divorce: 'You're not entitled to leave a
marriage that isn't working out [...] because at the end of the day it's
shameful, that's what it is, it's about shame.'[36]

These cultural features have been repeatedly mentioned in recent
reports and studies on domestic abuse and the sexual exploitation of
Asian girls and young women. For example, a study by Shayma Izzidien
published in 2008 by NSPCC, a leading charity working to end child
abuse, specifically mentioned *izzat* and *sharam* as two relevant social and
cultural patriarchal constructs used to socially control and silence
women within South Asian communities. Honour and shame are used to
control victims of abuse and protect the abusers and 'female oppression is
often – wrongly – justified by men on the basis of religious beliefs.'[37]

Significantly for our discussion, Bhardwaj highlighted how women
are taught that the public image of the family is more important than
their individual safety, and that the concepts of honour and
respectability are intrinsically dependent on a successful marriage.
As a result, women fear the 'dishonour and rejection from their
community if their marriage should fail'; they also fear that their actions
will have consequences for other family members including children and
especially daughters, and therefore they remain committed to their
marriage and tolerate abuse.[38]

Likewise, in her 2013 report on the sexual exploitation of Asian girls
and young women, Shaista Gohir specifically mentioned the cultural
attitudes towards girls and women within Asian and Muslim
communities as an underlying cause. In addition to the social control
related to *izzat* and *sharam*, the experiences of Muslim and Asian women
have shown that family and community expect them to suffer in silence
for the sake of family honour, even when subjected to abuse. They are
often blamed and stigmatised in family break-ups and divorce; and girls

and women are subjected to greater social restriction and expected to obey the males in the family, whether father, brother or husband. Finally, marital rape is considered normal, as wives are expected to respond to the sexual demands of their husbands.[39]

Women activists I interviewed, who work on a grassroots level, confirm that these features of patriarchal culture are common within Asian communities in general, regardless of religion. However, they also highlight the frequent use of religion to justify the control of women within closed communities of Muslim heritage. For example, Habiba Jaan, a women's activist and a mental health worker in closed communities, described it this way:

I think it stems from childhood. If you are born as a girl in a community, you are shown your place from day one when you are born. Does that make sense? As you are growing up, you know how to behave, you know what your place is, in your home as a sister, with your brothers and father, you have to address them in a certain way, you cannot raise your voice, you have to behave in a certain way, you have to give them dinner first, pick up their dishes, you have to cook and wash, and the women take up that role. So we actually grow up with that thinking and mentality, and then obviously we are told when we are going to our husband's house, respect your husband; if you do not sleep with your husband you will be thrown into hell.[40]

Because it is considered a religious duty to fulfil the husband's sexual demands, rape within marriage 'does not exist.' This view has been pulled into the theological mainstream by none other than the president of the Islamic Shari'a Council, Sheikh Maulana Abu Sayeed, who has allegedly been accused of war crimes in Bangladesh. His comments in an interview with the website Samosa explain this belief:

Clearly there cannot be any 'rape' within the marriage. Maybe aggression, maybe indecent activity. It is not an aggression, it is not an assault, it is not some kind of jumping on somebody's individual right. Because when they got married, the understanding was that sexual intercourse was part of the marriage, so there cannot be anything against sex in marriage.

Of course, if it happened without her desire, that is no good, that is not desirable. But that man can be disciplined and can be reprimanded.[41]

Abu Sayeed had to retract these comments after their publication created an uproar.[42] Yet what he said is indicative of a mentality that is predominant in his shari'a council and in closed communities in the UK. One woman I interviewed, whom I will call Reyhana, who asked to remain anonymous, recounted how, at age 15, she was bullied into marrying a cousin during a holiday in her father's village in Pakistan. On their wedding night, her husband raped her because she did not want to sleep with him. The next morning, when she told her family about what happened, the reaction was 'he is your husband; it is his right.' The attitude, she said, is not limited to her family.[43]

Similarly, Gina Khan, a well-known British women's activist with Pakistani roots and extensive experience in closed communities in Birmingham, described to me a case she was involved with – of a young woman, who had to flee her forced marriage:

Her mother took her to Pakistan after her father died, pulled this really bright and intelligent girl out of college, and forced her into marriage with a cousin. In the first night of wedding, he is gone into the room, and she said no. She did not know him. And her mother sent him back and said to him: you have got every right. And the man raped her.[44]

Fleeing the marriage she turned to several Shari'a Councils to get a divorce, but her account of the story did not matter: 'She went to several shari'a councils, and they did not care that she was forced to marry, they did not care that she is being raped in marriage, they do not see that as rape in marriage.'[45]

Usha Sood, a distinguished lawyer and head of Champers, is renowned for her decades of community work defending the human rights of women, men and children in Britain's Asian communities, particularly around dowry abuse, forced marriage, child abduction and immigration.[46] Describing the type of problems facing women within closed communities of Islamic heritage, she alluded first to the patriarchal structures and expectations:

The conflict of cultures is the most important. Women have to conform to family and social expectations and it does not matter if the woman is educated or not. We find that they have a lot of expectations placed on them and that sometimes it leads them to give up their dreams. At other times they are discreet in trying to break away – sometimes they live double lives.[47]

Within these structures, Sood continues, women are very fearful. Trapped in a hierarchical and gender-based order, they are less in control of their own lives and decision making.

Sood also articulated the problems of closed communities and the rise of an Islamic fundamentalism that seek to control the behaviour of community members:

I would go so far as to say that at present the Islamic communities are quite closed communities. There are those who call for change, or insist that they should enjoy the same rights as others in the UK but they are silenced and [are] lone voices. Just as in Iran and Saudi Arabia and their religious polices, there are moral police here. Even in this country there are police groups who are trying to redress inappropriate behaviour; how a woman is dressing would be commented on and the woman would be reproached. But there is the extreme case of a Muslim woman going with a non-Muslim; this can lead to both the man and the woman being beat up. The tip about the woman's behaviour may not even come from her family, but from moral guidance [social control of community elders and extremists].[48]

It is within this context of patriarchal structures, social control and the rise of Islamic fundamentalism that women of Muslim heritage are expected to exercise their 'choice'. A choice that is so constrained by such structures, values and norms may not be a choice after all. In other words, the exit option – that is, the right to exit from the jurisdiction of a legal order[49] – is not a realistic guarantee of individual rights in the UK. Not when the pressure to conform to tradition, the fear of bringing shame on the family, and the dread of losing one's family and being ostracised by the community are real consequences of one's choice.

It is the most vulnerable women who will fall victim to the introduction of Islamic law in a western society, not the articulate middle-class woman. And although women, regardless of their background, do exercise their agency even in the most delicate situations, they are often left to a system that will certainly exploit their vulnerability. The educated, strong and articulate middle-class woman, who is simply seeking a religious divorce to end a marriage, will not be manipulated into giving up her custody or financial rights to get a divorce; nor will she be blackmailed into a mediation that she does not want. But a woman trapped in a closed community will not be in a position to act similarly.

Profiles of Women Turning to Shari'a Courts

Profiles of the women who go to the shari'a courts highlight this vulnerability. The classification below is based on two sources. The first is a six-month examination of cases that went to trial conducted by Salma Dean, a survivor of a forced marriage, and a barrister working on human rights; she worked on Baroness Cox's team on the Equality Bill. The second source is Charlotte Proudman, a human rights barrister who researched the councils, provided a report in support of the Equality Bill, and shared some of the cases she addressed. Based on these two sources, three types of cases can be identified.[50]

First Type of Case: Religious Divorce

A woman seeks a religious divorce because she believes that a civil divorce does not suffice, as people have told her that under Muslim law she is not divorced.

Within this category is another subgroup: mainly first- or second-generation Muslim women, who were born and brought up in England and often have a strong Muslim identity. Others are women who converted to Islam and took on an Islamic mantle. For this group it is crucial to have a religious divorce, just as they desired a religious marriage.

Sonia Shah-Kazemi and Samia Bano each conducted studies on shari'a councils, interviewing 20 to 25 women each. They both highlighted how important it was to these women to get a religious divorce, as they consider that doing so is 'part of their religious identity'.[51]

Second Type of Case: Marriage Outside of the UK

These marriages may be either forced or arranged. The ceremony may have taken place in Pakistan, Bangladesh or India, and no civil marriage followed in the UK. Under international private law, the UK recognises a marriage conducted outside of the country and considers it legally binding, and therefore it is legally possible to dissolve it. Many women do not know this and think that the only place they can get help ending their marriage is a shari'a court.

Within this category are those who come to England on a spousal visa, often marrying a cousin or a member of a clan living in the UK. Usually they do not speak English, they have little if any formal education, and they are not aware of their legal rights in England. They live under the patriarchal regime in the family household, often in poverty in a ghettoised area of England. Women in this category 'genuinely believe that the community is the only option they have in England; they are not aware of the wider society in England.'[52]

Third Type of Case: UK Marriage not under Civil Law

Women in this category had a religious marriage but failed to register it. Such marriages, called *nikahs*, are not recognised under civil law, so these women must go to a shari'a court to get a divorce.

Despite the lack of reliable statistics and numbers, the failure to register an Islamic religious marriage is considered a widespread problem in the UK – alarming to the extent that the BBC reported on it and women's organisations launched campaigns to alert women about the consequences of not registering their marriages. Cassandra Balchin, the late president of the Muslim Women's Network, explained that *nikahs* are a matter of concern because the woman has little recourse to justice if she experiences discord in the relationship or her husband dies.[53]

There are many reasons why women fail to register their marriages. The most common is ignorance about the legal status of religious marriage, but sometimes women want to test a relationship before committing to a real civil marriage. Often the situation results when the husband makes a deliberate attempt to trick his wife out of registering a civil marriage and thus enjoying the rights that civil law affords to women.[54]

In her study *Untying the Knot,* Sonia Shah-Kazemi examined a total of 287 case files in one shari'a council in Ealing, West London. She found that 57 per cent of the women had a religious Islamic marriage but did not register it in the UK as required by civil law (not all of these religious marriages took place in the UK); 27 per cent who had religious marriages in the UK did not register them.[55]

Samia Bono also examined cases in various shari'a councils in the UK for her *Muslim Women and Shari'a Councils*. Most of those cases involved women whose religious marriages were not registered. This was not a matter of the women making a deliberate decision. In fact, the majority of these women expected that their religious marriages would be registered after they completed the religious ceremony and consummated the marriage. But some husbands simply refused to register, and thus formalise, the marriage as required by civil law. Bano concludes that it would be difficult to ignore the 'relations of power and the gendered cultural norms and values' that underline the decisions made by many husbands not to formalise the marriage. These women are left with a violation of their trust and a loss of decision making and autonomy in the marriage.[56]

Sometimes the husband has another motive for refusing to register the marriage: he is entering into a polygamous marriage.

In an interview with the BBC, Dr Siddiqui, whom I mentioned earlier, expressed his concern about the exploitation some women are subjected to. Their partners promise them a civil wedding after the religious marriage, and then refuse to go ahead with it after consummating the marriage:

> This allows Muslim men to control their wives because they can threaten to leave them and end the Islamic marriage by just saying the words 'divorce, divorce, divorce' to her. It also enables some men to commit polygamy. I know of cases where men have taken on several wives because they have just had the *nikah* with each partner.[57]

The rise of fundamentalist interpretations of Islam within some closed communities, some of my interviewees contend, has mainstreamed polygamy as part of an 'Islamic way of life'. It has also led 'women to be misled' that a religious marriage, a *nikah,* is the 'proper Muslim way'.[58] When they face troubles in their marriage they discover that they are left with no protection and are forced to go to a shari'a court.

Why Women Turn to the Shari'a Courts

The types of cases I outlined above, and the reasons why women turn to shari'a courts, highlight the social context within which they are often operating – a patriarchal order. Though their context may be similar, their backgrounds are diverse. Some are educated, and independent, with their own income, while many others have only a minimum of formal education, and are economically inactive and poverty stricken. Some are living in closed communities, while a few others are not constrained by such structures; this is especially true of converts.

Yet despite their diversity they share one common feature: what they often want is a *religious divorce.* This is important. They are not interested in mediation or arbitration; they want to end their marriage and get a religious divorce. The fact that the majority of women going to the shari'a courts have not registered or formalised their religious marriage according to civil law only highlights the legal loopholes that compel these women to seek the assistance of the shari'a courts. Once they go there, they enter into an inherently discriminatory process, in which they are pushed to seek mediation instead of divorce. Some are even forced to concede the rights they would be afforded by civil law, as their only means to get the religious divorce they desperately seek.

At the three shari'a councils I visited in London and Birmingham, the people I met all confirmed that women who resort to the shari'a councils are seeking a religious divorce.

Sister Sabah, the administrative coordinator of the Family Support Service at the Islamic shari'a Council in Birmingham told me that 9 out of 10 cases coming to the council are from women applying for divorce: 'obviously [...] if a man wants a divorce they can give it to themselves.' Women are given a choice: 'if they want to have a divorce privately, they are able to [be referred to a mosque]; if they want a certificate, then they have to follow the procedure.'[59]

The procedures will involve visiting the council's Family Support Service and Counseling Clinic, where female counsellors will listen to the case of the individual or couple. The counsellors will suggest reconciliation as a matter of Islamic principle. If the person insists on divorce, their case will be given a number. Once the case files are ready, the case will be put forward to the shari'a council, which will consider the case and deliver its final verdict on whether to grant the divorce, called a *talaq*, or a *khula*, a divorce initiated by the woman.[60]

Sheikh Mohammad Talha Bokhari, the coordinator of the Shari'a Council and one of its members, confirmed Sister Sabah's account. Asked about the types of cases that come to the council, he said they do not get many marriage cases; their mosque has a marriage bureau that deals with such cases. Rather, the council deals with divorce cases; in most of them, 'the wife does not want to live with him and the husband does not want to give her a divorce.'[61]

Dr Mohammad Shahoot Kharfan, the imam of the Muslim Welfare House in London, said that most of the cases he deals with are either to contract a marriage or to issue a divorce. What he usually does first is try mediation between the two partners; when this does not succeed he issues a divorce.[62]

Salim Leham, the legal director of the Muslim Welfare House in London, explained to me that most of those coming to the centre are refugees of Arab or Somali backgrounds. Very often they do not speak English and need assistance. His role is to help them in their communications with the local authorities. When it concerns family cases, specifically issues of *talaq* and *khula*, people are referred to the imam, in this case Dr Kharfan. Sometimes Leham translates for him if the applicant is a convert who does not speak Arabic. He added that the 'sheikh gives the Islamic perspective, but we live in a state that is not Muslim; its law should be implemented. So we explain the British divorce process to them, [...] and help them in the court system.'[63]

On the other hand, Sheikh Dr Suhaib Hasan, of the Islamic Shari'a Council in Leyton, stated that his council was created in 1982 to 'guide the Muslim community in all matters'; later the council recognised that there was a 'great field still not filled by any Muslim organisation: the field of matrimonial problems of *talaq* and *khula*. So then we said, all right, let us fill this vacuum.' Asked about the type of service the council is offering – mediation, arbitration, or family counselling services – Sheikh Dr Hasan answered:

We receive a lot of cases of women seeking *khula*. Now the very same woman might go to civil court as well. And civil courts do not try to mediate, they do not try to reconcile, but they try to give the decision regarding the case which is presented to them. But that is not the case with us. Here, whenever a woman applies for a divorce, we treat it as a case of *khula*, in which the man has to be persuaded to give his consent. If he is not ready, if he is not willing to give a *khula*, then it is not a proper *khula*. Then it becomes our responsibility as *qadis* [judges] to dissolve the marriage.

So in this way, we have to have a joint meeting for husband and wife, and when they come, we try to mediate between them. So this is part of our policy, that we should try to mediate between the two of them and try to explore if there are any avenues in which they can come together, they can minimise their differences, and they can live together. We ask a woman if she has any conditions, please lay down these conditions, and we say to the man, if you comply with these conditions, we will give you still another chance, two or three months, and if the man does not comply with these conditions, then we will award the woman the divorce she is seeking.

So we do try mediate in each and every case, except when it becomes very clear that the woman is a victim of violence, and there is no room for reconciliation at all. Then and only then we take the decision ourselves to dissolve the marriage because the man does not want a divorce, but if he is willing to divorce then the matter is very easy.[64]

Hence, mediation is almost always offered as an obligatory part of the process even if the woman has a clear objective of obtaining a religious divorce. This may lead to situations where women are forced to enter into mediation.

Sonia Shah-Kazemi and Samia Bano, in their two separate studies, have highlighted that the single most important reason why women turn to shari'a councils is to get a religious divorce – not a desire to save their marriage or enter mediation.[65] Shah-Kazemi, who favours the use of shari'a councils, asked her interviewees about their views on mediation. All talked about the positive aspect of mediators coming from backgrounds like their own. However, women who came from small, close-knit communities (from different regions in the UK) did express their concerns about confidentiality within the community. Only one interviewee had actually gone through the mediation process.

When mediation concerns their children, the positive attitude toward mediation evaporates.

Shah-Kazemi recognised that women who come to the Shari'a Council have made up their mind about the divorce. One of her interviewees put it this way:

> [The situation was] too far gone; if there had been any doubt in my mind I would not have started the procedure [...] I had thought about it: 'Is there any hope in this?'[66]

Samia Bano, who cautiously supports the use of what she calls the alternative dispute resolution mechanism, has observed that in some cases women were encouraged to reconcile even if they did not wish to do so. She is very much aware of the troubling context within which mediation takes place: it is riddled with dynamics of power emphasising what is described as the woman's divinely ordained obligation. It is also male dominated, and often imbued with conservative interpretations about the position of women in Islam.[67]

Bano describes one of the troubling findings of her study: ten of her interviewees reported that they had been 'coaxed' into participating in the reconciliation sessions with their husbands even though they were reluctant to do so. More troubling still, four of these women had existing injunctions against their husbands on the grounds of domestic violence and yet they were urged to sit only a few feet away from these men during the reconciliation sessions.[68]

Bano, who – I emphasise – is cautious about her support of Alternative Dispute Resolution Mechanism, came to this conclusion:

> Empirical findings in this study confirm the existence of intra-group inequalities and that Shari'ah councils construct boundaries for group membership that rely upon traditional interpretations of the role of women in Islam, primarily as wives, mothers and daughters. Under such conditions the multicultural accommodation of Muslim family law in Britain can lead to violations of human rights for Muslim women. In effect this privatised form of religious arbitration means the shifting of state regulation to the private domain thereby giving religious leaders greater power to dictate acceptable patterns of behaviour.[69]

Similarly, Charlotte Proudman, who provided evidence in support of Baroness Cox's bill, said that in all the cases she examined, women went to shari'a courts to end their marriages. Yet more often than not, these women were pushed to enter mediation in a process that was misogynistic and gender discriminatory. Proudman not only profiled cases she dealt with personally in her capacity as a lawyer. She also documented testimonies provided by nine reputable Muslim and women's organisations working within the communities, which handled cases of women turning to shari'a courts.[70]

Their accounts are important in illustrating the patriarchal social context of these women, the social control and pressure they endure while seeking to receive their religious divorce, and the lack of legal knowledge, combined with the system's legal loopholes, that are driving them to shari'a councils. Two testimonies are worth mentioning.

The first is of Jasvinder Sanghera, the president of Karma Nirvana – a renowned registered charity – which supports victims and survivors of forced marriage and honour-based abuse. Sanghera provides expert evidence and opinions in family law matters to UK courts of law. She gave this testimony:

> Many women telephoning Karma Nirvana are calling to ask how to obtain a sharia divorce. Karma Nirvana supports them with their application, often providing women with a letter of support. Once women begin the sharia divorce process, the sharia councils soon pressurise vulnerable and marginalised women to reconcile their marriage. Family members also become involved further adding to the pressure these women are under to return to the matrimonial home regardless of the abuse that they have, and will continue to, suffer. Where women refuse to return to their husband, sharia Councils have insisted that women return their children to their husbands. Once the child is returned to its father there is a high risk that the child will be abducted.[71]

The Henna Foundation, a national registered charity committed to strengthening families in Muslim communities, highlighted the legal misinformation that leaves these women vulnerable. Over the past 12 years one third of Henna's work involved Muslim women who were seeking an Islamic divorce and clarity on their Muslim marriage:

The lack of regulation and accountability of the Councils has caused undue stress and pressure particularly on Muslim women. This can be illustrated in the lack of acceptance of decree absolutes [civil divorce] as a valid and finalised divorce for Muslim women. A number of renowned scholars have made it clear that a decree absolute [civil divorce] is sufficient to fulfil the requirements of an Islamic divorce and technically Muslim women need not obtain a Sharia Council divorce. However due to community pressure, lack of understanding of divorce, and also for peace of mind, a large majority of Muslim women will apply for an Islamic divorce once given their decree absolute. The lack of understanding on the issue of divorce is particularly concerning as there are religious leaders and ex-husbands etc. who exploit this and tell vulnerable Muslim women that they are still married in Islam and that they have to continue to perform their duty/role as a wife.[72]

Remember the expression I used in Chapter 4: the *anthropological version of the law*? I defined it as a version of law void of any historical, political, or even legal context. Again, it is at play here in the contexts described above. Women are lost in a confusing system that persistently fails to address their needs.

Women are resorting to the shari'a courts because they need to obtain a religious divorce, but this need is complicated by three factors.

First, most women are ignorant about the legal status of marriage and divorce. On the one hand, most of these women are unaware that a marriage conducted outside of the UK is accepted as legally binding back in Britain. They can therefore obtain a civil divorce with the protection that comes with it. On the other hand, most are also unaware that a British civil divorce is religiously accepted as a valid divorce.

Second, the woman's religious marriage contracted in the UK may be not registered. As I described above, many women who seek divorce have contracted only religious marriages in the UK and have failed to register them. They need a divorce and to get that divorce they turn to the shari'a councils.

Third, the fundamentalist interpretation of Islam is being mainstreamed. The rise of fundamentalist interpretations of Islam, such as those in Salafi Islam, has mainstreamed and propagated the false assumption within closed UK communities that a Muslim woman is only divorced through an Islamic divorce. This opinion was strongly articulated by Haitham al-Haddad of the Shari'a Council, Leyton, who warned against accepting the 'judgment of non-Muslims' in a fatwa he issued in July 2010. He insisted that a 'divorce issued by the civil court in response to the wife's request is neither a valid divorce nor legitimate marriage dissolution.'[73]

Al-Haddad's opinion is in fact a fringe opinion – an extreme one. It contradicts the actual practice in many Islamic countries, including Pakistan, Bangladesh, Tunisia and Morocco, which do accept a civil divorce as a valid divorce. Sohail Akbar Warraich and Cassandra Balchin demonstrated this legal practice in their report *Recognising the un-Recognised*; they say that cases coming before courts in Bangladesh and Pakistan involving a British civil divorce always involve custody and property disputes, and neither party challenges the actual fact of the divorce.[74]

Al-Haddad's opinion also stands at odds with classical Islamic jurisprudence. In fact, Rashad Ali points out that Muslim scholars have traditionally advised Muslims to obtain divorces from courts within the legal system where they live. Such divorces would be legitimate divorces both on religious grounds and according to the law of the land. This position is not novel – it is part of classical Islamic jurisprudence and has long been advocated by pre-modern scholars for Muslims living in areas which have a majority non-Muslim population or even where non-Muslims were judges in Muslim-majority countries. Accordingly, it is religiously, morally and legally binding upon Muslims to adopt the prevailing legal norms and standards within their own contractual undertakings. One leading contemporary authority on Islamic law, Sheikh Abdullah Bin Mahfudh Bin Bayyah, explicitly states that you are married and divorced according to the laws of the country where you live.[75]

He is not alone in this. The Birmingham Council abides by this rule, as I showed in Chapter 4. Indeed, Sheikh Mohammad Talha Bokhari, the coordinator of that shari'a council and one of its members, explained to me that if a woman came with a civil divorce, she would not need a religious divorce from the council: 'Because when the [civil] divorce has come, issued from the civil court, then she is done. That is a divorce.'[76]

Both Islamists and essentialists reject this solid theological position and the modern practice of legal systems in Islamic countries; instead they argue for an *anthropological version of Islamic law*, demanding that a parallel legal order of shari'a courts be integrated into the Western legal system. This is a misrepresentation of the issue. Women are not seeking religious arbitration; what they need is a procedural measure that allows them to get a religious divorce without having to go to a religious court. The British authorities have so far failed to address this problem out of an absurd sense of political correctness. There are specific policy measures that can address the issue but doing so will require political will. I will describe them in the concluding chapter.

Shari'a Contested: A Discourse of Consequences

The essentialists' prism of the anthological version of Islamic law is void of context. It ignores the historical, political, social and even the legal context of what it is describing. Significantly, it also discounts the critical discourse on Islamic law that has been taking place in the Arab and Islamic countries since the early twentieth century. It is as if this critical discourse never existed. Likewise it disregards how Islamic law has been challenged and contested outside and inside of the UK.

As I said in the Introduction, many Arab and Islamic intellectuals and writers, both men and women, have made the point that the emancipation of women is a condition for the rise of their societies in general. This emancipation cannot be separate from the laws that govern their lives: specifically family laws, religious family laws.

Within an Arab context, in 1930, the Tunisian Al-Taher Al-Haddad was the first to specifically point to Islamic law as part of the problem, and to its reformation as part of the solution. In his book *Our Women in Shari'a and Life*, first published in 1930, he wrote, 'Quranic verses privileged the man over woman in explicit positions. This should not be a hindrance to accepting the principles of social equality between them as time progresses, since its [the Qur'an's] ultimate aim is total justice.'[77]

Social equality, he argued, can be achieved by implementing several measures. First, a woman should have an equal legal and civil identity to man. In addition, the practice of male guardianship over their female relatives should be ended and the marriage age should be set at 18 years. The male right to unilateral divorce should be abolished and only a civil court should decide between husband and wife in familial disputes. Polygamy should be prohibited because of the humiliation women endure and the family strife and disputes it causes. Finally, new provisions should allow for equality in inherence rights.[78]

The first measure that Habib Bourguiba (1903–2000), the president of Tunisia, took after independence in 1946 was introducing a civil family law that integrated all of Al-Haddad's measures, except for equality in inheritance. Bourguiba justified the law by saying that all the efforts to modernise Tunisian society would be rendered futile unless the country changed the inferior status of woman within the family structure. Changing the family law was the tool to correct this imbalance.

More than 75 years after Haddad's book was published, in 2005 to be precise, the Arab Human Development report, *Towards the Rise of Women in the Arab World*, dedicated to improving conditions for women in Arab societies, repeated the same argument. Many women, the report argues, continue to struggle for fair treatment; are left victim to conservative authorities, discriminatory religious family laws in legally pluralist systems, chauvinist male peers and tradition-minded kinsfolk, who regulate their aspirations, activities, and conduct.[79]

Most importantly, the report pointedly argued that Islamic family laws discriminate against women and should be changed. The authors put it this way:

> Most Arab legislation is characterised by a marked deficit in gender equality in family law. The notion that men are women's keepers and have a degree of command over them is sustained in Islamic scriptures. In legal practice, this has translated into laws requiring husbands to support their wives financially, laws ordaining wifely obedience, laws granting men alone the right to dictate divorce and laws granting men the right to the compulsory return of their wives in the event of a revocable divorce (*talaq raj'i*).[80]

Not surprisingly, the report singles out the Tunisian Personal Status Code (family law) as a model in the Arab world for promoting the principle of equality in marital relations in law by avoiding what it described as 'archaic interpretations of Shari'a prejudicial to the rights of women.'[81] Nor was the fact lost on the report's authors that the Tunisian family law is the 'only Arab personal status code that applies to all the country's citizens regardless of religious affiliations.'[82] As I showed in Chapter 3, one cannot overstate the significance of applying family law to all citizens regardless of religion or ethnicity to ensure the cohesion of national identity and equality between citizens.

Notice that this report was written by Arab scholars and experts, some of them of Islamic heritage, and not by Western experts. These Arab scholars had no trouble calling the problem by its name, stating that family laws derived from Islamic law discriminate against women in family affairs.

There is a critical discourse in the Arab and Islamic countries on Islamic law and the need to reform it. This discourse involves a combination of research-oriented activism and scholarly work. Moreover, at a time when the essentialists are pushing to introduce Islamic law in the Western legal systems, the trend in the Arab and Islamic countries is to push for the reform of Islamic law — not to insist on its application.

One famous example of research-oriented activism is Women Living Under Muslim Laws (WLUML), an international solidarity network that extends to more than 70 countries ranging from South Africa to Uzbekistan. It is a platform that provides information, support and collective space for 'women whose lives are shaped, conditioned or governed by laws and customs said to derive from Islam.'[83]

These women live in different contexts. They live in countries or states where Islam is the state religion; in secular states with Muslim majorities; in Muslim communities governed by minority religious laws; in secular states where Islamist groups are demanding religious laws; in migrant Muslim communities in Europe, the Americas and around the world; and in contexts where non-Muslim women may have Muslim laws applied to them directly or through their children. Finally, they may be women labelled as Muslims because they were born into Muslim communities or families, but they define themselves differently, either because they left the religion or because they prefer not to be identified in religious terms, preferring to highlight other aspects of their identity such as political ideology, profession, or sexual orientation.[84]

The founder of the network is Marieme Hélie-Lucas, an Algerian sociologist. She explains what brings all of these women together: women are oppressed all over the world in different societies just as are the women living under Muslim laws. However, the difference between them and women in other societies is the ways that this oppression is constructed and justified:

> We are told (or made to believe if not directly told) that the circumstances under which we live cannot be changed, because God said it should be like this. This is really what makes our situation specific. This is also what brings us together. We do have the same problems as other women around the world, except for the way it is constructed for us.[85]

The WLUML's mission was shaped by this difference and gained a reputation for shattering the essentialists' and Islamists' homogenisation of Muslim and shari'a law. The very name challenges what they describe as 'the myth of one, homogenous "Muslim world"'.[86] This 'Muslim world' is a construction, a 'deliberately created myth.' It fails to reflect the fact that laws said to be Muslim vary from one context to another and that they are derived from diverse sources: religious, customary, colonial and secular.

Variations and differences are a given. In fact, even when they share the same religious denomination and school of jurisprudence, they differ in the ways they apply its religious provisions. For example, Morocco and Kuwait share the same school of jurisprudence: the Sunni Maliki school. Yet in 2004 Morocco made use of an old Islamic provision from a different jurisprudence, stating that a woman who has come of age is entitled to guardianship as a right. In Kuwait this provision has been totally ignored. Instead, the male guardian has been given the authority to marry off his daughter, sister, etc., even without her knowledge. What compels one society to make use of one provision and another to ignore it? Again, it is the human and social context that makes the difference.[87]

By highlighting this political, social and cultural context and the political use of religion by both Islamists and political leaders, the WLUML Network has produced research that makes it clear that these laws 'are man made and not God given.' This has enormous implications for women's struggles, Marieme Hélie-Lucas contends, 'because if it is man made nobody will feel afraid to contest and confront these laws – while many people feel restricted if they look at it as God given.'[88]

These laws are indeed made by men (and a few women) – not by God. This view of Muslim law is reiterated, in a scholarly critical discourse on shari'a, by the Sudanese American Abdullahi Ahmed An-Na'im, a renowned professor of law at Emory University. In his famous book *Toward an Islamic Reformation: Civil Liberties, Human Rights and International Law,* he argues that shari'a is not the whole of Islam. Instead, shari'a is an interpretation of fundamental sources of Islamic law as understood in a particular historical context. In other words, shari'a was constructed by its founding jurists.[89]

Appreciating this aspect makes it possible to make a judgement based on today's norms. In fact, An-Na'im argues that historical shari'a is discriminatory towards women and religious minorities. This discrimination was the norm at the time when the shari'a provisions were promulgated, in the seventh through tenth centuries, though some aspects of shari'a did try to restrict and reduce the scope of this discrimination. Nonetheless, when viewed from a modern perspective, the principles of shari'a – sanctioning serious and unacceptable discrimination on grounds of gender and religion – are untenable today and violate the constitutional principle of equality before the law. A justification of this discrimination is unacceptable, An-Na'im contends. He uses the example of slavery: it may have been accepted as justifiable in the past. Today no one would accept it. By the same token, 'discrimination against women and non-Muslims can not be accepted as justifiable by the standards of justice and reasonableness prevailing today.'[90]

An-Naim is considered an authority in Islamic law and he speaks from within the Islamic tradition. In other words, he is not an ex-Muslim. Yet the conclusion he comes to is not just that Islamic law needs reform – an enterprise he sees as very necessary – but also that religion and state must be separated from the state. If a state professes to treat its citizens as equals, then it must separate itself from religion. An-Naim's position has profound relevance to our discussion of Islamic law in the UK because he contributed a chapter for the volume on *Islam and English Law,* edited by Robins Griffith-Jones and published as an intellectual debate on the speech by Rowan Williams, the former archbishop of Canterbury, on Islamic law in the UK.[91]

In it, An-Na'im argues that 'the state must be neutral regarding religion. That is, the state cannot deal with me *other* [italics in original] than by virtue of my citizenship. My religious affiliation has nothing to do with the state. It is not the business of the state to differentiate among its citizens on the basis of their religious affiliation.'[92]

He finds it very ironic that Europeans tend to treat Muslims as a community of believers – making people's affiliation to a religious community the means by which they and the state interact. It reminds him of the way the Ottoman Empire applied the 'millet' system to non-Muslim communities. The very Europe that dismantled the Ottoman Empire in the name of allowing citizenship to all its residents is now denying the same citizenship to believers by accepting that the state can deal with believers by referring to their belief. He insists that this is the wrong direction to go:

> There should be no accommodation here, on either side. The state should not deal with communities or with individuals other than by virtue of their citizenship, without reference to their religious affiliation; and citizens should interact with the state on the basis only of their citizenship.[93]

Many women's organisations and other groups working in the UK could not agree more.

Women's Organisations and Shari'a in the UK

Those working with vulnerable women in the UK are the least impressed by the demands of the essentialists and their Islamist allies. They know better than to be lured by a theoretical emphasis on choice, void of context.

Yet at first glance one would be excused for thinking that women's organisations in the UK were slow to raise the alarm on the issues of weak legal pluralism – the introduction of Islamic law into the British legal system – and its consequences for vulnerable women.

Compared with the reaction in Canada, that impression is certainly justified. There, a coalition of secular, humanist, and Muslim women's organisations joined forces to stop a Canadian proposal to establish in Ontario the first Islamic tribunal in a North American jurisdiction.

The call to use Islamic law in Ontario's legal system came from Mumtaz Ali, a retired Muslim lawyer. In 2003 he formed the Islamic

Institute of Civil Justice, enlisted a panel of arbitrators and demanded that shari'a law be used to resolve family disputes among Muslims. Hence the report by Marion Boyd, the former Attorney General, with the title *Dispute Resolution in Family Law: Protecting Choice, Promoting Inclusion,* released in December 2004. In it, Ms Boyd suggested introducing voluntary tribunals for Canadian Muslims based on shari'a jurisprudence to settle family disputes and offer binding arbitration. Her proposal for Islamic tribunals was made when the government tried to assess the permissibility of shari'a law under the Ontario Arbitration Act. The act allows religious and cultural groups to resolve their family and civil disputes through private and binding arbitration. When the act was introduced in 1991, only the rabbinical law for Jews came into force, whereas the Catholics and Protestants did not use it.[94]

To the government's surprise the outcry that greeted its proposal came from within this very religious minority – from the *minority* within the minority. It came from the Canadian Council of Muslim Women. The council reacted by saying that '(s)anctioning the use of religious laws under the Arbitration Act will provide legitimacy to practices that are abhorred by fair-minded Canadians, including Muslim women.'[95] Choice was not inclusive after all.

More specifically, the council submitted a counter position to that of Ms Boyd. In it, they explained that what the many forms of Muslim family law have in common is that they perpetuate a patriarchal model:

> The jurisprudence of fiqh does have some common understandings. It is based on a patriarchal model of community and of the family. It is generally accepted that men are the head of the state, the mosque and the family. The responsibilities outlined for males is that they will provide for their families and because they spend of their wealth, they have the leadership to direct and guide the members of their families, including the women. [...] Most proponents of Muslim law accept that men have the right to marry up to four wives; that they can divorce unilaterally; that children belong to the patriarchal family; that women must be obedient and seek the male's permission for many things; that if the wife is 'disobedient' the husband can discipline the wife; that daughters require their father's permission to marry and she can be married at any time after puberty. A wife does not receive any

maintenance except for a period of three months to one year and most agree that the children should go to the father usually at age 7 for boys and 9 for girls. If the wife wants a divorce she goes to court, while the husband has the right to repudiate the union without recourse to courts. Inheritance favours males, to the extent that the wife gets only a portion at the death of the husband.[96]

Similarly, the Muslim Canadian Congress pointed out the problem in allowing the use of Muslim law. Doing so:

> ghettoises the Muslim community, which otherwise spans five different continents covering 1.3 billion people, in an extensive array of sects languages, cultures, and customs, all into one second-class compartment in the determination of human and family law rights, which are of public importance and domaine. [...] all of this, behind the dishonest guise of religious tolerance and accommodation.[97]

Others disputed the system of religious and customary arbitration in general as favouring traditionalist male perspectives:

> Religious leaders (Christian, Jewish or Muslim) and community leaders (in the case of First Nations Canadians) are primarily male, and primarily traditionalists, who hold tightly to outdated beliefs and outdated laws that in some cases withhold the freedoms so held in esteem by Canadians. Traditional culture tends to be male dominated – the concept of women 'voluntarily' agreeing to faith-based arbitration will never be an option for many women, especially immigrants and First Nation women with lower levels of literacy and education and reduced self esteem and control over their own lives.[98]

Despite the strong opposition of many organisations, including the major Muslim women's organisations, Ms Boyd ignored their concerns and went ahead with a proposal that cherished a theoretical concept of 'choice and inclusion'.

Seeing this proposal for what it was – blatant discrimination against their rights in family affairs – the Canadian Council of Muslim Women joined forces with other Canadian organisations and launched an international public campaign. It succeeded in forcing the Canadian government to back off from its proposal and, significantly, it brought down the Arbitration Act itself. The outcry made it clear to Ontario Premier Dalton McGuinty that religious arbitration can threaten Canadian 'common ground'. Therefore he promised to introduce a bill banning all religious courts, vowing that 'There will be one law for all Ontarians.' On February 14, 2006 the Ontario government passed Bill 27, The Family Statute Law Amendment Act, which mandates that all family law arbitration be conducted only in accordance with Canadian law.[99]

'The key in that campaign is that it became a mass movement,' Maryam Namazie told me. She is the director of One Law for All; she participated in the Canadian campaign and has been one of the leading voices against shari'a councils in the UK. She explained, 'We all have made campaigns. But some make an impact; some reach large numbers of people and others don't [...] I think what was important in Canada, which we have seen less here, is that Muslim women groups went behind that campaign.'[100]

This situation has started to change in the UK, however. In fact, in June 2015 a coalition of 200 women's rights and secular campaigners, in addition to several reputable NGOs, alarmed at the increasing influence of shari'a courts over the lives of citizens of Muslim heritage, called for the UK government to stick to its pre-election promises to hold an inquiry into shari'a courts. The coalition brought together a diverse group of women's groups, along with secular, Muslim and ex-Muslim NGOs. Prominent Muslim organisations, such as British Muslims for Secular Democracy, Inspire, Women Living Under Islamic Law and the Quilliam Foundation, joined forces with secular, women's, and women's health organisations such as One Law for All, the Black Southhall Sisters, the Centre for Secular Space, the Iranian and Kurdish Women's Rights Organisation, the Kurdish and Middle Eastern Women's Organisation, and Aurat, a women's organisation supporting women in the Midlands.[101]

The bold call in 2015 stands in contrast to the silence that shrouded the issue in the 1980s and 1990s. In fact as recently as 2005 some women's and human rights groups were reluctant to scrutinise the effects of the shari'a courts for fear of interfering in the religious domain of minorities. The issue was sensitive, I was told in my field research.

The sensitivity was related to a culture of 'looking the other way' – part of the multicultural maxim of group difference and the collective cultural rights of others. As the fascination with multiculturalism as a state policy started to wane, the sensitivity shifted to a fear of providing the far right with fuel for its xenophobic agenda.

Maryam Namazi, who is known for her strong opposition to the far right, explained:

> Initially a lot of women's rights groups, while they were sympathetic, they did not officially join the One Law campaign [against the shari'a courts] because it is such a sensitive issue; there is so much of the far right taking advantage of this issue. And my argument was: if we do not say anything, we will leave it to them, and that is why we have to do it ourselves.[102]

At first, addressing the problem was not an option. The combination of cultural sensitivity and fear of the xenophobic agenda has proved to be very powerful. For example, amnesty International did not even mention the shari'a councils at all in its 2012 report on Muslims in Europe, which bore the title *Choice and Prejudice: Discrimination against Muslims in Europe.* Although the report did mention the importance of protecting 'Muslim women' from discrimination by non-state actors and their right to be free from gender-based discrimination, the bulk of it was dedicated to discrimination against Muslims in employment and to Muslim women's rights to wear the headscarf and burka![103] It did not address the discrimination against the minority within the minority: discrimination against women and children by their own male relatives, the pressure girls and women might endure to wear the headscarf and burka, and the ways that religious arbitration might affect vulnerable women in closed communities.

Amnesty, which says that fighting gender-based violence is one of its main goals, has yet to tackle the issue, but UK women's organisations began to become aware of the problem in the early 2000s. A woman's rights advocate I interviewed told me that these organisations' own experiences with women led to a growing concern that the services offered by faith groups might not be operating for the best interests of those women and might not be supporting their human rights.[104]

The faith groups this woman mentioned included Hindus, Jews and Christians. Some of these faith groups, I was told, were working within the UK human rights framework, but others were not. The concerns were not only related to Muslim arbitration – which has been receiving the bulk of criticism – but extended to other forms of arbitration, such as the Jewish Beth Din tribunals.[105]

As a result, some women's organisations started to launch a wider critical discussion of the government's faith-based approach. For example, Southall Black Sisters (SBS) showed that contrary to the popular view often promoted by state and religious leaders, the women they interviewed do not feel the need to be 'deferential' to religious leaders, nor do they want some form of religious laws. In fact, the SBS stated that once they were assured anonymity and felt safe to express themselves, these women 'have no problems in critiquing the idea of religious laws including sharia.'[106]

Women's views were tied directly to their negative experiences in religious institutions and at the hands of religious leaders: experiences of sexist and misogynistic discrimination, corruption and petty politics. Women expressed the view that religious institutions are corrupt and unaccountable places; they are divided over differences and fighting rival factions of trustees seeking to assert their authority and/or interest in financial gain. Divisions and discrimination based on religion, class and caste are common within these institutions. The lack of transparency and accountability of religious institutions only increased women's general distrust of faith-based organisations. These women have also raised cases of sexual abuse; some recounted cases where religious authorities had abused their positions of power and tried to sexually abuse the very women who turned to them for help.[107]

Similar testimonies about the abuse of power and sexual harassment have been reiterated by well-known women's rights activists within Muslim communities. For example, Gina Khan, whom I mentioned earlier, recounted to me how an imam tried to abuse his power when she needed a religious divorce:

> The first time I went to a small mosque in Birmingham – I went there and I remember I was crying; I was vulnerable, desperate; and this imam sent me to another old village man in his house to mediate. My father was staying with me at that time, and at 11 pm

at night, the imam rang me up drunk and made a pass at me. And my father asked me, 'who is that', and I said 'oh just the imam from your mosque, he just made a pass at me.'[108]

The SBS report concludes that far from inspiring trust, religious authority provoked multiple fears of discrimination and harassment and that this fear is even more clear when it came to the question of religious laws: 'Most interviewees made the obvious point that the concept of religious law is inseparable from its execution by religious leaders who were more often than not deeply conservative and even sexist when it came to women's rights.'[109]

Within this general critical discussion of the government's faith-based approach to minorities, women's organisations working on the front line were reporting specifically on the negative experiences of the women who turned to shari'a courts. In addition, human rights organisations began to become aware of this parallel legal system. One women's rights advocate put it this way:

That is how we found out about the impact [through the front line women's organisations]. It is when a woman has gone through an [Islamic] tribunal and has challenges around domestic violence or another form of domestic violence in the family or the community and as part of her journey comes to a refuge or a support service and then gives her history of what she had to deal with and if there is a kind of tribunal aspect to it. That is how we found out about it.[110]

This awareness was combined with recognition of how social pressure was, and remains, an integral feature of the mechanism that allows these courts to function, especially when they are embedded within closed communities. Contravening the norms in a closed community leads to 'ostracism and isolation and so many things that are not necessarily direct threats but can make your life hell,' Maryam Namazie told me.[111] If a woman does not dare to take off her veil in Tower Hamlets in London, Coventry in Birmingham, Little Horton in Bradford, or in some communities in Leicester, how is she supposed to insist on not turning to one of these courts or resist the bullying that takes place in them?

In cases where women turned to these courts of their own choice, women's organisations were alarmed by the discriminatory, misogynist process, imbued with a conservative if not reactionary interpretation of Islamic law, that sanctioned and belittled domestic violence. They also discovered a disregard of UK law as these courts often refused to grant a girl or woman a divorce even in cases of forced marriage and child marriage and in cases where the woman had a civil divorce.

These courts have also condoned and legitimised practices illegal under UK law such as polygamy. The number of polygamous cases is rising with the increasing numbers of unregistered religious marriages, and shari'a courts accept the practice. In fact, my research confirmed this situation. Amra Bone, the only female member of the Islamic Shari'a Council in Birmingham Central Mosque, described a case of polygamy in a matter of fact way:

> Amra Bone: I remember a particular case, a girl approached the council requesting us to resolve the issues in her marriage (the boy was from a different origin and cultural background).[112] It was only after their marriage she had found out he was already married. It was a clear case of deception and she had every right to dissolve this marriage, however she wanted to give him another chance. She suggested that as long as he was willing to tell his first wife about their marriage and treat them both equally, she would choose to remain in this marriage with him. The Panel decided to invite him with her to set up the conditions to which they both agreed and if he did not fulfil those conditions within the next few months then their marriage would be dissolved.[113]

The more the women's organisations and advocates became aware of the problematic nature of these religious courts and their consequences, the more they also recognised its political dimensions. In fact these women were the first to loudly alert the public that Islamists were promoting the implementation of shari'a law and a political agenda that is inherently discriminatory and totalitarian. The issue is not only about conservative clerics and imams, who are using the law in ways they have always known about. The issue is most significantly political, as these clerics and imams are very often members of Islamist organisations or fundamentalist groups.[114] One Law for All made this point clear in its campaign and other organisations followed; and so did famous women's rights advocates such as Gita Saghel and Pragna Patel, director of SBS.

The Islamists, argues Patel, are demanding religious and secular laws in the UK 'to operate in parallel universes, with the former applying to minorities and the latter to the white majority.'[115]

Indeed, women turned to the shari'a councils and Muslim arbitration tribunals to get a divorce, yet these organisations often function in a way that seals the social control over closed communities and contravenes their mandate.

The shari'a councils are operating as legal courts though they are not subject to any independent monitoring mechanism. Some are registered as charities and claim to provide mediation services. In reality, though, they issue 'court rules' and will often ask people to sign an agreement to abide by their decisions. Councils often call themselves 'courts' and the presiding imams are called 'judges'. No control is exercised over the appointment of 'judges'. People often have no access to legal advice and representation. The proceedings are not recorded and there is no right to appeal.[116]

The arbitration available at the Muslim arbitration tribunals (MATs) is recognised under the Arbitration Act 1996 and their rulings are binding in law, provided that both parties in the dispute agree to MATs arbitration. Under the act, all British citizens have the right to resolve civil disputes through arbitration. Civil disputes, such as contractual disputes, claims in tort, disputes concerning intellectual property rights and certain statutory claims, can legally be resolved by arbitration; but family law and criminal matters cannot. Although the 1996 Act was meant to allow multi-national companies to resolve disputes in the UK in accordance with the laws of other nations, faith groups have used it.[117]

MATs have admitted overseeing six cases of domestic violence, apparently working 'in tandem' with police investigations. In each case the women who had been abused withdrew her complaints to the police. MAT judges suggested that the husbands take anger-management classes and advice from Muslim elders but were given no further punishment.[118]

In our interview, Sheikh Faizul Aqtab Siddiqi, the director of the MAT in Nuneaton, confirmed that his tribunal deals with cases of domestic violence. He also said that in the experience of people running MATs, '95 per cent of those domestic violence [cases] do not occur again,' especially as MATs 'monitor and follow that'. When I asked how 'they follow that' he answered:

> We ask the community leaders in that area to visit that family regularly and to ask the person considered the victim and the perpetrator how this balance is going and we try to monitor it to make sure that it does not happen; and to continue to remind the man that he is being watched not just by the victim or the family but the community; and the community will stamp on him and shame him if he acts in that barbaric way again.[119]

Similarly, and most worryingly, he also boasted that they deal with cases of child abuse. The revelation came when I asked him if I could have access to the tribunal data. He answered:

Sheikh Siddiqi: We do not publish our cases; we do not publish our decisions. But the data I have given you [verbal description of women's profile] is probably the only data that we offer researchers. Because obviously some data, we are obligated not to disclose them [for] data protection reasons. And people come to us because they know they can ensure confidentiality. So therefore we do not give, you know some cases are very really very very difficult cases.

We get cases, where girls have been abused by their father or brother. So we say, look go to the police, and they say no, we do not want to. We say please go to the police, and they say no, we just want protection.

Manea: How do you offer that?

Sheikh Siddiqi: Well, you know. There are many ways to deal with such a situation. The first and foremost is the recognition that this man has done this wrong within the community. The first thing that is necessary is to name and shame that guy within the community.

Manea: And if she is living with this person?

Sheikh Siddiqi: It does not matter.

Manea: It will continue?

Sheikh Siddiqi: It will continue if we do not name and shame this person.

Manea: I mean, name and shame is one step of course but...

Sheikh Siddiqi: [interrupting] That is the first step; the second step is to take that person out of that family. And say you will not stay with this girl again. Because, why should the girl be taken out?

Manea: How can you enforce that without police?

Sheikh Siddiqi: The family will enforce it. The mother, she has to enforce it. The brothers, they have to enforce it. You know, the community leaders, they have to enforce it. There is a very big power called moral obligations.

Manea: Which community are we talking about here?

Sheikh Siddiqi: Our community here in the UK. Many times we have done this. I'll tell you one example. I had one case, this girl was abused by her brother for ten years. Since the age of 8 she was abused till 18. Father and mother and other siblings did not know that he sexually abused her. And you know he was like the breadwinner of the family, so the father and mother were like ooh, my son, he is earning so much money. So [he] was throwing his weight around and sexually abused his sister. So *Alhamdulillah* [Thank God], we were able to take the boy out of the house, we encouraged the girl many many times to go to the police, because she was victimised under age. And we finally managed to get her to speak to social services. Thank God she spoke to them but even they could not convince her, so the police got recordings of her, but she would not

give evidence in court for this. She said I will
speak with you but I will not give evidence in
court. Because you know, whatever her reasons,
we cannot force people to do that. And then we
got rid of the boy, not just from the house but
from the whole city. We have gotten him out of
there. We said, you cannot come back to the
city. Everybody in the city now knew that this is
a bad guy.

Women's groups opposing the shari'a courts do have a point when
they insist that the way they function creates de facto parallel legal
enclaves separate from the wider society with its own mechanisms of law
and order.

***

To recap, at first glance women's organisations in the UK may have been
slow to raise the alarm on the issue of weak legal pluralism, that is, on
the introduction of Islamic law in the British legal system and its
consequences for vulnerable women. But this was in fact connected to
the British context, which made it tantamount to 'racism' to offer any
critique of the closed communities or of the consequences of applying
religious laws for women's lives. The 7 July 2005 home-grown terrorist
attacks broke the wall of silence on many fronts. Closed communities
came under more scrutiny and so did practices that were otherwise
considered 'cultural'. Secular organisations paved the ground for a
critical discourse on shari'a law and courts and many women's
organisations followed.

This critical discourse was unimaginable in the UK in the early
2000s, as Baroness Caroline Cox correctly remarked in one of the first
meetings organised on the issue.[120] Given the silence that cloaked the
issue, an awareness campaign was necessary. The Arbitration and
Mediation Services (Equality) Bill was launched in 2010, Baroness Cox
told me, to raise this awareness, to 'let people out there in the wider
society know that there is a parliamentarian initiative' and alert them to
the 'suffering of women in closed communities'.[121]

Today, the silence of the 1980s and 1990s has ended. Women's
organisations and secular Muslim organisations have been highlighting

the consequences of applying Islamic law in the UK. Those engaged in this campaign are aware that some 'issues [...] are very hard to tackle legally' and have to be challenged 'culturally and through policies' that are specifically tailored to address them.[122] No one said it is easy to change the cultural and social norms that lead to discrimination. But they insist that treating individuals as citizens and applying one law for all citizens and members of a society is a first step in the right direction.

CONCLUSION

TIME FOR A PARADIGM SHIFT

A Consequence-Based Approach to Human Rights and Dignity

Academic discourses have an impact on our daily lives. They have consequences. They are not merely abstract discussions shared at closed conferences or published in peer-reviewed journals and books and read only by a privileged few. Opinions at the academic level frame our actions on the societal level. They influence policies, laws, politics, development aid and social services – and thus they shape our daily lives. Therefore social science has a function and a responsibility.

Nothing can highlight this importance or responsibility more than the role that the Essentialist Paradigm plays in our lives. This is the paradigm of thinking that has become characteristic of Western academic post-colonial and post-modernist discourse, dominating it for far too long. It has four specific ideological features.

The first is a combination of multiculturalism and legal pluralism in a social context. It divides people along cultural, religious and ethnic lines, setting them apart, and placing them in parallel legal enclaves. The second is group rights, perceiving rights from a group perspective – the group has the rights, not the individuals within it. It insists that each group has a collective identity and culture, an essential identity and culture, which should be protected and perpetuated even if doing so violates the rights of individuals within the group. The third is cultural relativism, dominated by a cultural relativist approach to rights, and arguing that rights – and other social practices, values and moral rules – are culturally determined. And the fourth is the white man's burden, the strong sense of shame and guilt over the Western colonial and imperial past, which drives a paternalistic desire to protect minorities or people from former colonies. It is a mindset that perceives the other, whether a member of a minority group or an entire developing country, as the oppressed, and human rights as the tools imposed by the Western oppressor. It considers that those who are fighting for universal human rights in their own societies are not authentic representatives of their own countries, and in the process it ignores or justifies dire human rights violations committed in the name of group rights or cultural and religious rights.

The Essentialist Paradigm

It is crucial that we identify the paradigm, name it and recognise its features. Because once we do, we will see its footprints all around us not only in academic circles, or in a given subject area – here, introducing Islamic law in Western legal systems – but also in the way policies are suggested and made on the international and domestic levels.

We see its imprint in transitional justice policies and development projects. When the United Nations and development and donor agencies claim they are bringing peace, stability, democracy and human rights to failed states or developing countries, what they are actually introducing are frameworks shaped by the markers of the Essentialist Paradigm. That is, they are advocating legal pluralism rather than a rule of law founded on sound functioning institutions. Such frameworks give tribal and sectarian leaders and their 'groups' the upper hand in any peace process that opts for a realist approach; they argue – not without merit – that peace is not possible without these strongmen. But that 'peace' remains precarious in many places like the Balkans and has turned out to be utterly unsustainable in countries such as Somalia, Iraq, Afghanistan and Yemen. This is not a naïve expectation about difficult situations; it is simply common sense. The fact that these policies have continued to fail in a wide range of international contexts begs for a paradigm change in international policies and approaches.

We also see the paradigm's footprints in international human rights campaigns. During the Iraq insurgency in 2004 academics and human rights campaigners refused to see the consequences of supporting what they called 'jihad in self-defence'. That groups allied with al-Qaeda launched this jihad, that they were made up of Sunni militants who practise sectarian violence, and that they directed their violence and campaigns of destruction mainly against Iraqis, and against women, minorities, LGBT persons and people with different political or ideological orientations: none of that seemed to be of any consequence. What mattered to these academics and campaigners were their ideological battles with their own countries (the enemy of my enemy is my friend), their white man's burden and their obsession with imperialism and Western hegemonic power.

And what happened to the voices of Iraqis opposed to the insurgencies from the left, and to feminists and intellectuals, and to the Shi'as and Kurds who together represent the majority of the Iraqi population? They were muted and silenced as not representative of their own society. The destruction that their society was experiencing, the bloodshed and the massacres? That did not seem relevant to the essentialists' ideological battles.

This alliance and support has now become embarrassment. Amnesty International has just decided to stop its 'cooperation' with the British Muslim Moazzam Begg, a former Guantanamo detainee lauded as a 'human rights defender', and with his pro-jihadi organisation the CagePrisoners.[1]

Obviously, then, the ideological prism of the Essentialist Paradigm has consequences for those fighting extremism in their own lands. Indeed, people in international human rights circles tend to ignore what Karima Bennoune correctly described in her much-acclaimed book *Your Fatwa Does Not Apply Here* as the 'most important – and overlooked – human rights struggles in the world': the struggles that intellectuals and activists are waging in Muslim majority societies in opposition to Islamist extremism.[2]

We also see the paradigm's footprints in the constant attempts by intellectuals, academics and politicians (liberal and leftist alike) to dilute, relativise and curtail core human rights in the name of respect for group rights and religious sensitivity. We see it in the attempts to restrict freedom of expression, opinion and the press in Europe and North America as the Mohammad cartoons controversies have shown. We see it in the refusal by the UK National Union of Students to condemn ISIS for fear that such an action would be construed as

'Islamophobic'. All of these attempts were made in the name of respecting a group's 'religious sensitivity'. But they ignore the fact that without the freedom of expression there is no freedom at all. If we think of all the authoritarian and theocratic states in the world we realise that the one thing that brings them together, in addition to their human rights violations, is the absence of any freedom of expression.[3]

Moreover, these attempts fail to achieve their objective. When we start to curtail freedom of expression and opinion we are not respecting 'Muslims', many of whom may disagree and even hate the depiction of their prophet but will nevertheless express these feelings peacefully. Instead, we are catering to the wishes of the violent Islamists, who are spreading their reign of terror and killing the artists and intellectuals who dare to contradict their opinions.

We also see the paradigm's footprints in Britain, where it clearly has wide influence after the essentialists successfully introduced the politics of difference and group rights. Losing faith in secular universalism and Enlightenment ideas of rationalism and humanism, they championed a multiculturalism of group rights and exceptionalism, in the process erecting walls around segregated closed communities. Britain today is paying a heavy price for these policies of difference.

And yes, we see its footprints in the subject matter of this book, in the suggestion by Christian Giordano, the Swiss professor of social anthropology, that the country introduce weak legal pluralism and with it Islamic law to regulate the affairs of the Muslim minority. And we see it in the passionate call by former UK Archbishop of Canterbury Rowan Williams that we all 'think a little harder about the role and rule of law in a plural society of overlapping identities.'[4]

As I said elsewhere in this book Giordano and Williams do not stand alone. Their suggestions are the tip of an iceberg, an expression of the Essentialist Paradigm.

I am aware that most proponents of legal pluralism and of introducing Islamic law in Western legal systems will strongly object to being called essentialists. After all, this expression has often been associated with racism. They do not consider themselves racists; how could they be, when their aim is 'protection'? But even though I recognise that their intentions are often noble – after all, they are suggesting ways to 'protect' the minorities – I also repeat that we must remember the prisms they look through as they develop this essentialist view. The first prism they use to look at society insists that a group of people have inherent unchanging characteristics because of their very religion or culture; they simply ignore the fact that any group is *constructed* through various political, social and religious factors. Looking through their second prism, they insist that a person is first and foremost a religious entity and part of another religious whole. That this person is a complex being with different layers of identity, that he or she may not subscribe to this religious identity in the first place: all this is swept aside as not sufficiently 'authentic' or 'representative'. The third prism is shaped by the insistence that the essentialists – and they alone – are in a position to protect this religious minority, understand what it wants, and designate who should speak on its behalf.

Most importantly, they are essentialist because they ignore the developments and struggles taking place in Islamic countries to change family laws based on shari'a law and the critical discourse contesting Islamic law by intellectuals and feminists of Islamic heritage. Instead, they introduce an 'anthropological version of law', a version that remains isolated from its social, political or historical contexts. This version reinforces the essentialists' expectation that 'Muslims' actually need this type of discriminatory law to regulate their affairs, and therefore we should leave them alone. Whatever they may claim, the fact is that culture, religion and also identity *do* change – they are not made of stone. But that point looks trivial if you are viewing the world through the essentialist ideological prisms.

In Chapters 2 and 5 I showed how the *Muslim community* was *constructed*. The community was in fact multiple communities – yet we failed to see how diverse and heterogeneous they are with multiple national, confessional, linguistic and regional lines of differentiation.

We only woke up to this fact after the London terrorist attacks of 2005. Three factors played roles in the construction of the so-called British Muslim community; together they succeeded in concealing the diversity of South Asian communities, instead lumping them together as one community. These were: (1) specific features of the British context; (2) measures that movements took to promote societal and political Islamism; and (3) British policies and the need for intermediaries to speak for and get the 'Asian vote'.

Together, all of these factors and measures provided the backbone of the British policies of multiculturalism. Given that these measures focused on separation and even tribalism, it was not surprising that they led instead to the reality of plural monoculturalism. Multiculturalism was well intentioned but the efforts to develop it actually ingrained differences rather than celebrating what brings together different people from different backgrounds. It focused on what makes them separate and that separateness was promoted in policy measures. And when these efforts concerned South Asian communities, they were made within a political and Islamist context that homogenised people and reduced them to their religious identity and promoted unelected Muslim/ Islamist leaders as speakers for the community. This policy has started to change recently as extremism has become a major problem in the UK.

If the essentialists' theoretical deliberations were simply theoretical and confined to their journals, books and conference rooms, I might not have minded. I would not have gone through the trouble of researching and travelling to write this book. But the problem is, this is not merely an intellectual exercise: their deliberations *lack context* and *have consequences*. And both ***context*** and ***consequences*** are indispensable for any research agenda that seeks to introduce policy recommendations.

Context allows us to judge the validity of the essentialists' theoretical deliberations and their calls to introduce Islamic law in Western legal systems. The essentialists ignore the contexts of countries that practice legal pluralism in different parts of the world. In Chapter 3 I showed that far from being a model to emulate, the system of legal pluralism is often connected to a pyramid based on a stratified citizenry and results in the double discrimination syndrome. It violates basic civil and human rights with impunity. I also highlighted how crucial it is to any functioning modern state to have a single secular democratic legal order as a minimum basis for respecting citizenship and human rights. And yes, I am deliberately using the word 'modern'. For I continue to believe that several aspects of modernity are important if we are to have a state that treats citizens as equal before the law: a *single, secular, democratic legal order based on respect for civil and human rights.* The essentialists would flinch at my use of 'secular', but I insist that a state that is not secular is in no position to be neutral in its treatment of its citizens. A state that is secular but not democratic and does not respect civil and human rights will ultimately abuse its power. And a secular state that is democratic and respects human rights but introduces plural legal orders will ultimately discriminate against some groups of its citizens. Hence, these qualities are mutually dependent: a single secular democratic legal order must be founded on norms of civil and human rights.

Moving away from this international level, I started to examine the British case not only for its relevance but also because it is being used by some essentialists – bizarre as this may sound now – as an 'example' of successful weak legal pluralism. I also deliberately chose to look at its practice in the UK because some may argue that even if legal pluralism did not work in other 'developing' countries, it might still be possible to introduce it successfully in a Western 'developed' context. I hope the latter three chapters have provided ample evidence that this is not the case. Weak legal pluralism has created a mess in the UK.

Context is also important to highlight the type of law that the essentialists want us to introduce to 'protect' Muslim group rights. It is a bad law. Full stop. We simply cannot dance around this issue. As I showed in Chapter 4, we can philosophise all we want about shari'a as a set of general principles that seek to bring justice. The fact remains that the religious laws governing family affairs and the lives of women and children are the rigid conservative religious laws written by medieval jurists; they treat women as minors, they provide the legal basis for child and forced marriages and polygamy, and they lead to grave violations of human rights. Protection is the last outcome that you would expect from such a legal framework. I have no problem stating that shari'a is bad law: by today's standards the current versions of shari'a violate the rights of women and children with impunity. I do not consider it God's Law, as the Islamists would like us to think of it. Instead I see it as manmade laws that can be changed and replaced with modern civil laws that respect the dignity and human rights of women and children.

The two go together: dignity and human rights. They should not be separated in any discussion of human rights. This point is significant, as I showed in Chapter 4. The term dignity is vague; it lacks substance and may be used to undermine the universality of human rights. Please do not forget how, in his speech, Rowan Williams ingeniously disconnected human dignity from human rights – just as Islamists do when they discuss women's rights.

I also said that dignity should be connected to rights if we are to defend the individual. In defending the individual, we will be in a position to guarantee the rights and equality of individual members of ethnic, religious and gender groups. This process works in only one direction: respecting the rights of the individual guarantees the overall protection of the group, and not the other way around.

Context is vital because it allows us to discern the political dimension of this issue and see how Islamists have been using it for their own political agendas. There is a political dimension here that we cannot ignore. Whether in Western or in Muslim majority countries, those who are calling for the application of Islamic law are Islamists who promote a totalitarian ideology of separation, which inherently discriminates against the rights not only of women but also of minorities, citizens, and LGBT people. I used the British context to show how advocates of two types of Islamism, societal and political, have been working consistently since the 1950s to essentialise Islam and Muslims, to insist on the homogeneity of Islam and Muslims, and to present their own Islamist demands as the demands of all Muslims and of Islam. And I showed how the British policies of monoculturalism have facilitated the *construction* of the *Muslim Community*: lumping diverse communities of people with different nationalities and religious affiliations into one homogenous entity that the essentialists simply call Muslims.

The two general groups that back societal and political Islamism share a similar worldview about creating an Islamist state and implementing shari'a law, and about the supremacy of Muslims and Islam. The two groups also share a way of narrating history that portrays Muslims and Islam as perpetual victims subject to hegemonic attacks and persecution.

I showed how Islamism relates to our discussion of weak legal pluralism and the introduction of shari'a law in the family affairs of Muslim communities in the UK and the West in general. The first link, a key one, is membership: many members of the shari'a courts belong to the various movements promoting societal and political Islamism. Second is ideology: those working in the shari'a courts often display the ideological and political features of Islamism. And third, Islamists have co-opted the idea of weak legal pluralism to suit their own political agenda. Many Western politicians and academics are aware of this connection but hesitate to voice their concerns for fear of being accused of being Islamophobic. The political dimension of the issue has significant implications not only for the fight against terrorism and extremism, but also for the cohesion of society and the successful integration into British society of Muslim migrants of very diverse backgrounds.

Context matters because it necessitates examining the situation of women: the first group to suffer under the essentialists' well-intentioned call to apply Islamic law in family affairs. It allows us to see that the 'choice' narratives of proponents of legal pluralism and the 'exit option' turn out to be hollow when we look closely at the daily reality of women living in closed communities: a reality formed by patriarchal structures, social control and the rise of Islamic fundamentalism. It is within this context that women of Muslim heritage are expected to exercise their 'choice'. A choice that is so constrained by such structures, values and norms is often no choice after all. In other words, the exit option – that is, the right to exit from the jurisdiction of a legal order[5] – is not a realistic guarantee of individual rights, not for women who face the pressure to conform to tradition, who realistically fear they will bring shame on the family, and who dread losing their family and being ostracised by the community.

Looking at the context of women's reality will also allow us to understand why women are turning to shari'a councils in the UK: they go to them because they want a *religious divorce*. Unlike what many claim, women can satisfy this demand within the British legal system; they do not need the shari'a courts.

Hence, *context* allows us to judge the validity of the essentialists' theoretical deliberations and their calls to introduce Islamic law in Western legal systems. And context shows us the landscape within which these theoretical deliberations will be implemented.

And so do *consequences*. Again, and I will not tire of repeating this: the moment the state starts to situate rights within a group rights frame rather than an individual frame, the outcome will likely be segregation, inequality and discrimination. The weakest will be left vulnerable, subject to abuse and discrimination. This is the main consequence of legal pluralism in its two forms: weak and strong.

A key consequence of introducing weak legal pluralism and with it Islamic law in Western legal systems will be a stratified citizenry, involving two types of women: Western women who can enjoy their rights based on the state's laws, and migrant women who cannot. The system in the UK has in effect created these two types of citizens; one enjoys equality before the law and the other does not because of their religious identity. These women suffer from the double discrimination syndrome: in addition to gender discrimination they are also denied access to their legal rights. Indeed, this stratification will only further cement the walls around the closed parallel societies.

In addition, the system is, de facto, legitimising polygamous marriages, and facilitating child marriage and forced marriage. Most significantly for the cohesion and unity of society and the fight against extremism, it has continued to separate minority groups from their wider society and has given Islamists a free hand in reinforcing their social control over closed communities.

Throughout this book I have taken a position that defends the universality of human rights. Using the words of Frank La Rue, the former UN Special Rapporteur on the Promotion and Protection of the Right to Freedom of Opinion and Expression, these universal human rights are simply the 'minimum standards for protection'[6] for every person in any society. They are the minimum that one should expect in any society. The struggles of men and women fighting for these universal rights in different societies of the globe testify to this fact.

I argue therefore that special treatments for specific groups and the introduction of religious laws will only undermine this very universality and the protection granted by the international standards of human rights. I maintain that, rather than deliberating about whether human rights are universal or culturally determined, we should use a consequence-based approach to add needed substance to the discussion. We must bring in the human face of the suffering that results when human rights are violated – whether those are the rights of individuals or a larger society.

Such an approach can illuminate the grave consequences of violating human rights and make the case that doing so is by nature *bad*. Once we establish this fact, we will dare to make the moral judgement that these violations are *wrong*. It will also help us turn the discussion around. Rather than making frantic efforts to answer the question of whether human rights are universal, which the essentialists deny, the question will be: why are these rights being violated in the first place?[7]

A consequence-based approach to human rights reflects the idea that from a moral point of view what is most important is to 'consider how one's actions are likely to affect others.' After all, 'It is the consequences of one's actions, not the intentions behind them, which form the most relevant benchmark for measuring the moral worth of an action.'[8] If we are to apply this approach in concrete steps to our subject matter, we should look at the consequences on two levels. On the *individual* level, what individual harm is being done to the girl or woman through the application of a parallel legal system (shari'a law)? And on the *societal* level, what are the general negative consequences for society of segregating groups and creating what Amartya Sen called the monoculturalism of closed communities?

Once we understand the consequences of the parallel religious legal orders in the UK and of efforts to introduce group and identity politics and policies based on difference, we see the need for specific policy recommendations.

Policy Recommendations

I suggest that the UK government consider six policy recommendations to address the problems that women endure when they turn to shari'a courts within the framework of the UK legal system. These recommendations are also very important and relevant to other European and North American countries.

1. Make it mandatory to have a civil marriage before contracting any religious marriage; implement this ruling with clear and harsh sanctions for any imams and individuals who violate it.
2. Launch a nationwide campaign to register all Islamic marriages. This will ultimately reveal many polygamous marriages. The women who are parties to these marriages, and their children, should be protected. But that protection should not entail recognising polygamy as a form of marriage, as some essentialist legal scholars are arguing.
3. Punish the Muslim man who is involved in polygamous marriages in the same way that the UK legal system would punish a Christian, Jewish or atheist man doing the same thing.
4. Attach to the British court system a unit (with local branches nationwide) that is authorised to automatically issue an Islamic divorce after the civil divorce has been issued: a decree absolute. In many Islamic countries, the religious authorities recognise a civil divorce as religiously valid; the situation should be the same in the UK.
5. Launch a nationwide campaign that reaches women within closed communities to inform them about their rights, the importance and

protection of civil marriage, the need to register their marriage and how the law functions in the UK.

6. Abolish the parallel religious legal systems in the UK, end the work of shariʿa courts, and treat citizens and migrants as equal before the law.

To European and North American governments, I recommend eight policies for treating citizens and migrants from Islamic countries:

1. Stop reducing this minority to its religious identity. In Europe in the 1950s and 1960s, Polish or Italian migrants in Switzerland, Germany or Britain were not referred to as Catholics or Christians; they were called by their nationality. Extend the same treatment to migrants from Asian, African and Arab countries.

2. Treat them as citizens equal before the law. Or as migrants whose rights are protected under constitutional and international law.

3. Treat them as individuals, not on the basis of their group identity.

4. Do not ignore the political context (especially regarding the two forms of Islamism) and the social context (especially the patriarchal and power structures) within which members of these communities are living.

5. Look closely at the demands presented as *religious* demands of the *Muslim minority* and make sure they are not demands that reflect the political agenda of Islamists.

6. To fight violent extremism, policies must confront the societal and political messages in schools, mosques, madrassas and religious classes. In charting these policies, it is important to avoid alliances with societal or political Islamist movements, however 'non-violent' their message may seem to be.[9]

7. While religious persons have the right to be respected, these rights should be extended on an individual level – not a group level – and they should not lead to violations of gender equality or human rights.

8. Recognise that in any society there are rules of the game: A single secular democratic legal order founded on norms of civil and human rights – and these rights should apply to everyone in society.

***

This book in your hands is a direct result of a media controversy in 2009. The catalyst was a short article by a Swiss professor of social anthropology suggesting special laws for Muslims and other groups: shari'a in the case of Muslims. Given the ramifications of his call and the implications for society in general, I thought it wise to research and produce a counterargument. In this journey I realised that we are dealing with a particular paradigm of thinking. I named it, highlighted its features, and discussed its consequences.

As a female Arab academic who considers Islam to be her religion and has extensively researched the conditions for people of all genders in the Arab Middle East and North Africa (MENA) region, as a women's rights activist who has been involved in various campaigns for gender justice, and as a woman who has seen the dire consequences of the application of shari'a law, I knew all too well what the essentialist suggestion would entail.

I have seen the dire consequences of Islamic law for the lives of women and children in Arab and Islamic countries and in closed communities in the European context. I also have first-hand knowledge of how Islamism works in different contexts, how it adapts to its different circumstances yet remains faithful to its totalitarian political agenda. In their call to introduce Islamic law in Western legal systems as a means of respecting religious rights, the essentialists play into the hands of Islamists and their political agenda while concurrently constructing a 'Muslim minority'. In reality, what they are suggesting is that nations legitimise systematic discrimination against women, children and LGBT people. Such discrimination will certainly not help people in Islamic migrant communities to integrate successfully. In fact it will only cement the social control of Islamists over the closed communities.

I took a stance against this call and pleaded that we look instead at the *context* and *consequences* of such proposals. Doing that will reveal the absurdity of such a proposition along with the dire consequences not only for the minority within the minority – the women, children and LGBT people – but also for the wider society and its long-term political stability. I did that knowing that scholars and activists of Muslim heritage, both men and women, and people who live/have lived under Muslim laws have a double responsibility. They must explain and clarify what such a proposal entails; and they must raise their own voices to defend their own rights and those of women who are shut away in closed communities unable to speak for themselves. They also have a responsibility towards the Western countries, new to them, that have offered them dignity and human rights. Once the voices of all these groups are included in this discourse, the essentialist academic circles will have to recognise that the time is ripe for a paradigm shift.

NOTES

Introduction: The Debate

1. Elham Manea, 'Islamisches Recht in der Schweiz wäre verheerend', *NZZ am Sonntag*, 4 January 2009.

2. Christian Giordano, 'Der Rechtpluralismus: Ein Instrument für den Multikulturalismus? Eidgenössische Kommission gegen Rassismus', *Bulletin TANGRAM*, no. 22 (Dec. 2008), pp. 74–77.

3. The first to introduce the binary distinction between strong and weak legal pluralism was anthropologist John Griffiths. See John Griffiths, "What is Legal Pluralism?", *Journal of Legal Pluralism*, 32 (24), 1986.

4. Sheikh Haitham al-Haddad, http://www.youtube.com/watch?v=thoP4EjtmzE (accessed 24 January 2014; video was later removed from YouTube). The video and its transcript can be found on Haitham al-Haddad's blog, The Islamic Far-Right in Britain, under Islamic Supremacy. http://tifrib.com/haitham-al-haddad/ (accessed 6 April 2015).

5. Elham Manea, 'Islamisches Recht in der Schweiz wäre verheerend'.

6. Tahmina Saleem, interview by author, Luton, 27 January 2013.

7. United Nations Development Program, *Arab Human Development Report 2005: Towards the Rise of Women in the Arab World* (New York: United Nations, 2006).

8. Elham Manea, 'Islamisches Recht in der Schweiz ist gefährlich', *NZZ am Sonntag*, 3 July 2011.

9. Elham Manea, *The Arab State and Women's Rights: The Trap of Authoritarian Governance* (London: Routledge, 2011), pp. 197–198.

10. Gita Sahgal, interview by author, London, 24 January 2013.

11. Martin Beglinger, 'Bis dass der Zwang euch Bindet', Das Magazin, *Tages-Anzeiger*, vol. 24 (2007), p. 18.

Chapter 1   A Critical Review of the Essentialist Paradigm

1. Kenan Malik, *Multiculturalism and its Discontents* (London: Seagull Books, 2013), pp. 7–8.

2. Anne Phillips, *Multiculturalism Without Culture* (Princeton and Oxford: Princeton University Press, 2007), pp. 162–163. I am aware of Phillips' supportive position of the Shari'a Councils in Britain but do not see this as a reason to discard her nuanced and superb discussion of multiculturalism.

3. Ibid.

4. Charles Taylor, 'The politics of recognition', in *Multiculturalism: Examining the Politics of Recognition* (Princeton, NJ: Princeton University Press, 1994), p. 25.

5. Ibid., p. 26.

6. Ibid., p. 30.

7. Ibid., pp. 30–33.

8. Ibid., p. 40.

9. Ibid., p. 61.

10. David Pilgrim, *What was Jim Crow?* (Big Rounds, MI: Jim Crow Museum, Ferris State University). Available at http://www.ferris.edu/jimcrow/what.htm (accessed 14 July 2015).

11. Ibid.

12. Ibid.

13. Taylor, 'The politics of recognition', pp. 26–30.

14. Imaan supports the efforts of LGBT Muslim people, and their families and friends, to address issues of sexual orientation within Islam. It provides a safe space and support network where people can address issues of common concern through sharing individual experiences and institutional resources. For more information see their website http://www.imaan.org.uk/about/about.htm

15. Taylor, 'The politics of recognition', p. 68.

16. *Unreported World: The Cursed Twins of Madagascar*, Channel 4 documentary, 9 May 2014; Kiki King, 'The cursed twins of Madagascar', Huffington Post Blog entry, 9 May 2014, available at http://www.huffingtonpost.co.uk/kiki-king/unreported-world-twins-in-madagascar_b_5293247.html?utm_hp_ref=uk&i r = UK&just_reloaded = 1 (accessed 14 July 2015); IRIN, 'Madagascar: Twins taboo splits a community', *IRIN News*, UN Office for the Coordination of Humanitarian Affairs, 3 November 2011. Available at http://www.irinnews. org/report/94124/madagascar-twins-taboo-splits-a-community (accessed 14 July 2015).

17. Jack Donnelly, 'Cultural relativism and universal human rights', *Human Rights Quarterly* vi/4 (Nov. 1984), p. 401.

18. Ibid.

19. Text of Resolution 16/3 'Promoting human rights and fundamental freedoms through a better understanding of traditional values of humankind', *Human Rights Council*, 8 April 2011, http://daccess-dds-ny.un.org/doc/RESOLUTION/

GEN/G11/124/92/PDF/G1112492.pdf?OpenElement (accessed 15 July 2015).

20. Graeme Reid, 'The trouble with tradition: When "values" trample over rights', *HRW World Report* 2013. Available at http://www.hrw.org/world-report/2013/essays/trouble-tradition (accessed 14 July 2015).

21. Reza Afshari, *Human Rights in Iran: The Abuse of Cultural Relativism* (Philadelphia: University of Pennsylvania Press, 2011), p. 5.

22. Ibid., p. xvi.

23. Ibid., p. 124.

24. Quoted in ibid., p. 123.

25. Graeme Reid, 'The trouble with tradition'.

26. 'Saudi Arabia: Shura Council approves sport for girls based on the fatwa [edict] of Sheikh Ibn Baaz and postpones [the issue of] female teachers teaching boys', *CNN Arabic*, 9 April 2014 (in Arabic). Available at http://arabic.cnn.com/middleeast/2014/04/07/saudi-shura-sport-vote (accessed 14 July 2015).

27. Text of Judiciary Decision N. 34184394 (07 May 2014), in Arabic, Criminal Court, Jeddah, Saudi Arabia; 'A thousand lashes and 10 years in prison for online Saudi Arabian activist', press release, Amnesty International, 7 May 2014. Available at http://www.amnestyusa.org/news/news-item/a-thousand-lashes-and-10-years-in-prison-for-online-saudi-arabian-activist (accessed 14 July 2015).

28. Ibid.

29. Roland Burke, *Decolonization and the Evolution of International Human Rights* (Philadelphia: University of Pennsylvania Press, 2010), p. 114.

30. Ibid.

31. The term white man's burden first appeared as the title of a 1899 poem by the English poet Rudyard Kipling, calling on the white man to colonise nations to help the people living in these nations; it became emblematic both of Eurocentric racism and of Western aspirations to dominate the developing world. William Easterly used the title for his book *The White Man's Burden* (Oxford University Press, 2007); in it he criticised aid work in developing nations, and chastised the complacent and patronising attitude of the West that attempts to impose solutions from above.

32. Taylor, 'The politics of recognition', pp. 63–64.

33. Adamantia Pollis and Peter Schwab, *Human Rights: Cultural and Ideological Perspectives* (New York, Praeger, 1979), pp. 1–17.

34. Ibid., p. 12.

35. Taylor, 'The politics of recognition', p. 65.

36. Pollis and Schwab, *Human Rights*, p. 10.

37. Feras Shamsan, interview by author, via Skype, 18 May 2014.

38. Adamantia Pollis, 'Cultural Relativism Revisited: Through a State Prism', *Human Rights Quarterly*, 18.2 (1996), p. 316.

39. Ibid., p. 320.

40. Meredith Tax, *Double Bind: The Muslim Right, the Anglo-American Left, and Universal Human Rights* (London: Centre for Secular Space, 2012), p. 99.
41. Ibid., p. 74.
42. Ibid., p. 96.
43. Agence France Presse AFP, 'A human rights organization demands the release of prisoners of conscience in Gulf Countries', *Swissinfo*, 16 May 2014, in Arabic. Available at http://www.swissinfo.ch/ara/detail/content.html?cid=38599094 (accessed 15 July 2015).

Chapter 2   Islamic Law in the West: The Case of Britain

1. Christian Giordano, 'Der Rechtpluralismus: Ein Instrument für den Multikulturalismus? Eidgenössische Kommission gegen Rassismus', *Bulletin TANGRAM*, no. 22 (Dec. 2008), p. 77.
2. Sternstunde Philosophie, 'Islamisches Recht in Europa? Die Zürcher Professorin Andrea Büchler im Gespräch mit Roger de Weck', programme on Sternstunde Philosophie, Swiss TV, 11 January 2009. Available at http://www.srf.ch/player/tv/sternstunde-philosophie/video/sternstunde-philosophie-islamisches-recht-in-europa-die-zuercher-professorin-andrea-buechler-im-gespraech-mit-roger-de-weck?id=2a039aea-b02e-489b-9984-3c4e80d885af (accessed 15 July 2015).
3. John R. Bowen, *Blaming Islam* (Cambridge, MA: Boston Review Books, 2012), p. 74.
4. Quoted in Laura Muchowiecka, 'The end of multiculturalism? Immigration and integration in Germany and the United Kingdom', *Student Pulse*, v/6 (2013). Available at http://www.studentpulse.com/a?id=735 (accessed 15 July 2015).
5. An additional 126,000 came from the Caribbean islands, 66,000 from Malta and Cyprus and 50,000 from China. Ibid.
6. Ibid.
7. A British far-right political party for Whites only, opposed to non-White immigration, and committed to a programme of repatriation. According to its webpage, 'Multiracialism has been a disaster for Britain – only a policy that enforces a total ban on immigration and the humane repatriation of all immigrants and their descendants to their ancestral homelands can save this country from chaos'. Available at http://www.britishnationalfront.net/whatwestandfor.html (accessed date 27 July 2015).
8. Ed Husain, *The Islamist* (London: Penguin Books, 2007), p. 2.
9. Kenan Malik, *From Fatwa to Jihad: The Rushdie Affair and its Aftermath* (Brooklyn, NY: Melville House Publishing, 2009), p. 18.
10. Ibid., p. xii.
11. Enoch Powell, 'Rivers of blood' speech, republished in the *Telegraph*, 6 Nov 2007. Available at http://www.telegraph.co.uk/comment/3643823/Enoch-Powells-Rivers-of-Blood-speech.html (accessed 15 July 2015).

12. Text of Roy Jenkins', speech 'This is the Goal', London, 23 May 1966, quoted in Brian MacArthur, *The Penguin Book of Twentieth-Century Speeches* (London: Penguin Books, 1999), p. 363.

13. Amartya Sen, 'The uses and abuses of multiculturalism', *The New Republic*, 27 February 2006.

14. Ibid.

15. BBC, '1969: Sikh busmen win turban fight', *BBC, On This Day*. Available at http://news.bbc.co.uk/onthisday/hi/dates/stories/april/9/newsid_2523000/2523691.stm (accessed 15 July 2015).

16. Ibid.

17. *Motor Cycles (Wearing of Helmets) Regulations 1973*. Statutory Instrument, 1973, No. 180.

18. 'Mandla (Sewa Singh) and another v Dowell Lee and and others [1983] 2 AC 548', House of Lords 24 March 1983. Available at http://www.equalrightstrust. org/ertdocumentbank/Micro %20Word%20-%20Mandla.pdf (accessed 15 July 2015).

19. Stonehouse statement quoted in Enoch Powell, 'Rivers of blood'.

20. Trevor Phillips, 'Not a river of blood, but a tide of hope', speech, 20 April 2008. Available at http://resources.cohesioninstitute.org.uk/Publications/Documents/Document/Default.aspx?recordId=44 (accessed 15 July 2015).

21. Malik, *From Fatwa to Jihad*, p. xix; Malik, *Multiculturalism and its Discontents* (London: Seagull, 2013), p. 19.

22. Munira Mirza, Abi Senthikumaran, and Zein Ja'far, 'Living apart together: British Muslims and the paradox of multiculturalism', *Policy Exchange Report*, 2007, pp. 23–24.

23. Ibid.

24. Ibid., p. 24.

25. Malik, *Multiculturalism*, pp. 58–59.

26. Ibid., p. 59.

27. Ibid., pp. 60–61.

28. Quoted in ibid., p. 62.

29. Phillips, 'Not a river of blood'.

30. Trevor Phillips, 'After 7/7: Sleepwalking to segregation', speech, 22 September 2005. Available at http://www.humanities.manchester.ac.uk/socialchange/research/social-change/summer-workshops/documents/sleepwalking.pdf.

31. Colin Brown, 'Let us adopt Islamic family law to curb extremists, Muslims tell Kelly', *The Independent*, 15 August 2006. Available at http://www.independent.co.uk/news/uk/politics/let-us-adopt-islamic-family-law-to-curb-extremists-muslims-tell-kelly-411954.html (accessed 15 July 2015).

32. Ihsan Yilmaz, *Muslim Laws, Politics and Society in Modern Nation States: Dynamic Legal Pluralism in England, Turkey and Pakistan* (Farnham, Surrey: Ashgate Publishing, 2005), p. 2.

33. See Ralph Grillo et al. (eds), *Legal Practice and Cultural Diversity* (Surrey: Ashgate, 2009); John Griffiths, 'What is Legal Pluralism?'; Ihsan Yilmaz,

'The challenge of post-modern legality and Muslim legal pluralism in England', *Journal of Ethnic and Migration Studies* xxvii/2 (April 2002); Yilmaz, *Muslim Laws*; Baudoiun Dupret, Maurits Berger, and Laila al-Zwaini (eds), *Legal Pluralism in the Arab World* (The Hague: Kluwer Law International, 1999); Michael Kemper and Maurus Reinkowski (eds), *Rechtspluralismus in der islamischen Welt: Gewohnheitsrecht zwischen Staat und Gesellschaft* (Berlin: Walter de Gruyter, 2005).

34. Ralph Grillo et al. (eds), pp. 25–26.

Chapter 3   Legal Pluralism in Practice

1. Albert Hourani, *Minorities in the Arab World* (London, New York: Oxford University Press, 1947), p. 22.

2. For example, while it is common knowledge that France's political and legal world was obsessed with cultural links and what it termed a *mission civilisatrice*, new research, like that by Mounira Charrad, has highlighted how France used different strategies to rule over each of its Maghribi colonies with varying 'implications for the degree of political centralization, strength of tribal solidarities, and the legal system of each country.' Mounira Charrad *States and Women's Rights: The Making of Postcolonial Tunisia, Algeria, and Morocco* (Berkeley: University of California Press, 2001), Chapter 6, pp. 114–144; Nazih H. Ayubi, *Over-Stating the Arab State: Politics and Society in the Middle East*, 3rd ed. (London: I.B.Tauris, 2006), pp. 89 ff.

3. Elham Manea, *The Arab State and Women's Rights: The Trap of Authoritarian Governance* (London: Routledge, 2011), pp. 35–41.

4. Ibid., p. 68.

5. Ibid., p. 42; Butrus Abu-Manneh, 'The Christians between Ottomanism and Syrian nationalism: The ideas of Butrus Al-Bustani', *International Journal of Middle East Studies*, xi/3 (May 1980), p. 287.

6. For example, Sheikh Abu Hamid al-Ghazali (1058–1111) determined that they 'apostatize in matters of blood, money, marriage, and butchering, so it is a duty to kill them'; and Sheikh Ahmad ibn Taymiya (1268–1238) considered that 'war and punishment [...] against them, are among the greatest of pious deeds and the most important obligations (for a Muslim)'. Manea, *The Arab State*, pp. 42–43; Eyal Zisser, 'The Alawis, lords of Syria', in Ofra Bengio and Gabriel Bendor (eds), *Minorities and the State in the Arab World* (London: Lynne Rienner, 1999), p. 130; Hourani, *Minorities in the Arab World*, p. 20.

7. Manea, *The Arab State*, p. 68; Stanford Jay Shaw, 'Ottoman Empire', *Encyclopedia Britannica Online*. Available at http://www.britannica.com/place/Ottoman-Empire (accessed 15 July 2015).

8. Quoted in Manea, *The Arab State*, p. 68. Fouad Shubat, *The Organization of Personal Status for Non-Muslims: Legislation and Judiciary in Syria and Lebanon*, in Arabic (Damascus: The Higher Institute for Arab Studies, 1966), p. 51.

9. Manea, *The Arab State*, pp. 41–42, 68–69; Abu-Manneh, 'The Christians'.

10. Hourani, *Minorities in the Arab World*.

11. Trevor Phillips, 'After 7/7: Sleepwalking to segregation', speech, 22 September 2005. Available at http://www.humanities.manchester.ac.uk/socialchange/res earch/social-change/summer-workshops/documents/sleepwalking.pdf

12. Manea, *The Arab State*, p. 190.

13. Ibid., pp. 256–257.

14. Amnesty International, 'Sudan: Mother at risk of flogging and death sentence: Meriam Yehia Ibrahim', Urgent Action, 13 May 2014. Available at http://www. amnesty.org/en/library/info/AFR54/006/2014/en (accessed 15 July 2015); Amnesty International, 'Sudan: Woman sentenced to death for her beliefs: Meriam Yehia Ibrahim' (16 May 2014). http://www.amnesty.org/en/library/asset/ AFR54/007/2014/en/ffc8916a-01f8-43f3-be3c-87c91360fecb/afr540072014en. html (accessed 15 July 2015); Nima Elbagir and Laura Smith-Spark, 'Sudanese Christian woman: "There's a new problem every day"', *CNN online*, 1 July 2014, available at http://edition.cnn.com/2014/07/01/world/africa/sudan-apostasy-case/index.html?hpt=hp_c6 (accessed 15 July 2015); Elham Manea, 'And yet it moves: One Meriam Yehia Ibrahim', *Modern Discussion*, 26 May 2014, available at http://www.ahewar.org/debat/show.art.asp?aid=416536 (accessed 15 July 2015).

15. This case is based on the research I conducted in Syria in 2007 and published in Chapter Nine of my book, *The Arab State and Women's Rights*, pp. 160–187.

16. Taken from Manea, *The Arab State*, p. 173.

17. Ibid., 171–172.

18. Ibid.

19. For more information see Elham Manea, *Regional Politics in the Gulf: Saudi Arabia, Oman, Yemen* (London: Saqi, 2005), pp. 21–22, 73–74.

20. Human Rights Watch (HRW), *Denied Dignity: Systematic Discrimination and Hostility toward Saudi Shia Citizens* (New York: HRW, 2009), p. 12.

21. Wajeha al-Huwaider, women's activist, email interview with author, June 2008.

22. The following section is based on a paper I published in July 2008: 'The Arab state and women's rights: The case of Saudi Arabia – The limits of the possible', *Orient – German Journal for Politics, Economics and Culture of the Middle East*, II/2008, pp. 15–25.

23. Manea, Ibid.; Saudi Women for Reform, *The Shadow Report for CEDAW* (Geneva: CEDAW, December 2007), pp. 13–14.

24. Manea, Ibid.; Saudi Women for Reform, *Shadow Report*.

25. May Yamani, *Cradle of Islam: The Hijaz and the Quest for an Arabian Identity* (London: I.B.Tauris, 2004).

26. Quoted in Manea, 'The case of Saudi Arabia', p. 23; Yamani, *Cradle of Islam*, pp. 80–81.

27. Manea, Ibid., pp. 23–24; Yamani, Ibid., p. 85.

28. Syrian interviewee no. 1, writer and journalist, interview by author, Syria, July 2007.

29. Gita Sahgal, interview by author, London, 24 January 2013.
30. Manea, 'The case of Saudi Arabia', p. 191.
31. Ibid., p. 198.
32. Human Rights Watch, *Denied Dignity*, pp. 12–13.
33. For more information on the systematic nature of this discrimination see Human Rights Watch, *Denied Dignity*; Nina Shea, *Saudi Arabia's Curriculum of Intolerance* (Washington, DC: Center for Religious Freedom Freedom House, and Institute of Gulf Affairs, 2006); Manea, *Regional Politics*, pp. 80–85.
34. Shea, *Saudi Arabia's Curriculum of Intolerance*, p. 13.
35. Field visit to Syria, 2007.
36. Syrian interviewee no. 2, writer and intellectual, interview by author, Syria, July 2007.
37. For more information see Manea, 'The case of Saudi Arabia', pp. 95–109.
38. Human Rights Watch, *Perpetual Minors: Human Rights Abuses Stemming from Male Guardianship and Sex Segregation in Saudi Arabia* (New York: HRW, 2008), p. 2.
39. Manea, 'The case of Saudi Arabia', p. 17.
40. Ibid., pp. 164–165.
41. Field visit to Syria, 2007.
42. Medhat Kalada, President of Copts United, an NGO that advocates for Copts' civil rights in Egypt: private telephone and email correspondence with author, 10–11 July 2014.
43. 'Names and details: Suspicious provisions of the customary session revealed by the lawyer of the accused Copts in Almataria avents', *Copts Today*, 18 June 2014 (in Arabic). Available at http://www.coptstoday.com/Copts-News/Detail.php?Id=78200 (accessed 15 July 2015); Egyptian Initiative for Personal Rights (EIPR), 'Part two: Sectarian tension and violence', *Quarterly Report on Freedom of Religion and Belief: April–June 2009*, in Arabic, EIPR website. Available at http://www.eipr.org/report/2009/12/12/286/290 (accessed 15 July 2015).
44. Mustafa Rahouma, 'Customary reconciliation: Treatment of sectarian strife through 'Sessions of humiliation and submission', *Al Watan News*, 6 January 2014, in Arabic. Available at http://www.elwatannews.com/news/details/387792 (accessed 15 July 2015). For another official position of the church towards customary law sessions see Alaa Aldin Al Minyawi, 'Bishop Makarios: Customary law sessions detract from state's status', in Arabic, *Al Bawaba News*, 16 December 2013, in Arabic. Available at http://www.albawabhnews.com/270124 (accessed 15 July 2015).
45. *Report on Sectarian Incidents in Egypt*. In Arabic. Egyptian Initiative for Personal Rights, 5 January 2012. Available at http://eipr.org/pressrelease/2012/01/05/1339 (accessed 15 July 2015). For a translation of the report please see http://sectarianviolenceegypt2012.blogspot.ch/2013/04/i-sectarian-violence-that-lead-to.html. (accessed 15 July 2015).
46. See for example Amira Hisham, 'Maspero Youth Union declares his rejection of customary reconciliation (session) in Alminia Events and describes it as

attempts to destroy state's sovereignty', *Ahram Gate*, 12 August 2013, in Arabic. Available at http://gate.ahram.org.eg/News/381765.aspx (accessed 15 July 2015). Medhat Kalada, President of Copts United, called customary sessions 'the reconciliation of humiliation' in his speech on Almataria events at the hearing of the Egyptian National Council for Human Rights on 2 July 2014; private telephone and email correspondence with author, 11 July 2014.

47. Rania Nabil, 'A human rights defender denounces the reconciliation between Muslims and Copts in Almataria and describes it as a shameful stigma', 14 June 2014, in Arabic. Available at http://www.altahrir.com/details.php?ID=29416 (accessed 15 July 2015).

48. Declaration of Israel's Independence 1948, Tel Aviv, 14 May 1948. Available at http://stateofisrael.com/declaration/ (accessed 15 July 2015).

49. Michael Mousa Karayanni, 'The separate nature of the religious accommodations for the Palestinian-Arab minority in Israel', *Northwestern Journal International of Human Rights* v/1 (Fall 2007), pp. 43–48.

50. Sarah Slan, *Arabisch-Jüdische Paare in Israel: Auswirkungen des Politischen Systems* (unpublished master's thesis, Zurich University, 2012), pp. 67–68.

51. Yüksel Sezgin, *Human Rights under State-Enforced Religious Family Laws in Israel, Egypt and India* (Cambridge, UK: Cambridge University Press, 2013), pp. 5–9.

52. Ibid., pp. 99–100.

53. Ibid., p. 97.

54. Ibid., pp. 97–98.

55. Werner Menski, *Comparative Law in a Global Context: The Legal Systems of Asia and Africa*, 2nd ed. (Cambridge, UK: Cambridge University Press, 2006), p. 356.

56. Ibid., p. 370.

57. Ibid.

58. Ibid.

59. Ibid., p. 373.

60. Encyclopedia Britannica (EB) editors, 'Ahmadiyyah', *Encyclopædia Britannica*. Available at http://www.britannica.com/EBchecked/topic/10189/Ahmadiyyah; Shahid Javed Burki, 'Pakistan', *Encyclopædia Britannica*. Available at http://www.britannica.com/EBchecked/topic/438805/Pakistan/23691/Religion (accessed 18 July 2015).

61. EB editors, 'Ahmadiyyah'; Burki, 'Pakistan'.

62. Shahid Khan, *Invisible Citizens of Pakistan: Minorities in Focus, Report 2013–2014* (Glasgow: Global Minorities Alliance, 2014). Available at http://www.globalminorities.co.uk/images/GMA%20Reports/Invisible%20Citizens%20of%20Pakistan%20Minorities%20in%20Focus%20Report%202013-2014.pdf (accessed 15 July 2015).

63. Sezgin, *Human Rights*, pp. 113–114.

64. Ibid., p. 71.

65. Naheda Mehboob Ellahi, *Family Laws and Judicial Protection*, p. 9. Available at Supreme Court of Pakistan, http://www.supremecourt.gov.pk/ijc/articles/21/1. pdf (accessed 15 July 2015).

66. Ibid.

67. Ibid., pp. 3, 11.

68. Participatory Development Initiatives (PDI), *Role of Tribal Jirga in Violence Against Women: A Case Study of Karo Kari in Sindh* (Karachi: PDI, 2005); Sherzaman Taizi, *Jirga System in Tribal Life* (Williamsburg, VA: Tribal Analysis Center, 2007). Available at http://www.tribalanalysiscenter.com/PDF-TAC/ Jirga%20System%20in%20Tribal%20Life.pdf (accessed 15 July 2015).

69. PDI, *Role of Tribal Jirga*, p. 23.

70. Ibid., pp. 26–27.

71. Ibid., p. 28.

72. Mukhtar Mai, *Die Schuld eine Frau zu sein* (Munich: Droemer, 2006), in German, pp. 5–18; Nicholas D. Kristof and Sheryl WuDunn, *Half the Sky: Turning Oppression into Opportunity for Women Worldwide* (New York & Toronto: Alfred Knopf, 2009), pp. 70–71; BBC News, 'Mukhtar Mai: History of a rape case', *BBC online*, 28 June 2005. Available at http://news.bbc.co.uk/2/hi/south_asia/ 4620065.stm (accessed 15 July 2015).

73. Human Rights Commission of Pakistan (HRCP), 'Conditions for fair elections', 3 May 2013. Available at http://hrcp-web.org/hrcpweb/conditions-for-fair-elections (accessed 15 July 2015). See also the HRCP report, *State of Human Rights in 2013*, which documented cases of Jirga verdicts against women: http://www.hrcp-web.org/hrcpweb/report14/AR2013.pdf (accessed 15 July 2015).

74. International Council on Human Rights Policy (ICHRP), *When Legal Worlds Overlap: Human Rights, State and Non-State Law* (Geneva, ICHRP, 2009). Available at http://papers.ssrn.com/sol3/papers.cfm?abstract_id=1551229 (accessed 15 July 2015).

75. James Anaya, *Report of the Special Rapporteur on the Rights of Indigenous Peoples: The Situation of Indigenous Peoples in Canada* (New York: UN General Assembly, Human Rights Council, 27th session, 4 July 2014), p. 4. Available at http://unsr. jamesanaya.org/docs/countries/2014-report-canada-a-hrc-27-52-add-2-en.pdf (accessed 15 July 2015).

76. Ibid., pp. 4–6. For more information on the Indian Act see Jay Makarenko, 'The Indian Act: Historical overview', *Mapleleafweb*, 2 June 2008. Available at http://mapleleafweb.com/features/the-indian-act-historical-overview (accessed 15 July 2015).

77. ICHRP, *When Legal Worlds Overlap*, p. 38.

78. Sandra Lovelace v. Canada, Communication No. R.6/24, U.N. Doc. Supp. No. 40 (A/36/40) at 166 (1981), view 9.2. Available at http://www1.umn.edu/hum anrts/undocs/session36/6-24.htm (accessed 15 July 2015).

79. ICHRP, *When Legal Worlds Overlap*, p. 38.

80. Ibid., p. 80.

Chapter 4   Islamic Law and Human Rights Between Theory and Reality: Britain as a Showcase

1. Archbishop Rowan Williams, 'Civil and religious law in England: A religious perspective' (lecture at the Royal Courts of Justice, 7 February 2008), p. 2. Available at http://rowanwilliams.archbishopofcanterbury.org/articles.php/1137/arc...re-civil-and-religious-law-in-england-a-religious-perspective#Lecture (accessed 16 July 2015).

2. Quoted in Dominic McGoldrick, 'The compatibility of an Islamic/shari'a law system or shari'a rules with the European Convention on Human Rights', in Robin Griffith-Jones (ed.), *Islam and English Law: Rights, Responsibilities and the Place of Sharia* (Cambridge: Cambridge University Press, 2013), p. 55.

3. Williams, 'Civil and religious law', pp. 1–2.

4. Ibid., p. 3.

5. Ibid., p. 3.

6. Ibid.

7. Interviews by author, London, St. Albans, Newcastle, August 2013.

8. International Council on Human Rights Policy (ICHRP), *When Legal Worlds Overlap: Human Rights, State and Non-State Law* (Geneva: ICHRP, 2009), p. 103.

9. Ibid.

10. Rajendra Pradhan, 'Negotiating multiculturalism in Nepal: Law, hegemony, contestation and paradox' (paper presented at conference, Constitutionalism and Diversity in Nepal, Kathmandu, 22–24 August 2007), p. 4. Available at http://www.uni-bielefeld.de/midea/pdf/Rajendra.pdf (accessed 16 July 2015).

11. Islamic Sharia Council, 'About us', available at http://test.islamic-sharia.org/?page_id=32 (accessed 16 July 2015).

12. Sheikh Haitham al-Haddad, http://www.youtube.com/watch?v=thoP4EjtmzE (accessed 24 January 2014; video was later removed from YouTube).

13. Baroness Caroline Cox, 'From a distinguished peer fighting to protect women... Sharia marriages for girls of 12 and the religious courts subverting British law', the *Daily Mail*, 14 September 2012. Available at http://www.dailymail.co.uk/news/article-2202991/Sharia-marriages-girls-12-religious-courts-subverting-British-law.html#ixzz38ruyG49M (accessed 16 July 2015).

14. Sheikh Dr Suhaib Hasan, interview by author, Leyton, London, 28 January 2013.

15. Haitham Al-Haddad, 'Why marriages fail? (WMF 1 of 7): The Scale of the Problem' YouTube video, available at https://www.youtube.com/watch?v=z37H-NuyY1c&list = PLA637A16BD2ABC692&index = 1 (accessed 16 July 2015).

16. Mona Mahmood and Richard Sprenger, 'Inside a sharia divorce court' (video), *The Guardian*, 9 March 2011, available at www.guardian.co.uk/law/video/2011/mar/09/islam-sharia-council-divorce (accessed 16 July 2015).

17. ICHRP, *When Legal Worlds Overlap*, pp. 107–108. For a refined theoretical discussion of the exit option see Phillips, *Multiculturalism without Culture*, pp. 166–176.

18. Ibid.
19. Field visit to the UK, January 2013.
20. Lord Stanley Kalms, statement during second reading in House of Lords of Arbitration and Mediation Services (Equality) Bill (19 October 2012), column 1703. Available at http://www.publications.parliament.uk/pa/ld201213/ldhansrd/text/121019-0002.htm (accessed 16 July 2015).
21. (ICHRP), *When Legal Worlds Overlap*, p. 108.
22. Gita Sahgal, interview by author, London, 24 January 2013.
23. Elham Manea (2010), 'Islam and human dignity: A consequence-based approach to human dignity and rights', in Dorothèe Deimann and Simon Mugier (eds), *Entgegensprechen: Texte zu Menschenwürde und Menschenrecht*, vol. 1 (Basel: edition gesowip, 2010).
24. Brian Orend, *Human Rights: Concept and Context* (Peterboro, Ontario, Canada: Broadview Press, 2002), p. 87. Quoted in Manea, 'Islam and human dignity', p. 500.
25. Ibid.
26. Mary Ann Glendon, *A World Made New: Eleanor Roosevelt and the Universal Declaration of Human Rights* (New York: Random House, 2011), p. 145, quoted in Manea, ibid., p. 500.
27. Examples are abundant. In 2008, the American President's Council on Bioethics tried, and failed, to reach a consensus about what dignity meant. The Council's chair explained that failure in a letter directed to the President of the United States, saying, 'there is no universal agreement on the meaning of the term, human dignity'. Quoted in Manea, ibid., p. 501.
28. UN General Assembly, Human Rights Council, *Draft Report of the Human Rights Council on its Tenth Session*, p. 79, quoted in Manea, Ibid., p. 502, available at http://www2.ohchr.org/english/bodies/hrcouncil/docs/10session/edited_versionL.11Revised.pdf (accessed 16 July 2015).
29. The Muslim World League, founded in Mecca in 1962 by Islamic religious leaders from 22 countries, is one of the largest Islamic/ist non-governmental organisations that promotes and propagates Wahhabi Islam worldwide. The Organization of the Islamic Conference is an intergovernmental organisation established in Rabat in 1969 and composed of 57 Muslim states. Manea, Ibid., p. 505; Karl Kreuzer, 'International instruments in human rights and shariah law', In Hélène Gaudemet-Tallon, T. Azzi et al. (eds), *Vers de nouveaux équilibres entre ordres juridiques. Liber amicorum* (Paris: Dalloz, 2008), pp. 345–364.
30. Manea, Ibid., pp. 505–506; Ebrahim Moosa, 'The dilemma of Islamic rights schemes', *Worlds & Knowledges Otherwise* (Fall 2004), pp. 8–9.
31. Manea, Ibid., pp. 508–509; Universal Islamic Declaration of Human Rights (UIDHR) (London: Islamic Council, 1981), available at http://www.alhewar.com/ISLAMDECL.html (accessed 16 July 2015); Cairo Declaration on Human Rights in Islam (CDHRI) (Cairo: The Conference of Islamic Countries, 1990). Available at http://www.arabhumanrights.org/publications/regional/islamic/cairo-declaration-islam-93e.pdf (accessed 16 July 2015).

32. Manea, ibid.; UIDHR.
33. Ibid. The CDHRI repeated the same parameters outlined above, restricting the political rights of minorities by the provisions of shari-a. Thus, it says in Article 23, Clause B: 'Everyone shall have the right to participate, directly or indirectly in the administration of his country's public affairs. He shall also have the right to assume public office in accordance with the provisions of Shari'ah'. Manea, ibid., pp. 509–510.
34. Williams, 'Civil and religious law in England'.
35. Ibid.
36. McGoldrick, 'The compatibility of an Islamic/shari'a law system', p. 46.
37. Sara Glazer, 'Are British sharia councils out of touch', *CQ Global Research*, vi/1 (3 January 2012), pp. 6–7.
38. Quoted in Glazer., ibid.
39. Tahmina Saleem, interview by author, Luton, 27 January 2013.
40. Werner Menski, *Comparative Law in a Global Context: The Legal Systems of Asia and Africa*, 2nd ed. (Cambridge, UK: Cambridge University Press, 2006), p. 372.
41. Cassandra Balchin, *Information and Advice on Muslim Marriages in Britain* (Birmingham: Muslim Women's Network UK, 2012), p. 12. Available at http://www.mwnuk.co.uk//go_files/factsheets/945946-MWNUKMarri ageBookletFinal-compressed.pdf (accessed 18 July 2015).
42. Sheikh Hasan, interview, January 2013.
43. Sheikh Faizul Aqtab Siddiqi, interview by author, Nuneaton, 15 January 2013.
44. Dr Mohammad Shahoot Kharfan, interview by author, London, 22 January 2013.
45. Sheikh Mohammad Talha Bokhari, interview by author, Birmingham, 23 January 2013.
46. Amra Bone, interview by author, Birmingham, 11 August 2013.
47. Sohail Akbar Warraich and Cassandra Balchin, *Recognizing the Un-recognized: Inter-country Cases and Muslim Marriages & Divorces in Britain* (London: Women Living Under Muslim Laws, 2006), p. 72.
48. Ihsan Yilmaz, 'The challenge of post-modern legality and Muslim legal pluralism in England', *Journal of Ethnic and Migration Studies* xxvii/2 (April 2002), p. 346.
49. Anver M. Emon, *Religious Pluralism and Islamic Law: Dhimmis and Others in the Empire of Law* (Oxford: Oxford University Press, 2012), pp. 8–9.
50. Shari-a is derived from four sources: 1) the Qur'an, compiled into a written text approximately 30 years after the death of Mohammad; 2) the Sunna, the sayings and deeds of Mohammad, compiled in a written form approximately 200 years after his death; 3) *Ijma*, the consensus of legal jurists on an issue; and 4) *Qiyas*, analogy: 'a jurist concluding from a given principle embodied in a precedent that a new case falls under this principle or is similar to this precedent on the strength of a common essential feature called the reason.' *Qiyas* is often considered similar to *ijtihad*, defined as independent juristic reasoning and a technique for such reasoning. However, the gates of *ijtihad* were supposed to

have been closed after the ninth century. For more information please see Abdullahi Ahmed An-Na'im, *Toward an Islamic Reformation: Civil Liberties, Human Rights, and International Law* (Syracuse, NY: Syracuse University Press, 1990), pp. 19–25.

51. Ibid.

52. Majid Khadduri, 'Human rights in Islam', *Annals of the American Academy of Political and Social Science* vol. 243 (January 1946), p. 79.

53. An-Na'im, *Toward an Islamic Reformation*', p. 171.

54. Ahmed Shukri, *Muhammedan Law of Marriage and Divorce* (New York: Ams Press, 1996), p. 21.

55. Ibid.

56. Yemen's Family Law No. 20, 1992 states in Article 1: 'Marriage is a union between the couple by a legal charter; it gives the man legal permission to access the woman (sexually), and together they establish a family based on good companionship'. Kuwaiti Personal Status Law, No. 51, 1984, states in Article 1: 'Marriage is a contract between a man and a woman. [With it] a woman becomes legally (sexually) accessible to the man; and its aim is settlement, chastity, and the strength of the nation. The Syrian Islamic Personal Status Law, No. 59, 1953, says in Article 1: 'Marriage is a contract between a man and a woman. [With it] a woman becomes legally accessible to the man (sexually); and its aim is building a mutual life bond and children'. This perception of marriage does change, however, when the Islamic law is reformed as with the case of the reformed Moroccan Family Code (*Moudawana*) of 2004, which states in Article 4 that 'Marriage is a legal contract by which a man and a woman mutually consent to unite in a common and enduring conjugal life. Its purpose is fidelity, virtue and the creation of a stable family, under the supervision of both spouses according to the provisions of this Moudawana.'

57. For more on this subject see Andrea Büchler and Christina Schlatter (2013), 'Marriage age in Islamic and contemporary Muslim family laws: A comparative survey', *Electronic Journal of Islamic and Middle Eastern Law*, vol. 1, pp. 37–74.

58. Elham Manea, *'Ich will nicht mehr schweigen': Der Islam, der Westen und die Menschenrechte* (Freiburg: Herder Verlag, 2009), p. 34.

59. Some of the Twelver Shi'a jurists added the condition that for a woman to enjoy this right, she should previously have been married. For more details on the jurisprudences positions on guardianship see Wael B. Hallaq, *Shari'a: Theory, Practice and Transformations* (Cambridge: Cambridge University Press, 2007), pp. 274–276.

60. Ahmed Shukri, *Muhammedan Law of Marriage and Divorce*, p. 97.

61. Ibid., p. 81; David Pearl, *A Textbook on Muslim Law* (London: Croom Helm, 1979), p. 65.

62. Manea, *'Ich will nicht mehr schweigen'*, pp. 141–143.

63. Imam Mohammad Abu Zahrah, *Ahkam Al Tirkat wa al Mawari'ith – Provisions for Legacies and Inheritances*, in Arabic (Beirut: Dar Al Fikr Al Arabi, 1963), pp. 122, 131; An-Na'im, *Toward an Islamic Reformation*, p. 176.

64. An-Na'im, ibid., p. 176.
65. Chibli Mallat, *Introduction to Middle Eastern Law* (Oxford: Oxford University Press, 2007), p. 357.
66. United Nations Development Program, *Arab Human Development Report 2005: 'Towards the Rise of Women in the Arab World'* (New York: United Nations Publications, 2006), p. 189, quoted in Manea, *The Arab State and Women's Rights*, p. 6.
67. UNDP, quoted in Manea, ibid.
68. UNDP, quoted in Manea, ibid., pp. 6–7.
69. For more information see Women Living Under Muslim Laws (WLUML), *Knowing our Rights: Women, Family, Laws and Customs in the Muslim World* (London: WLUML, 2006), pp. 65–93; and Farzaneh Roudi-Fahimi and Shaimaa Ibrahim, *Ending Child Marriage in the Arab Region* (Washington, DC: Population Reference Bureau, 2013), pp. 1–7.
70. WLUML, ibid.; Roudi-Famimi and Ibrahim, ibid.
71. Sheikh Mohammad Talha Bokhari, interview by author, ibid.

Chapter 5   Islamism and Islamic Law in the West: Stating the Obvious? Britain as an Example

1. Usama Hasan, 'A Submission regarding Baroness Cox's Arbitration & Mediation Services (Equality) Bill' (London: Quilliam Foundation, 17 October 2012), p. 1.
2. His exact quote was 'in retrospect we might have been more cautious about allowing the creation in the 1950s of substantial Muslim communities here, although when one observes the, in some ways, greater problems which France and Germany have in this respect, it is an illusion to believe that in the integrated world of today any major country can remain exclusively indigenous'; Roy Jenkins in the *Independent Magazine* (4 March 1989), p. 16.
3. Lorenzo Divino, *The New Muslim Brotherhood in the West* (New York: Columbia University Press, 2010), p. 115; Office for National Statistics (ONS), 'FOI request: Statistics of the Muslim population in the UK for 2011, 2012, 2013 (London: ONS, 16 May 2013).
4. Change Institute, *Summary Report: Understanding Muslim Ethnic Communities* (London: Change Institute, Department for Communities and Local Government, April 2009), pp. 19–23.
5. Ibid.
6. Change Institute, *The Pakistani Muslim Community in England: Understanding Muslim Ethnic Communities* (London: Change Institute, Department for Communities and Local Government, March 2009), p. 38. Sindhis are people from Sindh, the southeastern province of Pakistan. The region agreed to join Pakistan in 1947 as an 'autonomous and sovereign' state but it still does not have the provincial autonomy to govern its own affairs that was promised in

the Pakistan Resolution of 1940. This makes many Sindhis feel aggrieved and reflects on their identification with Pakistan. Balochis are from Baluchistan, a formerly independent nation that was annexed by Pakistan in 1948; nationalist movements have continued to struggle for autonomy and to protest against human rights abuses in the province.

7. Percentage of Cyprus-born population in England of Muslim heritage.

8. Elham Manea, *The Arab State and Women's Rights: The Trap of Authoritarian Governance* (London: Routledge, 2011), pp. 181–183.

9. Oliver Roy, *Islamic Radicalism in Afghanistan and Pakistan.* UNHCR Emergency and Security Service WRITENET Paper No. 06/2001 (Paris: CNRS, January 2002). Available at http://www.refworld.org/pdfid/ 3c6a3f7d2.pdf (accessed 1 July 2015).

10. Barbara D. Metcalf, *Traditionalist Islamic Activism: Deobandi, Tablighis, and Talibs* (Leiden: ISIM, 2002).

11. Roy, *Islamic Radicalism*, p. 4; Metcalf, *Traditionalist Islamic Activism*, p. 2.

12. Roy, ibid.

13. Ghaffar Hussain, interview by author, St. Albans, 6 August 2013.

14. Experts emphasise the recent convergence between Salafi theology and Deobandi sectarian political ideology. Roel Meijer (ed.), *Global Salafism: Islam's New Religious Movement* (London: Hurst & Company, 2009), p. 126.

15. Roy, *Islamic Radicalism*, p. 9; Kalim Bahadur, *The Jama'at-i-Islami of Pakistan: Political Thought and Political Action* (New Delhi: Chetana Publications, 1977), p. 4; Gilles Kepel, *Allah in the West: Islamic Movements in America and Europe* (Cambridge, UK: Polity Press, 1997), pp. 90–91.

16. For more information on Shah Waliullah's visit to Mecca and Medina and those who taught him see Jens Bakker, *Sah Waliy Allah ad-Dihlawiy (1703– 1762) und sein Aufenthalt in Mekka und Medina*, in German (Berlin: EB-Verlag, 2010).

17. Kepel, *Allah in the West*, pp. 88–89.

18. Ibid. For more information also see Innes Bowen, *Medina in Birmingham, Najaf in Brent: Inside British Islam* (London: Hurst & Company, 2014), pp. 12–14.

19. Kepel, *Allah in the West*, pp. 90–91.

20. Quoted in Bowen, *Medina in Birmingham*, p. 27; for the Wikileaks cable see 'Confidental cable written by Richard LeBaron, deputy chief of the US embassy in London. Passed by WikiLeaks to the *Daily Telegraph* and published by the *Telegraph* on 3 February 2011', http://www.telegraph.co.uk/news/wikileaks-files/ london-wikileaks/8304926/EUR-SENIOR-ADVISOR-PANDITH-AND-SP-ADVISOR-COHENS-VISIT-TO-THE-UK-OCTOBER-9-14-2007.html (accessed 11 March 2015).

21. Many books call on Muslims to separate themselves from their surroundings. See for example Husayn Bin 'Awadh Al-'Awaayishah, *A Conclusive Study on the Issue of Hijrah and Separating from the Polytheists* (New York: Sanatech Printers, 2006), author note p. 14; p. 37.

22. Bowen, *Medina in Birmingham*, p. 27.

23. Ibid.

24. Anya Hart Dyke, *Mosques Made in Britain* (London: Quilliam Foundation, 2009), pp. 5, 15–16; Change Institute, *Pakistani Muslim Community in England*, p. 39.

25. Elham Manea, '*Ich will nicht mehr schweigen*': *Der Islam, der Westen und die Menschenrechte* (Freiburg: Herder Verlag, 2009), p. 86; Author's Syria field visit, Summer 2007; Lawrence Ziring, *The Middle East: Political Dictionary* (Santa Barbara: ABC-CLIO, 1992), pp. 61–62.

26. Ishaan Tharoor, 'Can Sufism defuse terrorism?' *Time, 22* July 2009. Available at http://content.time.com/time/world/article/0,8599,1912091,00.html (accessed 1 July 2015).

27. Angel Rabasa, Cheryl Benard, Lowell H. Schwartz and Peter Sickle, *Building Moderate Muslim Networks* (Santa Monica: Rand Center for Middle East Public Policy, 2007), pp. 70, 73–74.

28. Kepel, *Allah in the West*, pp. 91–92; Bowen, *Medina in Birmingham*, pp. 115–116

29. Kepel, *Allah in the West*, p. 92; Bowen, *Medina in Birmingham*, ibid.

30. Bowen, *Medina in Birmingham*, p. 131.

31. Sheikh Faizul Aqtab Siddiqi, interview by author, Nuneaton, 15 January 2013.

32. Ibid.

33. Rashad Ali, email exchange with author, 31 January 2015.

34. Kepel, *Allah in the West*; Bowen, *Medina in Birmingham*, pp. 115–116; Arshad Alam, 'Competing Islams', *Outlook India*, 14 September 2006. Available at http://www.outlookindia.com/printarticle.aspx?232494 (accessed 1 July 2015); Anya Hart Dyke, *Mosques Made in Britain*, pp. 45–46. For more on the ideology of Shah Waliullah of Delhi, upon which the Deobandi movement was based, and his position of Sufi practices please see Abul A'la Maududi, *A Short History of the Revivalist Movement in Islam*, 3rd ed. (Lahore: Islamic Publications Ltd, 1979), pp. 82–103.

35. Kepel, *Allah in the West*, pp. 91–92.

36. Bowen, *Medina in Birmingham*, p. 49.

37. Kepel, *Allah in the West*.

38. Meijer, *Global Salafism*, pp. 126–129; p. 385 fn 5.

39. Sheikh Dr Suhaib Hasan, interview by author, Leyton], 28 January 2013.

40. 'Undercover Mosque', programme on *Dispatches*, Channel 4, 15 January 2007, minutes 9:48–10:54.

41. Suhaib Hasan, *An Introduction to the Sunnah* (London: Al-Quran Society, 2000), p. 6.

42. Hasan, on 'Undercover Mosque', minutes 17:34–19:19. When confronted with this video, Hasan told the Dispatches team that the word 'kuffaar' was 'not a racist or discriminatory term when heard in its Quranic sense'. He said he had stated many times that the re-establishment of a 'single Islamic state' would be peaceful. He said he had often praised the British welfare state, and

its judicial, health and education systems. He said: 'I have never promoted any form of extremism, whether religious or otherwise'.

43. Elham Manea, *Regional Politics in the Gulf: Saudi Arabia, Oman, Yemen* (London: Saqi, 2005), pp. 20–22, 73–74; for more information on Salifism and the principle of *al-wala' wa-lbara*, see Benham T. Said and Hazim Fouad (eds), *Salafismus: Auf der suche nach der wahren Islam* (Freiburg: Herder Verlag, 2014), pp. 64–74.

44. Manea, ibid.

45. Jonathan Brown, *Salafis and Sufis in Egypt* (Washington, DC: Carnegie Endowment for International Peace, 2011), p. 3.

46. Bowen, *Medina in Birmingham*, pp. 75–80.

47. The video of the interview and its transcript can be found on Haitham al-Haddad's blog, The Islamic Far-Right in Britain, under Islamic Supremacy. http://tifrib.com/haitham-al-haddad/ (accessed 6 April, 2015).

48. Bowen, *Medina in Birmingham*, pp. 58–59, 75, 80–81.

49. For more information on political Islam and the main writings of Islamist thinkers please see Barry Rubin (ed.), *Political Islam I* (London: Routledge, 2007), pp. 1–44; Wendell Charles (translator and annotator), *The Five Tracts of Hasan Al-Banna (1906–1949)* (Berkeley, CA: University of California Press, 1978), pp. 40–68, 133–161; John Calvert, *Sayyid Qutb and the Origins of Radical Islamism* (New York: Columbia University Press, 2010), chapter 6; Sayyid Qutb, *Milestones* (translated from Arabic) (Beirut: The Holy Koran House, 1978), chapters 1–5 & 12; Roy Jackson, *Mawlana Mawdudi and Political Islam* (London: Routledge, 2011), chapters 7–11; Ayatollah Ruhollah Khomeini, *Islamic Government*, 2nd ed. (Rome: European Islamic Cultural Centre, 1982), pp. 32–120.

50. Kepel, *Allah in the West*, pp. 109–125.

51. Charles, *The Five Tracts of Hasan Al-Banna*, pp. 46–47, 69–71, 74–75.

52. Rubin, *Political Islam I*, pp. 17–19.

53. Hassan Al-Banna, *Message for Youth*, translated from Arabic by Muhammad H. Najm (London: Ta-Ha Publishers Ltd, 1993), p. 6, quoted in Manea, *Ich Will Nicht Schweigen*, pp. 98–99.

54. Charles, *The Five Tracts of Hasan Al-Banna*, pp. 70–73.

55. Mohammad Khalaf Allah, 'Islamic Awakening in Egypt', in Ismael Sabri Abdullah and others (eds), *The Contemporary Islamic Movement in the Arab World*, in Arabic (Beirut: Center for the Studies of Arab Unity & United Nations Library, 1987), p. 53, quoted in Menea, *Ich will nicht schweigen*, pp. 99–100.

56. Hassan Al-Banna, 'On Jihad', in Charles, *The Five Tracts of Hasan Al-Banna*, p. 133, quoted in Manea, *Ich will nicht schweigen*, p. 101.

57. Ibid.

58. Quoted in John Clavert, *Sayyid Qutb and the Origins of Radical Islamism* (Oxford: Oxford University Press, 2013), p. 217.

59. Peter R. Demant, *Islam vs. Islamism: The Dilemma of the Muslim World* (Westport, CT: Praeger, 2006), p. 100.

60. Qutb, *Milestones*, pp. 16–140, John Clavert, *Sayyid Qutb and the Origins of Radical Islamism*, pp. 224–225.
61. Kepel, *Allah in the West*, p. 92.
62. Mawlana Maududi, *The Rights of non-Muslims (Dhmmis) in Islam*, in Arabic, 1947; Roy Jackson, *Mawlana Mawdudi and Political Islam* (London: Routledge, 2011), chapters 7–11.
63. Divino, *The New Muslim Brotherhood*, p. 116.
64. Kepel, *Allah in the West*, p. 122; Bowen, *Medina in Birmingham.* pp. 84–90.
65. Bowen, *Medina in Birmingham*, pp. 89–90.
66. Munira Mirza, Abi Senthikumaran, and Zein Ja'far, 'Living apart together: British Muslims and the paradox of multiculturalism', *Policy Exchange Report*, 2007, p. 6.
67. For more information see Martin Bright's report, *When Progressives Treat with Reactionaries: The British State's Flirtation with Radical Islamism* (London: Policy Exchange, 2006).
68. Manea, *Regional Politics*, p. 24; Manea, *The Arab State*, p. 59.
69. Kepel, *Allah in the West*, pp. 94–95.
70. David Page, *Prelude to Partition: The Indian Muslims and the Imperial System of Control (1920–1932)* (Delhi: Oxford University Press, 1982), p. 260, quoted in Kepel, *Allah in the West*, p. 95.
71. Manea, *The Arab State*, p. 63; Warren Hastings Act II of 1772, in Kashi Prasad Saksena, *Muslim Law as Administered in India and Pakistan*, 4th ed. (Lucknow: Eastern Book Company, 1963, p. 41; Rosemarie Zahlan Said, *The Making of the Modern Gulf States: Kuwait, Bahrain, Qatar, The United Arab Emirates and Oman* (London: Unwin Hyman, 1989); Karl Pieragostini, *Britain, Aden and South Arabia: Abandoning Empire* (New York: St. Martin's Press, 1991), p. 21; Maxine Molyneux, *State Policies and the Position of Women Workers in the People's Democratic Republic of Yemen, 1967–1977* (Geneva: International Labour Office, 1982), p. 246.
72. Z. H. Kour, *The History of Aden 1839–1872* (London: Frank Kass, 1981), p. 88.
73. Kepel, *Allah in the West*, p. 98.
74. Ibid., p. 108.
75. Ibid., pp. 110–111.
76. Muslim Educational Trust, 'About us', http://web-eab.wix.com/met#!__page-2 (accessed 1 July 2015).
77. Ibid.
78. Ibid.
79. Kepel, *Allah in the West*.
80. Gulam Sarwar, *Islam: Beliefs and Teachings*, 8th ed. (London: Muslim Educational Trust, 2006), p. 7.
81. Ed Husain, *The Islamist* (London: Penguin Books, 2007), pp. 20–21.
82. Rashad Ali, telephone conversation with author, 10 April 2015.
83. Sarwar, *Islam*, p. 169.
84. Ibid.

85. Ibid., p. 171.
86. Ibid., pp. 76–77. Below are the complete quotations. Sarwar says this on the political system of Islam:

> Politics is part of Islam. It cannot be separated from it. Indeed, the separation of religion and politics is meaningless in Islam. We have already learnt that Islam is a complete system of life, and politics is very much a part of our collective life. Just as Islam teaches us how to say Salah (prayer), observe Sawm (fasting), pay Zakah (Alms) and undertake Hajj (pilgrimage), so it teaches us how to run a state, form a government, elect representatives, make treaties and conduct trade. (p. 169).

Just as Sarwar emphasises Mawdudi's idea of the political system of Islam he reiterates his idea about the Sovereignty of Allah and that shari'a should be applied:

> Sovereignty means the source of power and authority. In Islam, Allah is the source of all powers and laws (3:154; 12:40; 25:2; 67:1). It is Allah who knows what is good and what is bad for His servants. His say is final. Human beings should not and must not change. For example, the Qur'an says *'As for the thief, male and female chip off their hands. It is the reward of their own actions and exemplary punishment from Allah. Allah is Mighty Wise'* (5:38). According to Islam, this order can not be changed by any ruler or government claiming to be Islamic (5:44; 2:229). There are many laws in the Qur'an concerning our life, and those laws must be put into practice by an Islamic state for the greater good of all human beings' (p. 169).

Needless to say jihad is very much part of this politicised worldview of Islam:

> Jihad is the use of all our energies and resources to establish the Islamic system of life, in order to gain Allah's favour. Jihad is an Arabic word which means to try one's utmost. It is a continuous process. In its first phase a Muslim learns to control his own passions and intentions. We need to strive hard to achieve this. This Jihad within ourselves is the basis for the comprehensive Jihad, which is concerned with establishing Ma'ruf (right) and removing Munkar (evil) from our lives and from society in which we live. It demands the use of all our material and mental resources. Eventually when the needs arise, we even have to give our life for Allah's sake. The Aim of Jihad is to seek the pleasure of Allah. This must not be forgotten because this purpose is the basis of all Islamic endeavours [...] Regular and conscious performance of the four basic duties should prepare and motivate us to live and die for the cause of Islam [...] In other words, all Islamic duties should prepare us to engage in Jihad. Jihad is the end result of our efforts in Salah (prayer), Zakat (Alms), Sawm (fasting) and Hajj (Pilgrimage). We cannot think of Islam without Jihad. We would like to see truth prevail and falsehood vanish, but we are aware that this can not happen on its own; we have to do our utmost to achieve it.

The performance of other Islamic duties will be meaningless if they do not motivate us to engage in Jihad. (pp. 76, 77)

Finally, Sarwar commended the efforts made by Islamist movements in establishing the Islamic state on earth. Hence he says:

> There is not a perfect Islamic state in the world today. There are many Muslim countries. An Islamic state is based on the model of the Prophet's state in Madinah while a Muslim state is one which has a majority Muslim population and some Islamic features. However, organised efforts are being made in many parts of the world to establish an Islamic system of government to implement the laws of the Qur'an and Suunah. Notable among the organisations which have been working to Islamic society are the Muslim Brotherhood in the Middle East, Jamaat-e-Islami in Pakistan, Bangladesh and Kashmir [...], Islamic salvation front in Algeria, [...] etc. (p. 171)

87. Ed Husain, *The Islamist*, p. 21.
88. Muslim Council of Britain, *Meeting the Needs of Muslim Pupils in State Schools: Information & Guidelines for Schools* (London: Muslim Council, 2007), pp. 38–58.
89. Ibid., p. 58.
90. Jack Barbalet, Adam Possamai, and Bryan S. Turner, *Religion and the State: A Comparative Sociology* (London: Anthem Press, 2013), p. 51.
91. Margaret Thatcher, 'My kind of Tory Party', *Daily Telegraph*, 30 January 1975. Available at http://www.margaretthatcher.org/document/102600 (accessed 1 July 2015). For more about how Thatcher perceived the state, government, and the church see also her speech at St Lawrence Jewry, 4th March 1981, available at http://www.margaretthatcher.org/document/104587 (accessed 1 July 2015).
92. Ghaffar Hussain, interview by author, St. Albans, 6 August 2013.
93. Mirza, Senthikumaran, and Ja'far, 'Living apart together', p. 25.
94. Kepel, *Allah in the West*, p. 112.
95. Malik, *From Fatwa to Jihad*, p. 68.
96. Ibid., p. 73.
97. Ibid., pp. 72–75.
98. Ibid., pp. 75–79.
99. Kepel, *Allah in the West*, pp. 114–115.
100 . Tehmina Kazi, interview by author, London, 14 January 2013.
101 . Change Institute, *Summary Report*, p. 6.
102. Usama Hasan, interview by author, Leytonstone, 9 August 2013.
103. Salman Rushdie, an Indian writer of Islamic heritage, was known for his harsh critique of the Jamaat-e-Islami agenda. When Penguin published his novel *Satanic Verses* in the UK in September 1988, representatives of political and societal Islamism launched a campaign against the book, saying it was blasphemous. The fatwa of Ayatollah Ruhollah Khomeini of Iran in 1989 ordering Muslims to kill Rushdie further politicised the situation. Iran was

competing against Saudi Arabia over the leadership of the 'Muslim world' and both used the affair as a proxy field for their rivalry.

104. Malik, *From Fatwa to Jihad*, pp. 1–36; Divino, *The New Muslim Brotherhood*, pp. 118–124.
105. Ghaffar Hussain, interview, August 2013.
106. Ibid.
107. Ibid.
108. Theresa May MP, Home Secretary, 'A stronger Britain, built on our values – A new partnership to defeat extremism' (Speech, 23 March 2015). Available at https://www.gov.uk/government/speeches/a-stronger-britain-built-on-our-values.ur (accessed 1 July 2015).
109. Ibid.
110. Ibid.
111. Ibid.
112. Maryam Namazie, interview by author, London, 19 January 2013.
113. Rashad Ali, interview by author, London, 18 January 2013.
114. http://www.islamic-sharia.org/aboutus/
115. See, for instance, Bangladesh Genocide Archive, *War Crimes File – A Documentary by Twenty Twenty Television*, available at http://www.genoci debangladesh.org/war-crimes-file-a-documentary-by-twenty-twenty-televisi on/ (accessed 1 July 2015); for more information on the Badr Squad see for instance Husain Haqqani, *Pakistan: Between Mosque and Military* (Washington, DC: Carnegie Endowment for International Peace, 2010), pp. 79–80.
116. Usama Hasan, interview, August 2013.
117. Ibid.
118. Rashad Ali, interview, January 2013.
119. Ibid.
120. Tahmina Saleem, written answers to author's questions, email exchange, 14 August 2014.
121. Usama Hasan, interview with author, August 2013.
122. See Islamopediaonline, 'European Council for Fatwas and Research (Dublin, Ireland)', available at http://www.islamopediaonline.org/websites-institutions/european-council-fatwas-and-research-dublin-ireland (accessed 1 July 2015).
123. European Council for Fatwa and Research, *Resolutions and Fatwas {edicts} of the European Council for Fatwa and Research*, in Arabic (Cairo: Islamic House for Distribution and Publication, 2002), p. 19.
124. Sheik Yousuf Al-Qaradhawi, 'Islam's "Conquest of Rome" will save Europe from its subjugation to materialism and promiscuity', *Qatar TV*, 28 July, 2007. The TV clip, no. 1592, translated and posted by *MERI TV, The Middle East Media Research Institute*, available at http://www.memritv.org/clip/en/1592.htm (accessed 1 July 2015).
125. Ikhwan Wiki, Federation of Islamic Organisations in Europe. In Arabic. Available at http://goo.gl/u57S2R (accessed 1 July 2015).
126. Ibid.

127. Muslim Council of Britain (MCB), *Fairness not Favours: British Muslims' Perspectives at the 2015 General Election* (London: MCB, 2015), p. 11. Available at http://www.mcb.org.uk/wp-content/uploads/2015/03/fairnessnotfavours-MCB. pdf (accessed 1 July 2015).
128. Ibid.
129. Arbitration and Mediation Services (Equality Bill), Baroness Cox, 7th June 2011, National Archive, Part 2, Article 4, p. 3.
130. Karen McVeigh and Amelia Hill, 'Bill limiting sharia law is motivated by "concern for Muslim women"', *The Guardian*, 8 June 2011. Available at http://www.theguardian.com/law/2011/jun/08/sharia-bill-lords-muslim-women (accessed 26 May 2015).
131. Usama Hasan, interview with author, August 2013.

Chapter 6   Contextualising the Debate in Women's Reality: Shari'a Law Contested

1. Quoted in Karen McVeigh and Amelia Hill, 'Bill limiting sharia law is motivated by "concern for Muslim women"', *The Guardian*, 8 June 2011. Available at http://www.theguardian.com/law/2011/jun/08/sharia-bill-lords-muslim-women (accessed 26 May 2015).
2. See Muslim Council of Britain (MCB), *Fairness not Favours: British Muslims' Perspectives at the 2015 General Election* (London: MCB, 2015), p. 11. Available at http://www.mcb.org.uk/wp-content/uploads/2015/03/fairnessnotfavours-MCB.pdf (accessed 9 July 2015).
3. Tariq Modood, 'Multicultural citizenship and the Shari'a controversy in Britain', in Rex Ahdar and Nicholas Aroney (eds), *Shari'a in the West* (Oxford: Oxford University Press, 2010), p. 34.
4. Ibid., p. 36.
5. Ibid., p. 40.
6. Ibid., pp. 40–41.
7. Dr Ghayasuddin Siddiqui, interview by author, London, 12 August 2013.
8. See the Muslim parliament website: http://www.muslimparliament.org.uk.
9. Ghayasuddin Siddiqui, interview, August 2013.
10. Ibid.
11. Ibid.
12. Sawsan Salim, interview by author, London, 12 January 2013.
13. Jenan Al Jabiri, interview by author, London, 12 January 2013.
14. Sarah Hall, 'Life for "honour" killing of pregnant teenager by mother and brother', *The Guardian*, 25 May 1999. Available at http://www.theguardian.com/uk/1999/may/26/sarahhall (accessed 9 July 2015).
15. Department of Justice, Canada, *Annotated Bibliography on Comparative and International Law Relating to Forced Marriage*, 'Selected Relevant Case Law'.

Available at http://www.justice.gc.ca/eng/rp-pr/fl-lf/famil/mar/chap8.html (accessed 9 July 2015).

16. Southall Black Sisters, *The Forced Marriage Campaign*. Available at http://www.southallblacksisters.org.uk/campaigns/forced-marriage-campaign/ (accessed 9 July 2015).

17. Purna Sen and Liz Kelly, *Cedaw Shadow Thematic Report on Violence Against Women in the UK* (London, 2007), p. 22. Available at http://www2.ohchr.org/english/bodies/cedaw/docs/ngos/UKThematicReportVAW41.pdf (accessed 9 July 2015).

18. Ibid.; UK Government, Foreign & Commonwealth Office and Home Office, *Forced Marriage: Information and Practice Guidelines for Professionals Protecting, Advising and Supporting Victims*. Available at https://www.gov.uk/forced-marriage (accessed 9 July 2015).

19. Ghayasuddin Siddiqui, interview, August 2013.

20. Tahmina Saleem, interview by author, Luton, 27 January 2013.

21. Elham Manea, *'Ich will nicht mehr schweigen': Der Islam, der Westen und die Menschenrechte* (Freiburg: Herder Verlag, 2009), p. 40.

22. Ibid.

23. Suad Joseph (ed.), *Citizenship and Gender in the Middle East* (Syracuse, NY: Syracuse University Press, 2000), p. xv.

24. Suad Joseph and Susan Slyomovics (eds), *Women and Power in the Middle East* (Philadelphia: University of Pennsylvania Press, 2001), p. 7.

25. For more information about gender and family values in a patriarchal structure see Joseph and Slyomovics, pp. 6–7.

26. Tahmina Saleem, interview, January 2013.

27. For a detailed summary of these findings see Alita Nandi and Lucinda Platt, *Ethnic Minority Women's Poverty and Economic Well Being* (London: UK Government Equalities Office, 2010). Available at https://www.gov.uk/government/uploads/system/uploads/attachment_data/file/85528/ethnic-minority-women_s-poverty.pdf (accessed 9 July 2015); Yaojun Li and Anthony Heath, *CSI 10: Are we becoming more or less ethnically-divided?* Briefing note (Oxford: Centre for Social Investigation, Nuffield College, March 2015). Available at http://csi.nuff.ox.ac.uk/wp-content/uploads/2015/03/CSI_10_Ethnic_Inequalities.pdf (accessed 9 July 2015); Anthony Heath and Yaojun Li, *Review of the Relationship between Religion and Poverty – An Analysis for the Joseph Rowntree Foundation*, CSI Working Paper 2015–01 (Oxford: Centre for Social Investigation, Nuffield College, 2015). Available at http://csi.nuff.ox.ac.uk/wp-content/uploads/2015/03/religion-and-poverty-working-paper.pdf (accessed 9 July 2015); UNHCHR, 'Special Rapporteur on violence against women finalizes country mission to the United Kingdom and Northern Ireland and calls for urgent action to address the accountability deficit and also the adverse impacts of changes in funding and services' (London, 15 April 2014). Available at http://www.ohchr.org/en/newsevents/pages/displaynews.aspx?newsid=14514& (accessed 9 July 2015).

28. UNHCHR, 'Special Rapporteur'.
29. Hannana Siddiqui and Meena Patel, *Safe and Sane: A Model of Intervention on Domestic Violence and Mental Health, Suicide and Self-harm Amongst Black and Minority Ethnic Women* (London: Southall Black Sisters, 2010), p. 9.
30. Anita Bhardwaj, 'Growing up young, Asian and female in Britain: A report on self-harm and suicide', *Feminist Review*, No. 68, Summer 2001.
31. Ibid., p. 56.
32. Ibid.
33. Ibid., pp. 58–59.
34. Ibid.
35. Ibid., p. 58.
36. Ibid., p. 59.
37. Shayma Izzidien, 'I cannot tell people what is happening at home – Domestic abuse within South Asian communities: The specific needs of women, children and young people', *NSPCC Inform: The Online Child Protection Resource*, June 2008, p. 21.
38. Ibid., pp. 21–22.
39. Shaista Gohir, 'Unheard voices: The sexual exploitation of Asian girls and young women', *Muslim Women's Network UK*, September 2013, p. 82. Available at http://www.mwnuk.co.uk/go_files/resources/UnheardVoices.pdf (accessed 17 July 2015).
40. Habiba Jaan, interview by author, Birmingham, 7 August 2013.
41. Quoted in Tahmina Kazi, 'Why the sheikh is wrong on rape', *The Samosa*, 25 October 2010. Available at http://www.thesamosa.co.uk/archive/thesamos a.co.uk/index.php/comment-and-analysis/society/437-why-the-sheikh-is-wrong-on-rape.html (accessed 9 July 2015).
42. Mark Hughes and Jerome Taylor, 'Rape "impossible" in marriage, says Muslim Cleric', *The Independent*, 14 October 2010. Available at http://www.independent.co.uk/news/uk/home-news/rape-impossible-in-marriage-says-muslim-cleric-2106161.html (accessed 9 July 2015).
43. 'Reyhana', interview by author, August 2013.
44. Gina Khan, interview by author, Birmingham, 10 August 2013.
45. Ibid.
46. For more about Sood see Louise Ridley, 'The trailblazing Hindu barrister who uses inner strength to win back abused women's dowries', *Huffington Post UK*, 5 November 2014. Available at http://www.huffingtonpost.co.uk/2014/11/03/usha-sood-dowry-abuse-forced-marriage-cases_n_6097448.html (accessed 9 July 2015).
47. Usha Sood, telephone interview by author, Nottingham, 14 August 2013.
48. Usha Sood, interview, August 2013.
49. International Council on Human Rights Policy (ICHRP), *When Legal Worlds Overlap: Human Rights, State and Non-State Law* (Geneva: ICHRP, 2009), pp. 107–108. Available at http://papers.ssrn.com/sol3/papers.cfm?abstract_id=1551229 (accessed 15 July 2015).

50. Salma Dean, interview by author, London: House of Lords, 9 August 2013; Charlotte Proudman, interview by author, London, 17 January 2013.
51. Samia Bano, *Muslim Women and Shari'ah Councils: Transcending the Boundaries of Community and Law* (London: Palgrave Macmillan, 2013), p. 186; Sonia Nurin Shah-Kazemi, 'Untying the Knot: Muslim Women, Divorce and the Shariah', *Nuffield Foundation* (London: Nuffield Foundation, 2001), p. 48
52. Charlotte Proudman, interview, January 2013.
53. Cassandra Balchin, 'Registering Muslim marriages' (London: *Critical Muslim* website, 2011). Available at http://criticalmuslim.com/upfront/religion/registering-muslim-marriages-cassandra-balchin (accessed 9 July 2015).
54. Field work in the UK in January and August 2013. See also Cassandra Balchin, 'Registering Muslim marriages'; Divya Talwa, 'Wedding trouble as UK Muslim marriages not recognised', *BBC News*, 3 February 2010. Available at http://news.bbc.co.uk/2/hi/uk_news/8493660.stm (accessed 9 July 2015).
55. Shah-Kazemi, *Untying the Knot*, p. 31.
56. Bano, *Muslim Women and Shari'ah Councils*, pp. 160–161.
57. Talwa, 'Wedding trouble'; on polygamous marriages in the UK also see Linda Serck, 'Polygamy in Islam: The women victims of multiple marriage', *BBC News*, 1 June 2012. Available at http://www.bbc.com/news/uk-england-berks hire-18252958 (accessed 9 July 2015).
58. Balchin, 'Registering Muslim marriages'.
59. Sister Sabah, interview by author, 23 January 2013.
60. Birmingham Mosque Trust (BMT), 'Islamic divorce (khula) procedure' (Birmingham: Birmingham Mosque Trust, 2015). Available at http://centralmosque.org.uk/downloads/62_Islamic%20Divorce-Procedure.pdf (accessed 9 July 2015).
61. Sheikh Mohammad Talha Bokhari, interview by author, Birmingham, 23 January 2013.
62. Dr Mohammad Shahoot Kharfan, interview by author, London, 22 January 2013.
63. Salim Leham, interview by author, London, 18 January 2013.
64. Sheikh Dr Suhaib Hasan, interview by author, London, 28 January 2013.
65. Bano, *Muslim Women and Shari'ah Councils*, p. 186; Shah-Kazemi, *Untying the Knot*, p. 34.
66. Shah-Kazemi, *Untying the Knot*, p. 35.
67. Bano, *Muslim Women and Shari'ah Councils*, pp. 210–212.
68. Ibid., p. 213.
69. Ibid.
70. Charlotte Rachael Proudman, *Equal and Free? Evidence in Support of Baroness Cox's Arbitration and Mediation Services (Equality) Bill* (London: House of Lords, May 2012), pp. 11–39.
71. Quoted in Ibid., p. 33.
72. Quoted in Ibid., p. 29.

73. Haitham al-Haddad, 'Fatwa: A civil divorce is not a valid religious divorce', Islam21c.com, 21 July 2010. Available at http://www.islam21c.com/fataawa/912-fatwa-a-civil-divorce-is-not-a-valid-islamic-divorce/ (accessed 9 July 2015).

74. Sohail Akbar Warraich and Cassandra Balchin, 'Recognizing the Un-recognized: Inter-country Cases and Muslim Marriages & Divorces in Britain', *Women Living Under Muslim Laws* (London: Women Living Under Muslim Laws, 2006), p. 3.

75. Rashad Ali, 'Islam, "Shari'ah courts, Islamisation and the far-right",' *Democratiya*, 16, Spring/Summer 2009, pp. 47–48. It is worth mentioning that even the European Council for Fatwa and Research (ECFR) – an affiliate of the global Muslim Brothers – reluctantly issued a religious decision acknowledging the validity of a divorce issued by a non-Muslim. ECFR, Fifth Regular Session, 4–7 May, Dublin, 2000. Available at http://goo.gl/hGOAeK (accessed 9 July 2015).

76. Sheikh Mohammad Talha Bokhari, interview by author, Birmingham, 23 January 2013.

77. Al Taher al Hadad, *Our Woman in Shari'a and Life*, in Arabic (Tunis: Tunisia's House for Publication, 1972), p. 40.

78. Ibid., pp. 27–82.

79. United Nations Development Program (UNDP), *Arab Human Development Report 2005: Towards the Rise of Women in the Arab World* (New York: United Nations, 2006), pp. 189–190.

80. Ibid., p. 191.

81. Ibid., p. 193.

82. Ibid., p. 194.

83. Women Living Under Muslim Laws (WLUML), 'About WLUML'. Available at http://www.wluml.org/node/5408 (accessed 9 July 2015).

84. Ibid.

85. Marieme Hélie-Lucas, *WLUML: Heart and Soul*. Transcribed from *Plan of Action, Dhaka 97*. Available at http://www.wluml.org/sites/wluml.org/files/Heart%20and%20Soul_Marieme%20Helie-Lucas.pdf (accessed 9 July 2015).

86. WLUML, 'About WLUML'.

87. Elham Manea, '*Ich will nicht mehr schweigen': Der Islam, der Westen und die Menschenrechte* (Freiburg: Herder Verlag, 2009), p. 34.

88. Hélie-Lucas, *WLUML: Heart and Soul*.

89. Abdullahi Ahmed An-Na'im, *Toward Islamic Reformation: Civil Liberties, Human Rights, and International* Law (Syracuse, NY: Syracuse University Press, 1990), p. xiv.

90. Ibid., pp. 89–91, 175–176.

91. Abdullahi Ahmed An-Na'im, 'Towards an Islamic society, not an Islamic state', in Robin Griffith-Jones (ed.), *Islam and English Law: Rights, Responsibilities and the Place of Shari'a* (Cambridge: Cambridge University Press, 2013), p. 242.

92. Ibid.

93. Ibid.
94. Manea, '*Ich will nicht mehr schweigen*', pp. 33–35.
95. Quoted in Manea, ibid, p. 34.
96. Marion Boyd, '*Dispute Resolution in Family Law: Protecting Choice, Promoting Inclusion*' (Toronto: Attorney General of Ontario, 2004), p. 48. Available at http://www.attorneygeneral.jus.gov.on.ca/english/about/pubs/boyd/ (accessed 10 July 2015).
97. Ibid., p. 52.
98. Ibid., p. 51.
99. Manea, '*Ich will nicht mehr schweigen*', pp. 35–36.
100. Maryam Namazie, interview by author, London, 19 January 2013.
101. Maryam Namazie, 'Nearly 200 Signatories call to Dismantle Parallel Legal Systems', *Freethought Blog*, 15 June 2015. Available at http://freethoughtblogs.com/maryamnamazie/2015/06/15/nearly-200-signatories-call-to-dismantle-parallel-legal-systems/ (accessed 9 July 2015); Emma Batha, 'Britain must ban Sharia 'Kangaroo Courts', say Activists', *Reuters*, 15 June 2015. Available at http://www.reuters.com/article/2015/06/15/us-britain-sharia-court-idUSKBN0OV2 EX20150615 (accessed 9 July 2015).
102. Maryam Namazie, interview, 19 January 2013.
103. Amnesty International (AI), *Choice and Prejudice: Discrimination Against Muslims in Europe* (Brussels: AI European Institutions Office, 2012), pp. 22–24.
104. Interviewee 2, anonymous women's rights advocate, interview by author, London, 16 January 2013. This person was not authorised to speak by the organisation and thus asked to remain anonymous.
105. Beth Dins are recognised as a form of civil arbitration under the Arbitration Act 1996. Their power, however, lies in their influence over family and other 'private' areas especially as they act as a formal religious court in matters of divorce and litigation. There is no overarching authority over the process; rather individual arbitrations are organised according to the broad lines of Orthodox and non-Orthodox Judaism.

      These tribunals serve several functions for members of the Jewish communities in the UK: they offer arbitration of civil disputes using Jewish law, and rule on religious matters such as designating religious holidays. Most importantly, they grant religious divorces for women.

      According to Jewish traditions, to pursue a religious divorce the husband must issue a 'get' – a written form of divorce – to his wife and the wife must accept it. If the husband is not co-operating or is refusing to provide a religious divorce, a Jewish woman turns to the Beth Dins. In Orthodox communities, a woman can suffer a considerable stigma if she remarries in a civil registry without a religious divorce. It can affect the future legitimacy of her children, who could be labelled illegitimate; this has profound implications for her access to both spaces and resources within the community. Although supporters and independent interviewees have insisted that the Beth Din does accept the UK civil law as the main reference for their dealings, critiques about the patriarchal nature of these tribunals persist. For instance, the *UK CEDAW Shadow Report* criticised some rabbinical courts: 'Whilst Jewish divorce is supposed to be based on the consent of both parties, rabbinical courts do issue a religious divorce to husbands where the wife does not consent (known as a Get Zikkui). Men and women start from an unequal legal standing but, moreover, Beth Dins have an inbuilt male bias because they usually comprise three men': three rabbis. Thus, the report argues, the system is inherently patriarchal. Centre for Social Cohesion (CSC), *The Beth Din: Jewish Courts in the UK* (London: CSC, 2009), pp. 1, 4; CEDAW Working Group, *UK CEDAW Shadow Report*, Appendix 31: Faith based organisations and legal arbitration (London: Women's Resource Centre, 2013). Available at http://thewomensresourcecentre.org.uk/our-work/cedaw/cedaw-shadow-report/ (accessed 9 July 2015); Arbitration and Mediation Services (Equality) Bill, House of Lords, May 2012, available at http://www.publications.parliam ent.uk/pa/bills/lbill/2012-2013/0007/13007.pdf (accessed 16 July 2015); Arbitration Act 1996; Interviewee no. 2, interview by author, January 2013; Judge Dawn Freedom, former circuit judge, telephone interview by author, 20 January 2013; David Frei, External and Legal Services Director of the United Synagogue, London, email written answers to author, 20 January 2013.

106. Pragna Patel and Uditi Sen, *Cohesion, Faith and Gender: A Report on the Impact of the Cohesion and Faith-based Approach on Black and Minority Women in Ealing* (London: Southall Black Sisters, 2010), p. 60. Available at http://www.southallblacksisters.org.uk/sbs/cfg-report-copyright-sbs.pdf (accessed 10 July 2015).

107. Ibid., pp. 58–63.

108. Gina Khan, interview by author, Birmingham, 10 August 2013.

109. Patel and Sen, *Faith and Gender*, p. 58.

110. Interviewee no. 3, interview, January 2013.

111. Namazie, interview, January 2013.

112. Details of the origins of the parties to the case were omitted for privacy protection.

113. Amra Bone, interview by author, Birmingham, 11 August 2013.

114. Gita Sahgal, interview by author, London, 24 January 2013.

115. Pragna Patel, '"Shariafication by stealth" in the UK', *50.50 Inclusive Democracy*, 17 October 2014. Available at https://www.opendemocracy.net/5050/pragna-patel/%27shariafication-by-stealth%27-in-uk (accessed 9 July 2015).

116. Maryam Namazie, *Sharia Law in Britain: A Threat to One Law for All and Equal Rights* (London: One Law for All, 2010), pp. 9–11; CEDAW Working Group, *Shadow Report*, 'Appendix 31.

117. Arbitration and Mediation Services Bill, May 2012; Arbitration Act 1996, available at http://www.legislation.gov.uk/ukpga/1996/23/data.pdf (accessed 17 July 2015); CEDAW Working Group, *Shadow Report*, Appendix 31; CSC, *The Beth Din*, pp. 1, 4.

118. Arbitration and Mediation Services (Equality) Bill, p. 1; CEDAW Working Group, *Shadow Report*, Appendix 31.

119. Sheikh Faizul Aqtab Siddiqi, interview by author, Nuneaton, 15 January.

120. Namazie, *Sharia Law in Britain*.

121. Baroness Caroline Cox, cross-bench Member of the British House of Lords, interviews by author, London, 28 January & 15 August 2013.

122. Ibid.

Conclusion: Time for a Paradigm Shift

1. Karima Bennoune, *Your Fatwa Does Not Apply Here: Untold Stories from the Fight against Muslim Fundamentalism* (New York: Norton, 2013), p. 22.

2. Ibid., p. 3.

3. Elham Manea, 'We are all in this together, like it or not': On Raif Badawi, Charlie Hebdo and non-violent Islamism', Qantara.de, 22 January 2015, available at http://en.qantara.de/content/on-raif-badawi-charlie-hebdo-and-non-violent-islamism-we-are-all-in-this-together-like-it-or (accessed 23 July 2015).

4. Archbishop Rowan Williams, 'Civil and religious law in England: A religious perspective', lecture at the Royal Courts of Justice, 7 February 2008, pp. 1–2. Available at http://rowanwilliams.archbishopofcanterbury.org/articles.php/1137/arc...re-civil-and-religious-law-in-england-a-religious-perspective#Lecture (accessed 16 July 2015).

5. International Council on Human Rights Policy (ICHRP), *When Legal Worlds Overlap: Human Rights, State and Non-State Law* (Geneva: ICHRP, 2009), pp. 107–108. Available at http://papers.ssrn.com/sol3/papers.cfm?abstract_id=1551229 (accessed 15 July 2015).

6. Frank La Rue, discussion with author by Skype, 23 July 2015.

7. Elham Manea, 'Islam and human dignity: A consequence-based approach to human dignity and rights', in Dorothèe Deimann and Simon Mugier (eds), *Entgegensprechen: Texte zu Menschenwürde und Menschenrecht*, vol. 1 (Basel: edition gesowip, 2010), p. 520.

8. Brian Orend, *Human Rights: Concept and Context* (Peterboro, Ontario, Canada: Broadview Press, 2002), p. 89, quoted in Manea, ibid, pp. 513–514.

9. Elham Manea, 'Tackling militant Islamism means also confronting its non-violent forms', *Europe's World*, 5 May 2015, available at http://europesworld.org/2015/05/05/tackling-militant-islamism-means-also-confronting-non-violent-forms/#.VbITcWDX_dv (accessed 24 July 2015).

BIBLIOGRAPHY

Abu-Manneh, Butrus, 'The Christians between Ottomanism and Syrian nationalism: The ideas of Butrus Al-Bustani', *International Journal of Middle East Studies*, xi/3 (May 1980).

Abu Zahrah, Mohammad, *Ahkam Al Tirkat wa al Mawari'ith – Provisions for Legacies and Inheritances*, in Arabic (Beirut: Dar Al Fikr Al Arabi, 1963).

AFP, 'A human rights organization demands the release of prisoners of conscience in Gulf Countries', *Swissinfo*, 16 May 2014, in Arabic. Available at http://www.swissinfo.ch/ara/detail/content.html?cid=38599094 (accessed 15 July 2015).

Afshari, Reza, *Human Rights in Iran: The Abuse of Cultural Relativism* (Philadelphia: University of Pennsylvania Press, 2011).

Al-'Awaayishah, Husayn Bin 'Awadh, *A Conclusive Study on the Issue of Hijrah and Separating from the Polytheists* (New York: Sanatech Printers, 2006).

Al-Banna, Hassan, *Message for Youth*, translated from Arabic by Muhammad H. Najm (London: Ta-Ha Publishers Ltd, 1993).

al Hadad, Al Taher, *Our Woman in Shari'a and Life*, in Arabic (Tunis: Tunisia's House for Publication, 1972).

al-Haddad, Haitham. Interview on YouTube. http://www.youtube.com/watch?v=thoP4EjtmzE (accessed 24 January 2014; video was later removed from YouTube).

———, 'Fatwa: A civil divorce is not a valid religious divorce', *Islam21c.com*, 21 July 2010. Available at http://www.islam21c.com/fataawa/912-fatwa-a-civil-divorce-is-not-a-valid-islamic-divorce/ (accessed 9 July 2015).

———, 'Why marriages fail? (WMF 1 of 7): The Scale of the Problem' YouTube video, available at https://www.youtube.com/watch?v=z37H-NuyY1c&list=PLA637A16BD2ABC692&index=1 (accessed 16 July 2015).

Al Minyawi, Alaa Aldin, 'Bishop Makarios: Customary law sessions detract from state's status', *Al Bawaba News*, 16 December 2013, in Arabic. Available at http://www.albawabhnews.com/270124 (accessed 15 July 2015).

Alam, Arshad, 'Competing Islams', *Outlook India*, 14 September 2006. Available at http://www.outlookindia.com/printarticle.aspx?232494 (accessed 1 July 2015).

Ali, Rashad, 'Islam, "Shari'ah Courts, Islamisation and the Far-Right"', *Democratiya*, 16, Spring/Summer 2009.

Al-Qaradhawi, Sheikh Yousuf, 'Islam's "Conquest of Rome" will save Europe from its subjugation to materialism and promiscuity', *Qatar TV*, 28 July, 2007. TV clip no. 1592, translated and posted by *MERI TV, The Middle East Media Research Institute*, available at http://www.memritv.org/clip/en/1592.htm (accessed 1 July 2015).

Amnesty International (AI), 'Sudan: Woman sentenced to death for her beliefs: Meriam Yehia Ibrahim' (16 May 2014). Available at https://www.amnestyusa. org/sites/default/files/uaa11814_0.pdf (accessed 15 July 2015).

———, 'Sudan: Mother at risk of flogging and death sentence: Meriam Yehia Ibrahim', AI Urgent Action, 13 May 2014. Available at http:// www.amnesty.org/en/library/info/AFR54/006/2014/en (accessed 15 July 2015).

———, 'A thousand lashes and 10 years in prison for online Saudi Arabian activist', press release, AI, 7 May 2014. Available at http://www.amnestyusa.org/news/ news-item/a-thousand-lashes-and-10-years-in-prison-for-online-saudi-arabian-activist (accessed 14 July 2015).

———, *Choice and Prejudice: Discrimination against Muslims in Europe* (Brussels: AI European Institutions Office, 2012).

Anaya, James, *Report of the Special Rapporteur on the Rights of Indigenous Peoples: The Situation of Indigenous Peoples in Canada* (New York: UN General Assembly, Human Rights Council, 27th session, 4 July 2014). Available at http://unsr. jamesanaya.org/docs/countries/2014-report-canada-a-hrc-27-52-add-2-en.pdf (accessed 15 July 2015).

An-Na'im, Abdullahi Ahmed, 'Towards an Islamic society, not an Islamic state', in Robin Griffith-Jones (ed.), *Islam and English Law: Rights, Responsibilities and the Place of Shari'a* (Cambridge: Cambridge University Press, 2013).

———, *Toward Islamic Reformation: Civil Liberties, Human Rights, and International Law* (Syracuse, NY: Syracuse University Press, 1990).

Arbitration Act 1996, available at http://www.legislation.gov.uk/ukpga/1996/23/ data.pdf (accessed 17 July 2015).

Arbitration and Mediation Services (Equality) Bill, House of Lords, May 2012, available at http://www.publications.parliament.uk/pa/bills/lbill/2012-2013/0007/13007.pdf (accessed 16 July 2015).

Ayubi, Nazih H., *Over-Stating the Arab State: Politics and Society in the Middle East*, 3rd ed. (London: I.B.Tauris, 2006).

Bahadur, Kalim, *The Jama'at-i-Islami of Pakistan: Political Thought and Political Action* (New Delhi: Chetana Publications, 1977).

Bakker, Jens, *Sah Waliy Allah ad-Dihlawiy (1703–1762) und sein Aufenthalt in Mekka und Medina*, in German (Berlin: EB-Verlag, 2010).

Balchin, Cassandra, *Information and Advice on Muslim Marriages in Britain* (Birmingham: Muslim Women's Network UK, 2012). Available at http://www.mwnuk.co.uk// go_files/factsheets/945946-MWNUKMarriageBookletFinal-compressed.pdf (accessed 18 July 2015).

———, 'Registering Muslim marriages' (London: *Critical Muslim* website, 2011). Available at http://criticalmuslim.com/upfront/religion/registering-muslim-marriages-cassandra-balchin (accessed 9 July 2015).

Bangladesh Genocide Archive, *War Crimes File – A Documentary by Twenty Twenty Television*, available at http://www.genocidebangladesh.org/war-crimes-file-a-documentary-by-twenty-twenty-television/ (accessed 1 July 2015).

Bano, Samia, *Muslim Women and Shari'ah Councils: Transcending the Boundaries of Community and Law* (London: Palgrave Macmillan, 2013).

Barbalet, Jack, Adam Possamai, and Bryan S. Turner, *Religion and the State: A Comparative Sociology* (London: Anthem Press, 2013).

Batha, Emma, 'Britain must ban sharia "kangaroo courts"', say activists', *Reuters*, 15 June 2015. Available at http://www.reuters.com/article/2015/06/15/us-britain-sharia-court-idUSKBN0OV2EX20150615 (accessed 9 July 2015).

BBC News, 'Mukhtar Mai: History of a rape case', *BBC online*, 28 June 2005. Available at http://news.bbc.co.uk/2/hi/south_asia/4620065.stm (accessed 15 July 2015).

———, '1969: Sikh busmen win turban fight', *BBC, On This Day*. Available at http://news.bbc.co.uk/onthisday/hi/dates/stories/april/9/newsid_2523000/2523691.stm (accessed 15 July 2015).

Beglinger, Martin, 'Bis dass der Zwang euch Bindet', Das Magazin, *Tages-Anzeiger*, vol. 24 (2007), p. 18.

Bennoune, Karima, *Your Fatwa Does Not Apply Here: Untold Stories from the Fight against Muslim Fundamentalism* (New York: Norton, 2013).

Bhardwaj, Anita, 'Growing up young, Asian and female in Britain: A report on self-harm and suicide', *Feminist Review*, No. 68, Summer 2001.

Birmingham Mosque Trust (BMT), 'Islamic Divorce (Khula) Procedure' (Birmingham: BMT, 2015). Available at http://centralmosque.org.uk/down loads/62_Islamic%20Divorce-Procedure.pdf (accessed 9 July 2015).

Bowen, Innes, *Medina in Birmingham, Najaf in Brent: Inside British Islam* (London: Hurst & Company, 2014).

Bowen, John R., *Blaming Islam* (Cambridge, MA: Boston Review Books, 2012).

Boyd, Marion, *Dispute Resolution in Family Law: Protecting Choice, Promoting Inclusion* (Toronto: Attorney General of Ontario, 2004). Available at http://www.attorneygeneral.jus.gov.on.ca/english/about/pubs/boyd/ (accessed 10 July 2015).

Bright, Martin, *When Progressives Treat with Reactionaries: The British State's Flirtation with Radical Islamism* (London: Policy Exchange, 2006).

Brown, Colin, 'Let us adopt Islamic family law to curb extremists, Muslims tell Kelly', *The Independent*, 15 August 2006. Available at http://www.independent.co.uk/news/uk/politics/let-us-adopt-islamic-family-law-to-curb-extremists-muslims-tell-kelly-411954.html (accessed 15 July 2015).

Brown, Jonathan, *Salafis and Sufis in Egypt* (Washington: Carnegie Endowment for International Peace, 2011).

Büchler, Andrea and Christina Schlatter, 'Marriage age in Islamic and contemporary Muslim family laws: A comparative survey', *Electronic Journal of Islamic and Middle Eastern Law*, vol. 1 (2013), pp. 37–74.

Burke, Roland, *Decolonization and the Evolution of International Human Rights* (Philadelphia: University of Pennsylvania Press, 2010).

Burki, Shahid Javed, 'Pakistan', *Encyclopædia Britannica*. Available at http://www.britannica.com/EBchecked/topic/438805/Pakistan/23691/Religion (accessed 18 July 2015).

Cairo Declaration on Human Rights in Islam (CDHRI) (Geneva: United Nations, 1993), available at http://www.arabhumanrights.org/publications/regional/islamic/cairo-declaration-islam-93e.pdf (accessed 16 July 2015).

Calvert, John, *Sayyid Qutb and the Origins of Radical Islamism* (New York: Columbia University Press, 2010).

CEDAW Working Group, *UK CEDAW Shadow Report*, Appendix 31: Faith based organisations and legal arbitration (London: Women's Resource Centre, 2013). Available at http://thewomensresourcecentre.org.uk/our-work/cedaw/cedaw-shadow-report/ (accessed 9 July 2015).

Centre for Social Cohesion (CSC), *The Beth Din: Jewish Courts in the UK* (London: CSC, 2009).

Change Institute, *Summary Report: Understanding Muslim Ethnic Communities* (London: Change Institute, Department for Communities and Local Government, April 2009).

———, *The Pakistani Muslim Community in England: Understanding Muslim Ethnic Communities* (London: Change Institute, Department for Communities and Local Government, March 2009).

Charles, Wendell (translator and annotator), *The Five Tracts of Hasan Al-Banna (1906–1949)* (Berkeley, CA: University of California Press, 1978).

Charrad, Mounira, *States and Women's Rights: The Making of Postcolonial Tunisia, Algeria, and Morocco* (Berkeley: University of California Press, 2001).

'Confidential cable written by Richard LeBaron, deputy chief of the US embassy in London. Passed by WikiLeaks to the *Daily Telegraph* and published by the *Telegraph* on 3 February 2011', http://www.telegraph.co.uk/news/wikileaks-files/london-wikileaks/8304926/EUR-SENIOR-ADVISOR-PANDITH-AND-SP-ADVISOR-COHENS-VISIT-TO-THE-UK-OCTOBER-9-14-2007.html (accessed 11 March 2015).

Cox, Baroness Caroline, 'From a distinguished peer fighting to protect women... Sharia marriages for girls of 12 and the religious courts subverting British law', the *Daily Mail*, 14 September 2012. Available at http://www.dailymail.co.uk/news/article-2202991/Sharia-marriages-girls-12-religious-courts-subverting-British-law.html#ixzz38ruyG49M (accessed 16 July 2015).

Demand, Peter R., *Islam vs. Islamism: The Dilemma of the Muslim World* (Westport, CT: Praeger, 2006).

Department of Justice, Canada, *Annotated Bibliography on Comparative and International Law Relating to Forced Marriage*, 'Selected Relevant Case Law'. Available at http://www.justice.gc.ca/eng/rp-pr/fl-lf/famil/mar/chap8.html (accessed 9 July 2015).

Divino, Lorenzo, *The New Muslim Brotherhood in the West* (New York: Columbia University Press, 2010).

Donnelly, Jack, 'Cultural relativism and universal human rights', *Human Rights Quarterly* vi/4 (Nov. 1984), pp. 400–419.

Dupret, Baudoiun, Maurits Berger, and Laila al-Zwaini (eds), *Legal Pluralism in the Arab World* (The Hague: Kluwer Law International, 1999).

Dyke, Anya Hart, *Mosques Made in Britain* (London: Quilliam Foundation, 2009).

Egyptian Initiative for Personal Rights (EIPR), 'Part two: Sectarian tension and violence', *Quarterly Report on Freedom of Religion and Belief: April–June 2009*, in Arabic. Available at http://www.eipr.org/report/2009/12/12/286/290 (accessed 15 July 2015).

Elbagir, Nima and Laura Smith-Spark, 'Sudanese Christian woman: "There's a new problem every day"', *CNN online*, 1 July 2014, available at http://edition.cnn. com/2014/07/01/world/africa/sudan-apostasy-case/index.html?hpt=hp_c6 (accessed 15 July 2015).

Ellahi, Naheda Mehboob, *Family Laws and Judicial Protection*. Available at Supreme Court of Pakistan, http://www.supremecourt.gov.pk/ijc/articles/21/1.pdf (accessed 15 July 2015).

Emon, Anver M., *Religious Pluralism and Islamic Law: Dhimmis and Others in the Empire of Law* (Oxford: Oxford University Press, 2012).

Encyclopedia Britannica (EB) editors, 'Ahmadiyyah', *Encyclopædia Britannica Online*. Available at http://www.britannica.com/EBchecked/topic/10189/Ahmadiyyah.

European Council for Fatwa and Research (ECFR), *Resolutions and Fatwas {edicts} of the European Council for Fatwa and Research*, in Arabic (Cairo: Islamic House for Distribution and Publication, 2002).

———, Fifth Regular Session, 4–7 May, Dublin, 2000. Available at http://goo.gl/ hGOAeK (accessed 9 July 2015).

Giordano, Christian, 'Der Rechtpluralismus: Ein Instrument für den Multikulturalismus? Eidgenössische Kommission gegen Rassismus', *Bulletin TANGRAM*, no. 22 (Dec. 2008).

Glazer, Sara, 'Are British sharia councils out of touch?', *CQ Global Research*, vi/1 (3 January 2012), pp. 6–7.

Glendon, Mary Ann, *A World Made New: Eleanor Roosevelt and the Universal Declaration of Human Rights* (New York: Random House, 2011).

Gohir, Shaista, 'Unheard voices: The sexual exploitation of Asian girls and young women', *Muslim Women's Network UK*, September 2013. Available at http://www. mwnuk.co.uk/go_files/resources/UnheardVoices.pdf (accessed 17 July 2015).

Griffiths, John, 'What is Legal Pluralism?', *Journal of Legal Pluralism*, vol. 32, no. 24 (1986).

Hall, Sarah, 'Life for "honour" killing of pregnant teenager by mother and brother', *The Guardian*, 25 May 1999. Available at http://www.theguardian.com/ uk/1999/may/26/sarahhall (accessed 9 July 2015).

Hallaq, Wael B., *Shari'a: Theory, Practice and Transformations* (Cambridge: Cambridge University Press, 2007).

Haqqani, Husain, *Pakistan: Between Mosque and Military* (Washington, DC: Carnegie Endowment for International Peace, 2010).

Hasan, Suhaib, *An Introduction to the Sunnah* (London: Al-Quran Society, 2000).

Hasan, Usama, 'A submission regarding Baroness Cox's Arbitration & Mediation Services (Equality) Bill' (London: Quilliam Foundation, 17 October 2012), p. 1.

Heath, Anthony and Yaojun Li, *Review of the Relationship between Religion and Poverty – An Analysis for the Joseph Rowntree Foundation*, CSI Working Paper 2015-01 (Oxford: Centre for Social Investigation, Nuffield College, 2015). Available at http://csi.nuff.ox.ac.uk/wp-content/uploads/2015/03/religion-and-poverty-working-paper.pdf (accessed 9 July 2015).

Hélie-Lucas, Marieme, 'WLUML: Heart and Soul'. Transcribed from *Plan of Action, Dhaka 97*. Available at http://www.wluml.org/sites/wluml.org/files/Heart% 20and%20Soul_Marieme%20Helie-Lucas.pdf (accessed 9 July 2015).

Hisham, Amira, 'Maspero Youth Union declares his rejection of customary reconciliation (session) in Alminia Events and describes it as attempts to destroy state's sovereignty', *Ahram Gate*, 12 August 2013, in Arabic. Available at http://gate.ahram.org.eg/News/381765.aspx (accessed 15 July 2015).

Hourani, Albert, *Minorities in the Arab World* (London, New York: Oxford University Press, 1947).

Hughes, Mark and Jerome Taylor, 'Rape "impossible" in marriage, says Muslim cleric', *The Independent*, 14 October 2010. Available at http://www.independent.co.uk/news/uk/home-news/rape-impossible-in-marriage-says-muslim-cleric-2106161.html (accessed 9 July 2015).

Human Rights Commission of Pakistan, 'Conditions for fair elections', 3 May 2013. Available at http://hrcp-web.org/hrcpweb/conditions-for-fair-elections (accessed 15 July 2015).

———, *State of Human Rights in 2013*. Available at http://www.hrcp-web.org/hrcpweb/report14/AR2013.pdf.

Human Rights Watch (HRW), *Denied Dignity: Systematic Discrimination and Hostility toward Saudi Shia Citizens* (New York: HRW, 2009), p. 12.

———, *Perpetual Minors: Human Rights Abuses Stemming from Male Guardianship and Sex Segregation in Saudi Arabia* (New York: HRW, 2008).

Husain, Ed, *The Islamist* (London: Penguin Books, 2007).

Ikhwan Wiki, 'Federation of Islamic Organisations in Europe'. In Arabic. Available at http://goo.gl/u57S2R (accessed 1 July 2015).

International Council on Human Rights Policy (ICHRP), *When Legal Worlds Overlap: Human Rights, State and Non-State Law* (Geneva, ICHRP, 2009). Available at http://papers.ssrn.com/sol3/papers.cfm?abstract_id=1551229 (accessed 15 July 2015).

IRIN, 'Madagascar: Twins taboo splits a community', *IRIN News*, UN Office for the Coordination of Humanitarian Affairs, 3 November 2011. Available at http://www.irinnews.org/report/94124/madagascar-twins-taboo-splits-a-community (accessed 14 July 2015).

Islamic Sharia Council (ISC), 'About us', available at http://test.islamic-sharia.org/?page_id=32 (accessed 16 July 2015).

Islamopediaonline, 'European Council for Fatwas and Research (Dublin, Ireland)', available at http://www.islamopediaonline.org/websites-institutions/european-council-fatwas-and-research-dublin-ireland (accessed 1 July 2015).

Izzidien, Shayma, 'I cannot tell people what is happening at home – Domestic Abuse within South Asian communities: The specific needs of women, children and young people', *NSPCC Inform: The Online Child Protection Resource*, June 2008.

Jackson, Roy, *Mawlana Mawdudi and Political Islam* (London: Routledge, 2011).

Jenkins, Roy, article in *Independent Magazine*, 4 March 1989.

Joseph, Suad (ed.), *Citizenship and Gender in the Middle East* (Syracuse, NY: Syracuse University Press, 2000).

Joseph, Suad and Susan Slyomovics (eds), *Women and Power in the Middle East* (Philadelphia: University of Pennsylvania Press, 2001).

Kalms, Lord Stanley, statement during second reading in House of Lords of Arbitration and Mediation Services (Equality) Bill (19 October 2012), column 1703. Available at http://www.publications.parliament.uk/pa/ld201213/ldhansrd/text/121019-0002.htm (accessed 16 July 2015).

Karayanni, Michael Mousa, 'The separate nature of the religious accommodations for the Palestinian-Arab minority in Israel', *Northwestern Journal International of Human Rights* v/1 (Fall 2007), pp. 43–48.

Kazi, Tahmina, 'Why the sheikh is wrong on rape', *The Samosa*, 25 October 2010. Available at http://www.thesamosa.co.uk/archive/thesamosa.co.uk/index.php/comment-and-analysis/society/437-why-the-sheikh-is-wrong-on-rape.html (accessed 9 July 2015).

Kemper, Michael and Maurus Reinkowski (eds), *Rechtspluralismus in der islamischen Welt: Gewohnheitsrecht zwischen Staat und Gesellschaft* (Berlin: Walter de Gruyter, 2005).

Kepel, Gilles, *Allah in the West: Islamic Movements in America and Europe* (Cambridge, UK: Polity Press, 1997).

Khadduri, Majid, 'Human rights in Islam', *Annals of the American Academy of Political and Social Science*, vol. 243 (Jan. 1946).

Khalaf Allah, Mohammad, 'Islamic Awakening in Egypt', in Ismael Sabri Abdullah and others (eds), *The Contemporary Islamic Movement in the Arab World*, in Arabic (Beirut: Center for the Studies of Arab Unity & United Nations Library, 1987).

Khan, Shahid, *Invisible Citizens of Pakistan: Minorities in Focus, Report 2013–2014* (Glasgow: Global Minorities Alliance, 2014). Available at http://www.globalminorities.co.uk/images/GMA%20Reports/Invisible%20Citizens%20of%20Pakistan%20Minorities%20in%20Focus%20Report%202013-2014.pdf (accessed 15 July 2015).

Khomeini, Ayatollah Ruhollah, *Islamic Government*, 2nd ed. (Rome: European Islamic Cultural Centre, 1982).

King, Kiki, 'The cursed twins of Madagascar', Huffington Post blog entry, 9 May 2014, available at http://www.huffingtonpost.co.uk/kiki-king/unreported-world-twins-in-madagascar_b_5293247.html?utm_hp_ref=uk&ir=UK&just_reloaded=1 (accessed 14 July 2015);

Kour, Z. H., *The History of Aden 1839–1872* (London: Frank Kass, 1981).

Kreuzer, Karl, 'International instruments in human rights and shariah law', in Hélène Gaudemet-Tallon, T. Azzi et al. (eds), *Vers de nouveaux équilibres entre ordres juridiques. Liber amicorum* (Paris: Dalloz, 2008), pp. 345–364.

Kristof, Nicholas D. and Sheryl WuDunn, *Half the Sky: Turning Oppression into Opportunity for Women Worldwide* (New York & Toronto: Alfred Knopf, 2009).

Li, Yaojun and Anthony Heath, *CSI 10: Are we becoming more or less ethnically-divided?* Briefing note (Oxford: Centre for Social Investigation, Nuffield College, March 2015). Available at http://csi.nuff.ox.ac.uk/wp-content/uploads/2015/03/CSI_10_Ethnic_Inequalities.pdf (accessed 9 July 2015).

Mahmood, Mona and Richard Sprenger, 'Inside a sharia divorce court' (video), *The Guardian*, 9 March 2011, available at www.guardian.co.uk/law/video/2011/mar/09/islam-sharia-council-divorce (accessed 16 July 2015).

Mai, Mukhtar, *Die Schuld eine Frau zu sein* (Munich: Droemer, 2006).

Makarenko, Jay, 'The Indian Act: Historical overview', *Mapleleafweb*, 2 June 2008. Available at http://mapleleafweb.com/features/the-indian-act-historical-overview (accessed 15 July 2015).

Malik, Kenan, *Multiculturalism and its Discontents* (London: Seagull Books, 2013).

———, *From Fatwa to Jihad: The Rushdie Affair and its Aftermath* (Brooklyn, NY: Melville House Publishing, 2009).

Mallat, Chibli, *Introduction to Middle Eastern Law* (Oxford: Oxford University Press, 2007).

'Mandla (Sewa Singh) and another v Dowell Lee and and others [1983] 2 AC 548', House of Lords 24 March 1983. Available at http://www.equalrightstrust.org/

ertdocumentbank/Microsoft%20Word%20-%20Mandla.pdf (accessed 15 July 2015).

Manea, Elham, 'Tackling militant Islamism means also confronting its non-violent forms', *Europe's World*, 5 May 2015, available at http://europesworld. org/2015/05/05/tackling-militant-islamism-means-also-confronting-non-violent-forms/#.VbITcWDX_dv (accessed 24 July 2015).

————, '"We are all in this together, like it or not": On Raif Badawi, Charlie Hebdo and non-violent Islamism', *Qantara.de*, 22 January 2015, available at http://en. qantara.de/content/on-raif-badawi-charlie-hebdo-and-non-violent-islamism-we-are-all-in-this-together-like-it-or (accessed 23 July 2015).

————, 'And yet it moves: One Meriam Yehia Ibrahim', *Modern Discussion*, 26 May 2014, available at http://www.ahewar.org/debat/show.art.asp?aid=416536 (accessed 15 July 2015).

————, *The Arab State and Women's Rights: The Trap of Authoritarian Governance* (London: Routledge, 2011).

————, 'Islamisches Recht in der Schweiz ist gefährlich', *NZZ am Sonntag*, 3 July 2011.

————, 'Islam and human dignity: A consequence-based approach to human dignity and rights', in Dorothèe Deimann and Simon Mugier (eds), *Entgegensprechen: Texte zu Menschenwürde und Menschenrecht*, vol. 1 (Basel: edition gesowip, 2010).

————, '*Ich will nicht mehr schweigen': Der Islam, der Westen und die Menschenrechte* (Freiburg: Herder Verlag, 2009), p. 34.

————, 'Islamisches Recht in der Schweiz wäre verheerend', *NZZ am Sonntag*, 4 January 2009.

————, 'The Arab state and women's rights: The case of Saudi Arabia–The limits of the possible', *Orient–German Journal for Politics, Economics and Culture of the Middle East*, July 2008.

————, *Regional Politics in the Gulf: Saudi Arabia, Oman, Yemen* (London: Saqi, 2005).

Maududi, Abul A'la, *A Short History of the Revivalist Movement in Islam*, 3rd ed. (Lahore: Islamic Publications Ltd, 1979).

Maududi, Mawlana, *The Rights of non-Muslims (Dhmmis) in Islam*, in Arabic, 1947.

May, Theresa, MP, Home Secretary, 'A stronger Britain, built on our values – A new partnership to defeat extremism', speech, 23 March 2015. Available at https:// www.gov.uk/government/speeches/a-stronger-britain-built-on-our-values.ur (accessed 1 July 2015).

McGoldrick, Dominic, 'The compatibility of an Islamic/shari'a law system or shari'a rules with the European Convention on Human Rights', in Robin Griffith-Jones (ed.), *Islam and English Law: Rights, Responsibilities and the Place of Sharia* (Cambridge: Cambridge University Press, 2013).

McVeigh, Karen and Amelia Hill, 'Bill limiting sharia law is motivated by "concern for Muslim women",' *The Guardian*, 8 June 2011. Available at http://www. theguardian.com/law/2011/jun/08/sharia-bill-lords-muslim-women (accessed 26 May 2015).

Meijer, Roel (ed.), *Global Salafism: Islam's New Religious Movement* (London: Hurst & Company, 2009).

Menski, Werner, *Comparative Law in a Global Context: The Legal Systems of Asia and Africa*, 2nd ed. (Cambridge, UK: Cambridge University Press, 2006).

Metcalf, Barbara D., *Traditionalist Islamic Activism: Deobandi, Tablighis, and Talibs* (Leiden: ISIM, 2002).

Mirza, Munira, Abi Senthikumaran, and Zein Ja'far, 'Living apart together: British Muslims and the paradox of multiculturalism', *Policy Exchange Report*, 2007.

Modood, Tariq, 'Multicultural citizenship and the shari'a controversy in Britain', in Rex Ahdar and Nicholas Aroney (eds), *Shari'a in the West* (Oxford: Oxford University Press, 2010).

Molyneux, Maxine, *State Policies and the Position of Women Workers in the People's Democratic Republic of Yemen, 1967–1977* (Geneva: International Labour Office, 1982).

Moosa, Ebrahim, 'The dilemma of Islamic rights schemes', *Worlds & Knowledges Otherwise* (Fall 2004), pp. 8–9.

Motor Cycles (Wearing of Helmets) Regulations 1973. Statutory Instrument, 1973, No. 180.

Muchowiecka, Laura, 'The end of multiculturalism? Immigration and integration in Germany and the United Kingdom', *Student Pulse*, v/6 (2013). Available at http://www.studentpulse.com/a?id=735 (accessed 15 July 2015).

Muslim Council of Britain (MCB), *Fairness not Favours: British Muslims' Perspectives at the 2015 General Election* (London: MCB, 2015), p. 11. Available at http://www.mcb.org.uk/wp-content/uploads/2015/03/fairnessnotfavours-MCB.pdf (accessed 1 July 2015).

———, *Meeting the Needs of Muslim Pupils in State Schools: Information & Guidelines for Schools* (London: Muslim Council, 2007).

Muslim Educational Trust, 'About us', available at http://web-eab.wix.com/met#!__page-2 (accessed 1 July 2015).

Nabil, Rania, 'A human rights defender denounces the reconciliation between Muslims and Copts in Almataria and describes it as a shameful stigma', 14 June 2014, in Arabic. Available at http://www.altahrir.com/details.php?ID=29416 (accessed 15 July 2015).

Namazie, Maryam, 'Nearly 200 signatories call to dismantle parallel legal systems', *Freethought Blog*, 15 June 2015. Available at http://freethoughtblogs.com/maryamnamazie/2015/06/15/nearly-200-signatories-call-to-dismantle-parallel-legal-systems/ (accessed 9 July 2015).

———, *Sharia Law in Britain: A Threat to One Law for All and Equal Rights* (London: One Law for All, 2010).

'Names and details: Suspicious provisions of the customary session revealed by the lawyer of the accused Copts in Almataria avents', *Copts Today*, 18 June 2014 (in Arabic). Available at http://www.coptstoday.com/Copts-News/Detail.php?Id=78200 (accessed 15 July 2015).

Nandi, Alita and Lucinda Platt, *Ethnic Minority Women's Poverty and Economic Well Being* (London: UK Government Equalities Office, 2010). Available at https://www.gov.uk/government/uploads/system/uploads/attachment_data/file/85528/ethnic-minority-women_s-poverty.pdf (accessed 9 July 2015).

Office for National Statistics (ONS), 'FOI request: Statistics of the Muslim population in the UK for 2011, 2012, 2013 (London: ONS, 16 May 2013).

Orend, Brian, *Human Rights: Concept and Context* (Peterboro, Ontario, Canada: Broadview Press, 2002).

Page, David, *Prelude to Partition: The Indian Muslims and the Imperial System of Control (1920–1932)* (Delhi: Oxford University Press, 1982).

Participatory Development Initiatives (PDI), *Role of Tribal Jirga in Violence Against Women: A Case Study of Karo Kari in Sindh* (Karachi: PDI, 2005).

Patel, Pragna, '"Shariafication by stealth" in the UK', *50.50 Inclusive Democracy*, 17 October 2014. Available at https://www.opendemocracy.net/5050/pragna-patel/%27shariafication-by-stealth%27-in-uk (accessed 9 July 2015).

Patel, Pragna and Uditi Sen, *Cohesion, Faith and Gender: A Report on the Impact of the Cohesion and Faith-based Approach on Black and Minority Women in Ealing* (London: Southall Black Sisters, 2010). Available at http://www.southallblacksisters.org.uk/sbs/cfg-report-copyright-sbs.pdf (accessed 10 July 2015).

Pearl, David, *A Textbook on Muslim Law* (London: Croom Helm, 1979).

Phillips, Anne, *Multiculturalism without Culture* (Princeton and Oxford: Princeton University Press, 2007).

Phillips, Trevor, 'Not a river of blood, but a tide of hope', speech, 20 April 2008. Available at http://resources.cohesioninstitute.org.uk/Publications/Documents/Document/Default.aspx?recordId=44 (accessed 15 July 2015).

———, 'After 7/7: Sleepwalking to segregation', speech, 22 September 2005. Available at http://www.humanities.manchester.ac.uk/socialchange/research/social-change/summer-workshops/documents/sleepwalking.pdf

Pieragostini, Karl, *Britain, Aden and South Arabia: Abandoning Empire* (New York: St. Martin's Press, 1991).

Pilgrim, David, *What was Jim Crow?* (Big Rounds, MI: Jim Crow Museum, Ferris State University). Available at http://www.ferris.edu/jimcrow/what.htm (accessed 14 July 2015).

Pollis, Adamantia, 'Cultural Relativism Revisited: Through a State Prism', *Human Rights Quarterly*, 18.2 (1996).

Pollis, Adamantia and Peter Schwab, *Human Rights: Cultural and Ideological Perspectives* (New York, Praeger, 1979).

Powell, Enoch, 'Rivers of blood' speech, republished in the *Telegraph*, 6 Nov 2007. Available at http://www.telegraph.co.uk/comment/3643823/Enoch-Powells-Rivers-of-Blood-speech.html (accessed 15 July 2015).

Pradhan, Rajendra, 'Negotiating multiculturalism in Nepal: Law, hegemony, contestation and paradox'. Paper presented at conference, Constitutionalism and Diversity in Nepal, Kathmandu, 22–24 August 2007. Available at http://www.uni-bielefeld.de/midea/pdf/Rajendra.pdf (accessed 16 July 2015).

Proudman, Charlotte Rachael, *Equal and Free? Evidence in Support of Baroness Cox's Arbitration and Mediation Services (Equality) Bill* (London: House of Lords, May 2012).

Qutb, Sayyid, *Milestones* (Beirut: The Holy Koran House, 1978).

Rabasa, Angel, Cheryl Benard, Lowell H. Schwartz and Peter Sickle, *Building Moderate Muslim Networks* (Santa Monica: Rand Center for Middle East Public Policy, 2007).

Rahouma, Mustafa, 'Customary reconciliation: Treatment of sectarian strife through 'Sessions of humiliation and submission', *Al Watan News*, 6 January 2014, in Arabic. Available at http://www.elwatannews.com/news/details/387792 (accessed 15 July 2015).

Reid, Graeme, 'The trouble with tradition: When "values" trample over rights', *HRW World Report* 2013. Available at http://www.hrw.org/world-report/2013/essays/trouble-tradition (accessed 14 July 2015).

Report on Sectarian Incidents in Egypt. In Arabic. Egyptian Initiative for Personal Rights, 5 January 2012. Available at http://eipr.org/pressrelease/2012/01/05/1339 (accessed 15 July 2015); translation at http://sectarianviolenceegypt2012. blogspot.ch/2013/04/i-sectarian-violence-that-lead-to.html (accessed 15 July 2015).

Ridley, Louise, 'The trailblazing Hindu barrister who uses inner strength to win back abused women's dowries', *Huffington Post UK*, 5 November 2014. Available at http://www.huffingtonpost.co.uk/2014/11/03/usha-sood-dowry-abuse-forced-marriage-cases_n_6097448.html (accessed 9 July 2015).

Roudi-Fahimi, Farzaneh and Shaimaa Ibrahim, *Ending Child Marriage in the Arab Region* (Washington, DC: Population Reference Bureau, 2013).

Roy, Oliver, *Islamic Radicalism in Afghanistan and Pakistan*. UNHCR Emergency and Security Service, WRITENET Paper No. 06/2001 (Paris: CNRS, January 2002). Available at http://www.refworld.org/pdfid/3c6a3f7d2.pdf (accessed 1 July 2015).

Said, Benham T. and Hazim Fouad (eds), *Salafismus: Auf der suche nach der wahren Islam* (Freiburg: Herder Verlag, 2014).

Said, Rosemarie Zahlan, *The Making of the Modern Gulf States: Kuwait, Bahrain, Qatar, The United Arab Emirates and Oman* (London: Unwin Hyman, 1989).

Saksena, Kashi Prasad, *Muslim Law as Administered in India and Pakistan*, 4th ed. (Lucknow: Eastern Book Company, 1963).

Sandra Lovelace v Canada, Communication No. R.6/24, U.N. Doc. Supp. No. 40 (A/36/40) at 166 (1981), view 9.2. Available at http://www1.umn.edu/humanrts/undocs/session36/6-24.htm (accessed 15 July 2015).

Sarwar, Gulam, *Islam: Beliefs and Teachings*, 8th ed. (London: Muslim Educational Trust, 2006).

'Saudi Arabia: Shura Council approves sport for girls based on the fatwa [edict] of Sheikh Ibn Baaz and postpones [the issue of] female teachers teaching boys', *CNN Arabic*, 9 April 2014 (in Arabic). Available at http://arabic.cnn.com/middleeast/2014/04/07/saudi-shura-sport-vote (accessed 14 July, 2015).

Saudi Women for Reform, *The Shadow Report for CEDAW* (December 2007).

Sen, Amartya, 'The uses and abuses of multiculturalism', *The New Republic*, 27 February 2006.

Sen, Purna and Liz Kelly, *Cedaw Shadow Thematic Report on Violence Against Women in the UK* (2007), p. 22. Available at http://www2.ohchr.org/english/bodies/cedaw/docs/ngos/UKThematicReportVAW41.pdf (accessed 9 July 2015).

Serck, Linda, 'Polygamy in Islam: The women victims of multiple marriage', *BBC News*, 1 June 2012. Available at http://www.bbc.com/news/uk-england-berkshire-18252958 (accessed 9 July 2015).

Sezgin, Yüksel, *Human Rights under State-Enforced Religious Family Laws in Israel, Egypt and India* (Cambridge, UK: Cambridge University Press, 2013).

Shah-Kazemi, Sonia Nurin, *Untying the Knot: Muslim Women, Divorce and the Shariah* (Detroit: Signal Press, 2001).

Shaw, Stanford Jay, 'Ottoman Empire', *Encyclopedia Britannica Online*. Available at http://www.britannica.com/place/Ottoman-Empire (accessed 15 July 2015).

Shea, Nina, *Saudi Arabia's Curriculum of Intolerance* (Washington, DC: Center for Religious Freedom, Freedom House, and Institute of Gulf Affairs, 2006).

Shubat, Fouad, *The Organization of Personal Status for Non-Muslims: Legislation and Judiciary in Syria and Lebanon*, in Arabic (Damascus: The Higher Institute for Arab Studies, 1966).

Shukri, Ahmed, *Muhammedan Law of Marriage and Divorce* (New York: Ams Press, 1996).

Siddiqui, Hannana and Meena Patel, *Safe and Sane: A Model of Intervention on Domestic Violence and Mental Health, Suicide and Self-harm Amongst Black and Minority Ethnic Women* (London: Southall Black Sisters, 2010).

Slan, Sarah, *Arabisch-Jüdische Paare in Israel: Auswirkungen des Politischen Systems* (unpublished master's thesis, Zurich University, 2012).

Southall Black Sisters, *The Forced Marriage Campaign*. Available at http://www.southallblacksisters.org.uk/campaigns/forced-marriage-campaign/ (accessed 9 July 2015).

State of Israel, Declaration of Israel's Independence 1948, Tel Aviv, 14 May 1948. Available at http://stateofisrael.com/declaration/ (accessed 15 July 2015).

Sternstunde Philosophie, 'Islamisches Recht in Europa? Die Zürcher Professorin Andrea Büchler im Gespräch mit Roger de Weck', programme on Sternstunde Philosophie, Swiss TV, 11 January 2009. Available at http://www.srf.ch/player/tv/sternstunde-philosophie/video/sternstunde-philosophie-islamisches-recht-in-europa-die-zuercher-professorin-andrea-buechler-im-gespraech-mit-roger-de-weck?id=2a039aea-b02e-489b-9984-3c4e80d885af (accessed 15 July 2015).

Taizi, Sherzaman, *Jirga System in Tribal Life* (Williamsburg, VA: Tribal Analysis Center, 2007). Available at http://www.tribalanalysiscenter.com/PDF-TAC/Jirga%20System%20in%20Tribal%20Life.pdf (accessed 15 July 2015).

Talwa, Divya, 'Wedding trouble as UK Muslim marriages not recognised', *BBC News*, 3 February 2010. Available at http://news.bbc.co.uk/2/hi/uk_news/8493660.stm (accessed 9 July 2015).

Tax, Meredith, *Double Bind: The Muslim Right, the Anglo-American Left, and Universal Human Rights* (London: Centre for Secular Space, 2012).

Taylor, Charles, 'The politics of recognition', in *Multiculturalism: Examining the Politics of Recognition* (Princeton, NJ: Princeton University Press, 1994), p. 25.

Text of Judiciary Decision N. 34184394 (07 May 2014), in Arabic, Criminal Court, Jeddah, Saudi Arabia.

Tharoor, Ishaan, 'Can Sufism defuse terrorism?' *Time*, 22 July 2009. Available at http://content.time.com/time/world/article/0,8599,1912091,00.html

Thatcher, Margaret, speech at St Lawrence Jewry, 4th March 1981, available at http://www.margaretthatcher.org/document/104587 (accessed 1 July 2015).

———, 'My kind of Tory Party', *Daily Telegraph*, 30 January 1975. Available at http://www.margaretthatcher.org/document/102600 (accessed 1 July 2015).

UK Government, Foreign & Commonwealth Office and Home Office, *Forced Marriage: Information and Practice Guidelines for Professionals Protecting, Advising and Supporting Victims*. Available at https://www.gov.uk/forced-marriage (accessed 9 July 2015).

UN General Assembly, Human Rights Council, *Draft Report of the Human Rights Council on its Tenth Session*, available at http://www2.ohchr.org/english/bodies/hrcouncil/docs/10session/edited_versionL.11Revised.pdf (accessed 16 July 2015).

UNHCHR, 'Special Rapporteur on violence against women finalizes country mission to the United Kingdom and Northern Ireland and calls for urgent action to address the accountability deficit and also the adverse impacts of changes in funding and services' (London, 15 April 2014). Available at http://www.ohchr. org/en/newsevents/pages/displaynews.aspx?newsid=14514& (accessed 9 July 2015).

'Undercover Mosque', programme on *Dispatches*, Channel 4, 15 January 2007, at 9.48 to 10.9 minutes into the programme.

United Nations Development Program, *Arab Human Development Report 2005: Towards the Rise of Women in the Arab World* (New York: United Nations, 2006).

Universal Islamic Declaration of Human Rights (UIDHR) (London: Islamic Council, 1981), available at http://www.alhewar.com/ISLAMDECL.html (accessed 16 July 2015).

Unreported World: The Cursed Twins of Madagascar, Channel 4 documentary, 9 May 2014.

Warraich, Sohail Akbar and Cassandra Balchin, *Recognizing the Un-recognized: Inter-country Cases and Muslim Marriages & Divorces in Britain* (London: Women Living Under Muslim Laws, 2006).

Warren Hastings' Act II of 1772, in Kashi Prasad Saksena, *Muslim Law as Administered in India and Pakistan*, 4th ed. (Lucknow: Eastern Book Company, 1963).

Williams, Archbishop Rowan, 'Civil and religious law in England: A religious perspective', lecture at the Royal Courts of Justice, 7 February 2008. Available at http://rowanwilliams.archbishopofcanterbury.org/articles.php/1137/arc...re-civil-and-religious-law-in-england-a-religious-perspective#Lecture (accessed 16 July 2015).

Women Living Under Muslim Laws (WLUML), 'About WLUML'. Available at http://www.wluml.org/node/5408 (accessed 9 July 2015).

———, *Knowing our Rights: Women, Family, Laws and Customs in the Muslim World* (London: WLUML, 2006).

Yamani, May, *Cradle of Islam: The Hijaz and the Quest for an Arabian Identity* (London: I.B.Tauris, 2004).

Yilmaz, Ihsan, *Muslim Laws, Politics and Society in Modern Nation States: Dynamic Legal Pluralism in England, Turkey and Pakistan* (Farnham, Surrey: Ashgate Publishing, 2005).

———, 'The challenge of post-modern legality and Muslim legal pluralism in England', *Journal of Ethnic and Migration Studies* xxvii/2 (April 2002).

Ziring, Lawrence, *The Middle East: Political Dictionary* (Santa Barbara: ABC-CLIO, 1992).

Zisser, Eyal, 'The Alawis, lords of Syria', in Ofra Bengio and Gabriel Bendor (eds), *Minorities and the State in the Arab World* (London: Lynne Rienner, 1999).

INDEX